THE SECOND GENERATION OF
AFRICAN AMERICAN
PIONEERS IN
ANTHROPOLOGY

The lives and work of
James Lowell Gibbs Jr.
Charles Preston Warren II
William Alfred Shack
Diane K. Lewis
Delmos Jones
Niara Sudarkasa
Johnnetta Betsch Cole
John Langston Gwaltney
Ira E. Harrison
Audrey Smedley
George Clement Bond
Oliver Osborne
Anselme Remy
Vera Mae Green
Claudia Mitchell-Kernan

THE SECOND GENERATION OF AFRICAN AMERICAN PIONEERS IN ANTHROPOLOGY

EDITED BY
Ira E. Harrison, Deborah Johnson-Simon,
and Erica Lorraine Williams

Publication of this book was supported in part by the
University of Illinois Press Fund for Anthropology.
© 2018 by the Board of Trustees
of the University of Illinois
All rights reserved
1 2 3 4 5 C P 5 4 3 2 1
♾This book is printed on acid-free paper.

Cataloging data available from the Library of Congress
ISBN 978-0-252-04202-7 (hardcover : alk.)
ISBN 978-0-252-08371-6 (paper : alk.)
ISBN 978-0-252-05076-3 (ebook)

Contents

Introduction. Celebrating Triumphs,
Overcoming Challenges, and Charting a Course
for Institutional Transformation   ix
Erica Lorraine Williams, Deborah Johnson-Simon,
and Ira E. Harrison

1. *James Lowell Gibbs Jr.: A Life of Educational Achievement*
   and Service   1
   Dallas L. Browne

2. *Charles Preston Warren II: Military Forensic Anthropologist,*
   Scholar, and Applied Scientist   15
   Alice Baldwin-Jones

3. *William Alfred Shack: An Unacknowledged Giant*   27
   Dallas L. Browne

4. *Diane K. Lewis and the Transformation of Anthropology:*
   An Ideology of Radical Change   37
   Cheryl R. Rodriguez

5. *Delmos Jones and the End of Neutrality*   52
   Elgin L. Klugh

6. *Niara Sudarkasa: Inspiring Black Women's Leadership*   68
   Erica Lorraine Williams

7. *Johnnetta Betsch Cole: Eradicating Multiple Systems*
   of Oppression   84
   Riché J. Daniel Barnes

8. *John Langston Gwaltney: The Development of a Core Black Ethnography and Museology* 99
   Deborah Johnson-Simon

9. *Ira E. Harrison: Activist, Scholar, and Visionary Pioneer* 114
   Alisha R. Winn

10. *Audrey Smedley: A Pioneers' Pioneer Anthropologist* 126
    Janis Faye Hutchinson

11. *George Clement Bond: Anthropologist, Africanist, Educator, and Visionary* 141
    Rachel Watkins

12. *Oliver Osborne: African American Nurse-Anthropologist Pioneer* 165
    Bertin M. Louis Jr.

13. *Anselme Remy and the Anthropology of Liberation* 174
    Angela McMillan Howell

14. *Vera Mae Green: Quaker Roots and Applied Anthropology* 191
    Antoinette Jackson

15. *Claudia Mitchell-Kernan: Sociolinguistic Anthropologist, Administrator, and Innovator* 200
    Betty J. Harris

Notes on Contributors 215

Index 221

INTRODUCTION

Celebrating Triumphs, Overcoming Challenges, and Charting a Course for Institutional Transformation

ERICA LORRAINE WILLIAMS, DEBORAH JOHNSON-SIMON, AND IRA E. HARRISON

African-American Pioneers in Anthropology introduced the world to a pantheon of African American intellectuals who had been drawn to the field of anthropology from the 1920s to the early 1950s. Through intellectual biographies, the volume shared the marginalized and invisibilized stories of black anthropologists, and, as Faye V. Harrison and Ira E. Harrison note in the introduction, "Anthropology, African Americans, and the Emancipation of a Subjugated Knowledge," repositioned "the African American intellectual lineage within the history of anthropology" (2). They assert that "any genuinely critical project designed to reinvent, decolonize, and transform anthropology" must first recapture "subjugated knowledges" (2). These words still ring as true today as they did in 1999 when the volume was first published.

The first cohort of African American pioneers in anthropology lived and worked through the periods of the Harlem Renaissance (New Negro Movement), World War I, the Great Depression, and the post–World War II era. While anthropology has historically been called "a child of Western imperialism," A. Lynn Bolles emphasizes that anthropology also has the "ability to serve as a positive social force for advancing equality among people" ("Seeking the Ancestors," 27). Black women in particular were drawn to the study of anthropology between 1915 and the 1950s because they saw anthropology as a "tool to locate the sources of inequality, and . . . as a place where one could participate in finding the 'cure'" (27).

African American pioneers in anthropology were not necessarily all part of the same generation, but they did belong to the first cohort of black pioneers in our field who were previously unrecognized and unacknowledged by the discipline.[1] The intellectual biographies in *African-American Pioneers in Anthropology* document those anthropologists' personal and intellectual trajectories and their scholarly and activist pursuits and detail how "their lives and work reflected the institutional structures of professional anthropology at the time" (Harrison and Harrison, Introduction to *African- American Pioneers in Anthropology*, 7). Moreover, the contributors were concerned with uncovering the pioneers' strategies for dealing with anthropology's ideological and institutional racism and sexism and exploring how they resisted victimization and expressed agency. Not only does the volume explore the pioneers' contributions to the field but it also shows how they paved the way for a new generation of black anthropologists. It is the generation *after* the pioneers that is the focus of this volume. In this volume emerging leaders and scholars in the field reflect on the challenges and triumphs of the intellectual trajectories of fifteen African American anthropologists who earned their doctorates in anthropology between 1960 and 1969. Following in the footsteps of the first book, this volume continues the quest for knowledge, respect, truth, and value in the inspiring legacy of the next generation of black anthropologists.

In "Anthropology, African Americans, and the Emancipation of a Subjugated Knowledge," Harrison and Harrison discuss three "generations" of black anthropologists: the pioneers, the second generation, and a third generation:

> The conditions for a second generation of professional anthropologists were set in 1953 when the Ford Foundation, responding to the forces of decolonization and the resultant shifts in international affairs, established a fellowship fund to increase the number of Africanists across several disciplines. This led to the emergence of a group of well-trained black experts on Africa, at least a dozen of whom were anthropologists, (e.g., Niara Sudarkasa [Gloria Marshall], Johnnetta Cole, James Gibbs, and William Shack). (10)

Sudarkasa, Cole, Gibbs, and Shack are just a few of the scholars whose intellectual biographies are featured in this volume. Their stories attest to the fact that Africanist scholarship became a significant, even if contentious, intellectual home for many black anthropologists.

According to Harrison and Harrison, the second generation was trained between the mid-1950s and 1968.[2] The much larger third generation emerged from the "watershed year" of 1968, when many more "historically white universities began accepting black students in record numbers" (10). In this volume, we use the term "next" as a way to bridge the second and third generations and refer to black anthropologists who earned their degrees between 1960 and 1969 as a cohort.

Establishing these "generations" or "cohorts" is an important tool in the recuperative project of uncovering, documenting, and making visible our "hidden figures" in the field. Jafari Sinclaire Allen and Ryan Cecil Jobson take this periodization even further when they refer to what they call the "decolonizing generation"—"the cohort of Black, allied antiracist, feminist, and political economy-oriented scholars" who conducted research "in the aftermath of the revolutionary socialist projects and in the throes of revolutionary projects forced to contend with economic sanctions and imperial containment" ("The Decolonizing Generation," 129, 134). They argue that "to invoke the language of generations—as opposed to that of schools, groups, or approaches, for example—is to indulge the 'structures of the conjuncture' that frame knowledge production itself as a temporal experience that reflects the societal exigencies of a particular moment" (130). Thus, while the idea of generations, cohorts, and periods is a useful framework for situating and understanding the contributions of these scholars, it is also important to note the continuities, overlaps, and blurred boundaries among these groupings.

In this book, chapters are presented in chronological order according to the year the each anthropologist earned his or her doctoral degree. There are seven major questions that the contributors to this volume are concerned with: Who is the next generation of African American anthropologists? What, if any, are their relationships with the African American pioneer anthropologists? What lessons can we learn from their personal and intellectual trajectories? What are their contributions to the field of anthropology, to academia, and to society in general? What kinds of research topics have members of this cohort pursued, and what kinds of theoretical contributions have they made? What, if anything, sets them apart from the pioneers? In what ways do they build on the first cohorts' contributions?

In their introduction, Harrison and Harrison point out that Columbia University and the University of Chicago long served as "gatekeepers of African American anthropology," since more than half of the pioneers studied at those institutions ("Anthropology, African Americans, and the Emancipation of a Subjugated Knowledge," 23). In this next generation, only three of the fifteen anthropologists featured in this volume studied at these institutions (Sudarkasa and Gwaltney at Columbia and Warren at the University of Chicago). The rest earned their degrees at other leading institutions of higher learning in the world, including the London School of Economics (Bond), the University of Manchester (Smedley), Northwestern University (Cole), Harvard University (Gibbs), the University of Arizona (Green), Syracuse University (Harrison), Cornell University (Lewis, Jones), the University of California at Berkeley (Kernan), and Michigan State University (Osborne). While Warren and Remy did not complete their doctoral degrees, this did not prevent them from having successful careers. They went on to teach at universities that include the University of California (Shack at Berkeley, Mitchell-Kernan at Los Angeles), San Francisco State University (Lewis), Stanford (Gibbs), the University of Chicago (Warren), the University of Michigan (Sudarkasa), SUNY Cortland and Syracuse University (Gwaltney), the University of Tennessee at Knoxville (Harrison), SUNY Binghamton and Virginia Commonwealth University (Smedley), Columbia University (Bond), Wayne State University and the University of Washington (Osborne), Fisk University and the University of the District of Columbia (Remy), and Harvard University (Mitchell-Kernan).

The anthropologists in this cohort pursued research spanning the diverse subfields of public anthropology, native anthropology, sociolinguistics, military forensic anthropology, medical anthropology, applied anthropology, public health, legal anthropology, intellectual activism, museum anthropology, and many other areas. Most of the anthropologists of this cohort focused on cultural anthropology, which is not surprising, since even as of 1997, a survey of anthropology PhDs found that "most minority PhDs are in cultural anthropology" (Givens, Evans, and Jablonski, "American Anthropological Association Survey of PhDs," 3).[3] This next generation of black anthropologists engaged in ethnographic and archival fieldwork on issues ranging from families, HIV/AIDS and black women, and the black church to interethnic relations in Aruba and Curaçao and many other topics. The diverse geographical areas of expertise of this next generation of black anthropologists represents a marked shift from the pioneers, who were often expected to study "their own or similar cultures" due to "anthropology's racial division of labor" (Harrison and Harrison, "Anthropology, African Americans, and the Emancipation of a Subjugated Knowledge," 19). Thus, while several members of this next generation chose to focus on the African diaspora, there was more opportunity for them to focus on other parts of the world as well. Members of this cohort conducted fieldwork in Asia and the Pacific Islands (Thailand, the Philippines, Malaysia, American Samoa), Africa (Nigeria, Ghana, Benin, Liberia, Ethiopia, Rwanda), and Latin America and the Caribbean (Aruba, Curaçao, Mexico, Cuba).

It is impossible to discuss this next generation of black anthropologists without also discussing the Association of Black Anthropologists (ABA), which they created. The next section gives an overview of the efforts of the American Anthropological Association (AAA) to be more attentive to racial and ethnic diversity and inclusion, as well as black anthropologists' agency in creating an autonomous space where they could connect, support each other, and thrive as a community.[4]

Carving Out a Space for People of Color in the AAA

The inspiration for this book project came from Ira E. Harrison—himself a member of this cohort of black anthropologists and one of the founders of the ABA.[5] At his first AAA meeting in 1962 in Chicago, Illinois, Harrison was shocked to only see three other black people— William Shack, Diane Lewis, and Delmos Jones (Winn, this volume). In his 1987 article "The Association of Black Anthropologists: A Brief History," Harrison issued a clarion call for remedying the "fundamental lack of knowledge about Afro-American anthropologists" within the discipline, contending that "there needs to be a general history and profiling of Afro-American anthropologists, past and present" and that "there needs to be a critical analysis of their works and their contributions to anthropology" (17). Harrison was determined to carry on the important project of "rehistoricization" that began with the publication of *African American Pioneers in Anthropology*. As he points out, it was this generation that gave birth to the ABA. Harrison says that the ABA provided "visibility and vitality to brothers and sisters to pursue anthropology as a valuable profession."[6]

The 1968 AAA annual meeting in Seattle was a key turning point in the development of the ABA.[7] After a panel on black curriculum in anthropological studies featuring Council Taylor, Delmos Jones, Diane Lewis, Johnnetta B. Cole, and Oliver Osborne, twenty-one anthropologists signed an agreement that led to the emergence of the Minority Caucus in the AAA (Harrison, "The Association of Black Anthropologists," 17).[8] The ABA emerged from the Minority Caucus in 1975, and founding members included Ira E. Harrison, Vera Green, Sheila Walker, and Glenn Jordan (Winn, this volume). A few of the notable ABA presidents are Vera Green (1977–78), Anselme Remy (1978–79), Johnnetta B. Cole (1979–80), and Ira E. Harrison (1985–87).[9] In 1986, the ABA became an official subsection of the American Anthropological Association. Reflecting on the legacy of ABA leadership, Harrison asserts that under Vera Green, the association earned "legitimacy and respectability in anthropological circles" and that through Sheila Walker's tireless efforts on ABA publications, including *Notes from the Natives*, which later became *Notes from the ABA*, the ABA assumed "vitality and visibility" (Harrison, "The Association of Black Anthropologists," 19). Looking ahead, much work still needs to be done to continue the work that the

Themes

ABA began to ensure the retention and relevance of black anthropologists. The remainder of the chapter explores some of the shared themes in the intellectual biographies of this cohort of black anthropologists and also provides an overview of the chapters.

Themes

There are many salient themes and connections that emerge when we put these intellectual biographies into conversation with each other. First, many members of this cohort had strong connections with the pioneers. Several of the scholars featured in this volume were mentored or inspired by the likes of St. Clair Drake, Elliott Skinner, and Allison Davis. For instance, Dallas Browne notes the profound influence that Allison Davis had on James Gibbs while he was a student at Harvard, even though Gibbs never met the man in person. Gibbs felt as if he were "the beneficiary of Davis's sterling performance as a student and professor" and acknowledged that Davis "made it easier for him to pursue his dreams by opening the way for him" (Browne, this volume). When Gibbs applied for a Ford Foundation Foreign Area Fellowship to study Liberian traditional law, the legendary St. Clair Drake served on his panel. Ultimately, Gibbs won the award to travel to Liberia and to study the Kpelle, and he kept in touch with Drake for many years.

Other themes that unite the chapters include military service, prestigious awards, connections to historically black colleges and universities (HBCUs), and international training. Several members of this cohort had experiences with military service—whether serving in the Vietnam War, the Air Force (Warren), or Coast Guard (Shack). Several members of this cohort received Fulbright, Ford Foundation, and other prestigious fellowships. For instance, Warren won a Fulbright for research in the Philippines, Diane Lewis won a Ford fellowship to conduct in a small Malaysian village, and Smedley won a Ford fellowship to study the history of race, just to name a few. Several members of this cohort also had important connections to HBCUs. For example, James Gibbs's family in Ithaca, New York, regularly invited visiting HBCU professors to dinner when he was a child (Browne, this volume). Ira E. Harrison is a 1955 graduate of Morehouse College and conducted research at Hampton University in 1984 (Winn, this volume). Anselme Remy taught at Fisk University, where he found a vibrant "multidisciplinary pan-Africanist community" of young black scholars (Howell, this volume). Finally, another common theme is that several members of this cohort pursued graduate training abroad, including William Shack, George Clement Bond, and Audrey Smedley, while at the urging of Meyers

Forte, James Gibbs spent a semester studying at Cambridge to train with leading Africanists in the United Kingdom.

Despite the common threads connecting their lives and intellectual pursuits, there were also significant class differences among the next generation. While several of these anthropologists were from working-class backgrounds, others were from long lines of esteemed educators and professionals. For instance, George Clement Bond was the son of a sociology professor (father) and prominent educator and civic leader (mother) (Watkins, this volume). His uncle, Horace Mann Bond, was the president of Lincoln University, and George Bond spent periods of his childhood in Haiti, Liberia, and Afghanistan (Watkins, this volume). Johnnetta B. Cole was the great-granddaughter of the first African American millionaire in Florida (Barnes, this volume).[10] Others experienced significant financial difficulties and constraints. For example, William Shack never received a scholarship and had to work full time throughout his graduate career (Browne, this volume). This is a theme that persists today. As Karen Brodkin, Sandra Morgen, and Janis Hutchinson point out in their article "Anthropology as White Public Space?," "students of color are disproportionately from working-class backgrounds, and institutional blindness to the concomitants of class works against them. Because levels of financial support are seldom adequate, students without family resources are disadvantaged. Many have to take nonacademic jobs, which restricts study time and participation in departmental social-professional life" (553). Students can surely benefit from learning about the historical struggles and challenges that this generation of black anthropologists faced and how they handled them.

It is also important to contextualize these scholars within the historical context of the tumultuous and turbulent 1960s—a time of continued vindicationism, shifting worldviews, and social activism. In the 1960s, the field of anthropology changed significantly as a result of the impact of anticolonial and US social movements (Brodkin, Morgen, and Hutchison, "Anthropology as White Public Space?," 546). The field became "more reflexive about its racial and colonial politics and its self-construction as a scientific enterprise carried out by objective researchers" (Brodkin, Morgen, and Hutchison, "Anthropology as White Public Space?," 546). In this way, the discipline of anthropology was finally catching up with some of the tenets long held by African American scholars—vindicationism in particular.

The tradition of vindicationism is a dominant theme of *African-American Pioneers in Anthropology*. Harrison and Harrison state, "Perhaps the clearest continuity in African American intellectual history over the past few centuries is a tradition of racial vindication." They go on to explain that "vindicationism emerged in reaction to racist assertions that Africans are degraded as savages, that Africans and African Americans have no culture, that blacks were inherently inferior, and that miscegenation was degenerative to whites and white culture. African American intellectuals have developed a deeply rooted humanistic tradition that directly opposes such ideas ("Anthropology, African Americans, and the Emancipation of a Subjugated Knowledge," 12). A. Lynn Bolles elaborates on the African American intellectual tradition as a framework that is concerned with correcting dominant paradigms, focusing on accurate descriptions, and reclaiming the history of cultures ("Seeking the Ancestors," 28). This tradition has several other characteristics as well, according to Bolles. Research in this tradition relies on alternative theories and methods, especially historical and comparative ones, and is conceived and conducted as form of activism. Furthermore, the African American intellectual tradition sees racism as a central problem in the contemporary world—a world in which race intersects with class on national and international levels ("Seeking the Ancestors," 41).

Harrison and Harrison point out that "the pioneers' shared commitment to fighting racism and instigating meaningful social change is also reflected in the contents of their scholarship" ("Anthropology, African Americans, and the Emancipation of a Subjugated Knowledge," 17). Many members of the next generation of black anthropologists also did research that drew on and contributed to the African American intellectual tradition and vindicationism in particular. Ira E. Harrison refers to this next generation of anthropologists as the "ABC's: Activists, Brave, and Committed." They were committed to studying and eliminating racism in the United States and beyond. For example, Audrey Smedley's classic book *Race in North America* has gone through four editions, and she also contributed to the video *Race: The Power of an Illusion*.

In *African-American Pioneers in Anthropology*, there is a common thread of activism, advocacy, and public service that unites the group, and it likewise connects the next cohort. As activists, they marched, protested, and were sometimes arrested in the struggle for justice. Ira E. Harrison participated in the March on Washington. James Gibbs was active in the civil and human rights movements in the San Francisco Bay area and also served on the advisory board of the NAACP Legal Defense Fund, as a volunteer consultant for the Museum of the African Diaspora, and as a tutor for a reading program in the economically depressed area of East Palo Alto (Browne, this volume). Delmos Jones was an active member of the American Anthropological Association (AAA) Task Force on Poverty and Homelessness. It is abundantly clear that these anthropologists took their engagements with scholar activism very seriously.

These anthropologists were brave because the academic institutions that they were invested in did not always support them. As members of this cohort navigated the difficult waters of academia in pursuing their doctoral degrees and establishing their careers, they dealt with rejection from those who were supposed to advise and guide them. For instance, pioneer military forensic anthropologist Charles Preston Warren II was refused membership into the Association of American Physical Anthropologists (Baldwin-Jones, this volume). After conducting two years of research on the Gurage in Ethiopia, William Shack wrote to the University of Chicago expressing his desire to enter into the PhD program. However, Robert Redfield said that the department decided that he was not PhD quality for Chicago, which was why he ended up pursuing his degree at the London School of Economics.

This cohort's stories are also a testament to how committed its members were to the field of anthropology. They did not abandon anthropology, even when it showed itself to be a field that did not always love them back. These anthropologists had to work "twice as hard," as the popular African American adage puts it, to prove themselves. For instance, Diane Lewis's professor told her that she "had too many strikes against" her to "earn a PhD and become a professional anthropologist" (Rodriguez, this volume). Of course, those "strikes" were her race and gender. Even as an undergraduate at UCLA in the late 1940s, Lewis was often the only black student in her classes. A southern white professor at UCLA discouraged her from majoring in Spanish by telling her that "Negroes could not learn foreign languages," and so she would not be able to earn above a C in her class (Rodriguez, this volume). Even today, scholars have shown that "anthropology departments have not done well when it comes to decolonizing their own practices around race" (Brodkin, Morgen, and Hutchison, "Anthropology as White Public Space?," 545). Despite these challenges, this next generation of black anthropologists tried to make the discipline better than it was when they entered it.

In their introduction to *African-American Pioneers in Anthropology*, Harrison and Harrison claim that several African American pioneers were either unable (Caroline Bond Day and Louis Eugene King) or chose not to work in the field of anthropology for various reasons (Arthur Huff Fauset, Manet Fowler, Katherine Dunham, and Zora Neale Hurston) (11). Sometimes, they had to fulfill their anthropological aspirations elsewhere, where they would be welcomed and appreciated. As St. Clair Drake pointed out decades ago, black scholars "lacked the institutionalized recognition, support, and power for producing and reproducing their work as 'anthropology'" (11). Ultimately, Harrison and Harrison assert that black anthropologists were "denied entrance into the fraternity of anthropologists because of the constraints of a racially segmented intellectual labor market" (11). Unfortunately, this is something that the next generation of pioneers in anthropology also confronted. Moreover, as Bolles points out, having one's work cited by colleagues, getting financial support, and being referred to as a scholar in a positive way is "what counts" in the academy ("Seeking the Ancestors," 26). While the pioneers suffered in this regard, this next generation fared a little better in terms of recognition in the field and institutional success, though their journeys to obtaining a PhD were often still precarious.

Despite these obstacles, this generation of black anthropologists still managed to have agency and autonomy over their work and to create dynamic and inspiring career paths for themselves. Ethics and integrity were at the heart of many of their life and career decisions. For example, Delmos Jones chose to stop collecting data and discontinue further publishing about the Lahu of Thailand in the mid-1960s once he became aware that his research could contribute to CIA counterinsurgency agendas (Klugh, this volume). Jones was even commended by the AAA Ethics Committee for his personal sacrifice.

There are many firsts in this cohort. Warren was one of the first African American faculty members at the University of Illinois, Chicago (Baldwin-Jones, this volume). Niara Sudarkasa was the first black woman to teach at New York University, the first African American woman to teach anthropology at the University of Michigan, the first African American woman to earn tenure in the arts and sciences at the University of Michigan, and the first African American woman to earn tenure in the arts and sciences (Williams, this volume). James Gibbs was the first African American to earn a degree from Cornell University, and the first person to hold the position of Martin Luther King Jr. Centennial Professor of Anthropology Emeritus at Stanford University (Browne, this volume). William Shack published the first social anthropological monograph on any Ethiopian society (Browne, this volume). Johnnetta B. Cole was the first black woman president of Spelman College. Oliver Osborne was part of the first generation of nurse-anthropologists in the United States (Louis, this volume), and John Langston Gwaltney was the first anthropologist of color to conduct independent fieldwork among Chinantec-speaking people in Oaxaca, Mexico (Johnson-Simon this volume). Finally, Diane Lewis's article "A Response to Inequality: Black Women, Racism, and Sexism" (1977) was "among the first publications in the social sciences to declare, discuss, and describe black women's feminist consciousness" (Rodriguez this volume).

Finally, many members of this cohort went on to pursue careers in higher education administration, such as Johnnetta B. Cole and Niara Sudarkasa, who became presidents of Spelman College, Bennett College, and Lincoln University, respectively. Furthermore, William Shack served as the dean of UC Berkeley's Graduate Division for six years (McBroom, "Anthropologist William Shack, Prominent African Scholar and Graduate Dean Emeritus, Dies at 76"), and James Gibbs served as chair of Stanford's Anthropology Department from 1987 to 1990, dean of undergraduate studies from 1970 to 1976), and codirector of the Stanford-Berkeley Joint Center for African Studies from 1985 to 1987. The next section provides an overview of the chapters in this volume.

Overview of Chapters

The first chapter by Dallas Browne focuses on Africanist anthropologist James Gibbs, who conducted fieldwork in Liberia and taught at Stanford for many years. Alice Baldwin-Jones's chapter explores the life and work of Charles Preston Warren II., highlighting his contributions to forensic anthropology, Philippine studies, and the University of Chicago. While most black anthropologists pursued cultural anthropology, Warren was a pioneer theoretical and applied military forensic anthropologist. As the longest-serving military forensic anthropologist, he identified deceased American soldiers from World War II, the Korean War and the Vietnam War.

The second contribution by Dallas Browne focuses on William Shack, who conducted fieldwork in Ethiopia. Shack made significant contributions to higher education. He served as a dean at the University of California at Berkeley, established a student exchange program with French universities, helped establish a department of sociology and anthropology at Haile Selassie 1 University in Ethiopia, chaired the International African Institute in London for ten years, and was conferred a Berkeley Citation in 1991 (McBroom, "Anthropologist William Shack, Prominent African Scholar and Graduate Dean Emeritus, Dies at 76").[11]

Cheryl Rodriguez documents the life of Diane K. Lewis, a black woman anthropologist who was undaunted by the explicit racism and sexism of her time. Lewis's experiences with blatant discrimination inspired a fiery intellectual activism. Her most influential work addressed the intersections of race, gender, and class and the impact of AIDS on black communities, and she made significant contributions to humanistic feminism and insider/native perspectives in anthropology.

Elgin Klugh's chapter on Delmos Jones explores Jones's quest for an anthropology of equality and social justice. Jones made significant contributions to discussions on the ethics of anthropological research and to native anthropology. Erica L. Williams's chapter on Niara Sudarkasa outlines her trajectory as a scholar, activist, and higher education administrator. It describes her contributions to scholarship on feminist anthropology, African studies, gender and migration, black women's leadership, and extended families in the African diaspora.[12] Riché J. Daniel Barnes's chapter on Johnnetta B. Cole explores Cole's life as an educator, president of two historically black colleges for women, and the director of the Smithsonian Museum of African Art. Barnes refers to Cole as "the consummate public anthropologist." Cole trained as an Africanist with Melville Herskovits at Northwestern University, and she was involved in efforts to develop some of the first black studies and African diaspora programs in the country.

Deborah Johnson-Simon's chapter takes up John Langston Gwaltney's career as a scholar, teacher, writer, ritual wood carver, and native anthropologist. She explores the complex factors that enabled Gwaltney to overcome the challenges of being blind from birth to conduct fieldwork under the guidance of Margaret Mead. His iconoclastic ethnography of African Americans' social exclusion is featured in his book *Drylongso* (1993). Alisha Winn's chapter details Ira E. Harrison's personal and professional journey as an advocate for civil and human rights, researcher in applied and medical anthropology, and cofounder of the Association of Black Anthropologists. Janis Faye Hutchinson's contribution focuses on the making of an antiracist anthropologist through the life experiences of the eminent race scholar, Audrey Smedley. Rachel Watkins's chapter documents the life of George Clement Bond, whose research in Zambia made significant contributions to both African studies and anthropology.

Bertin Louis's chapter covers Oliver Osborne, a nurse-anthropologist who developed interests in the burgeoning anthropological subdiscipline of medical anthropology. Osborne conducted his dissertation research in Nigeria, focusing on traditional African health care systems and their relationship to Western biomedical systems. More specifically, his study focused on how Yoruba villages served as therapeutic communities for the mentally ill. In her chapter on Anselme Remy, Angela McMillian Howell highlights Remy's identity as a Haitian scholar and his effort to use his research to improve the lives of Haitians. After teaching at Northeastern State University, Clark Atlanta University, Fisk University, and the University of the District of Columbia, he is now a professor of sociology and anthropology at the State University of Haiti Port-au-Prince, Haiti.

Antoinette Jackson's chapter covers Vera Green's life and work, which sits at the intersection of applied anthropology, African diaspora research, and community engagement. This chapter provides an overview of her intellectual contributions to the discipline, as well as a discussion of influences in Green's life that shaped her approach to applied anthropology, including her Quaker roots. Finally, Betty Harris's chapter on Claudia Mitchell-Kernan explores significant aspects of her academic career. Mitchell-Kernan's early sociolinguistic research focused on African Americans in northern California. She taught at Harvard and UCLA and served as director of the Ralph Bunche Center for African American Studies and dean of the UCLA Graduate School. In this capacity, she made important contributions to a national model for achieving diversity in graduate education, despite voter support for an anti–affirmative action proposition.

Conclusion

The intellectual biographies in this book help us to understand where African diaspora anthropology has been and where it is going. These chapters shed light on how this second generation of anthropologists has expanded and built on the contributions of the early pioneers and how they have left their own legacy for generations to come. Their work has had a long-standing impact on the academy. For instance, William Shack was instrumental in creating the Chancellor's Postdoctoral Fellowship Program to support women and people of color within the University of California system. This fellowship has had a significant impact on increasing diversity in the professoriate and has been replicated around the country. This volume also makes a significant contribution to the history of anthropology. It is timely and relevant to our students—particularly students of color, first-generation college students, and those from working-class backgrounds or immigrant families. Students whose identities have been stigmatized or marginalized in society can find sources of inspiration in the stories of the next generation of black anthropologists.

So, what is the state of the field of anthropology now as it relates to black anthropologists? To be sure, African American scholars in anthropology have made great strides, but we still have a long way to go. Diversity and inclusion efforts within the AAA began with twenty-one members who signed an agreement to create the Minority Caucus and led to the creation of the Association of Black Anthropologists that will soon be celebrating its fiftieth anniversary. The ABA now has approximately 313 members, a Facebook page with over 1700 members, and a Twitter handle with over 1380 followers.[13] We have gone from a time when black anthropologists were forgotten and invisible to a time in which there is a Mapping Black Anthropology website that features profiles of current ABA members.[14] Visitors to the website can search by research topic and see black anthropologists' research sites on a map of the world.

Increasing the racial diversity of anthropological practitioners as well as diversifying "the perspectives from which its theory comes" are two goals that the field has set for itself (Brodkin, Morgen, and Hutchison, "Anthropology as White Public Space?," 554). In 1973, the Committee on Minorities and Anthropology (CMA) documented the disparity between how white and black graduate students were trained in the field. While white graduate students were "trained for full professorial careers," students of color were trained "for secondary tracks as applied researchers or as informants and research assistants to white professionals" (Brodkin, Morgen, and Hutchison, "Anthropology as White Public Space?," 551).

Even today, anthropologists of color are often encouraged to leave anthropology and move to ethnic studies (Brodkin, Morgen, and Hutchison, "Anthropology as White Public Space?," 552). Allen and Jobson reflect on this "partial exodus" of black scholars in anthropology, arguing that their "entrée into the professorate has involved 'getting out,' that is, leaving the field of anthropology as a professional site or primary department, to establish homes in interdisciplinary programs and research units" ("The Decolonizing Generation," 137). For example, Allen and Jobson note that only four of twenty anthropology PhD recipients from the African diaspora graduate program in anthropology at UT Austin in the past eighteen years have primary appointments in anthropology departments (137).

Furthermore, there are still practices in anthropology that function as both racial exclusion and "theoretical and topical gate keeping" (Brodkin, Morgen, and Hutchison, "Anthropology as White Public Space?," 552). Before the late 1950s, black anthropology students were discouraged from conducting research in Africa—even Melville Herskovits allegedly thought that black Americans could not be objective in their study of African societies (Bolles, "Seeking the Ancestors," 45). Brodkin, Morgen, and Hutchison discuss the "modest progress" anthropology has made "in racially diversifying its faculties and Ph.D. cohorts since the late 1970s" (554). However, the authors emphasize that while "there is a general perception among anthropologists that the discipline has become more racially diverse since the 1960s," after a sharp rise in the number of faculty of color in the 1980s, these numbers stagnated in the 1990s, and the discipline remains "overwhelmingly white" (548). According to data from the AAA, African Americans made up 3 percent of full-time anthropology faculty between 1988 and 1998 (548).

Nonetheless, we have gone from a time when the work of black anthropologists was marginalized and invisibilized because the African American intellectual tradition was not valued by the academy to a time when *Cultural Anthropology* published a series entitled "#BlackLivesMatter: Anti-Black Racism, Police Violence, and Resistance."[15] As Allen and Jobson astutely note, "the ardent calls of the decolonizing generation and the Association of Black Anthropologists can be ignored only at the peril of the discipline" ("The Decolonizing Generation," 136).

Anthropology now has a vibrant presence on social media, and more public forms of writing like blogs are popular among anthropologists. The AAA also created the Committee on Minority Issues in Anthropology, the Commission on Race and Racism in Anthropology, and the Working Group on Racialized Police Brutality/Extrajudicial Violence to "track the historical and contemporary trajectory of racialized police brutality and extrajudicial violence in the United States, and develop resources to help mitigate its impact."[16] Next generation cohort member Audrey Smedley was integral in the process of drafting the AAA statement on race.[17] Thus, the argument that Bolles makes about the predecessors of black feminist anthropology can also be applied more broadly to the next generation. Bolles asserts that "what is most valuable is that even in the silence to which they were relegated by the discipline, the fact of their presence unlocked the door for subsequent generations of Black women intellectuals, trained as anthropologists and following in the African American vindicationist intellectual tradition, to enter the room and create their own place" ("Seeking the Ancestors," 43). Clearly, the next and current generations of black anthropologists have done just that. Following in the footsteps of the pioneers and the next generation, two black women anthropologists have served as past presidents of the AAA: Yolanda Moses (1995–97) and Leith Mullings (2011–13). At the 2016 AAA meetings in Minneapolis, the ABA hosted panels on the anthropology of white supremacy and on anthropologists of color in diversity leadership roles on campus as well as a late-breaking session called "Toward an Unapologetically Black Anthropology: Reflections on Grief and Rage."[18] It appears that black anthropologists today have boldly embraced the lessons from our predecessors and moved forward to carve out a space for an activist, engaged, "unapologetically black" anthropology.

Acknowledgments from Erica L. Williams

Five years after agreeing to contribute a chapter on Niara Sudarkasa for this volume in 2012, Ira Harrison invited me to serve as a coeditor for this volume to help bring this long-awaited project to completion. I would like to thank Ira and Deborah for giving me this opportunity, and I would also like to acknowledge the tireless efforts of the contributing authors, who have turned their attention back to chapters that they drafted so many years ago in order to respond to my emails and requests. I would also like to thank

Marika Christofides, who has walked us through this process with grace. On a personal note, I must thank my colleagues in the Department of Sociology and Anthropology at Spelman College and my partner, Terence Courtney, for his consistent support and love.

Notes

1. In this volume, we use "African American" and "black" interchangeably, with an awareness that these terms can and should also encompass black anthropologists from other parts of the African diaspora, such as Anselme Remy (from Haiti) and Oliver Osborne (a descendant of immigrants from Barbados).

2. A. Lynn Bolles points out that by 1967, only eight black women held a PhD in anthropology—Irene Diggs, Manet Fowler, Diane Lewis, Audrey Smedley, Vera Green, Johnnetta B. Cole, Claudia Mitchell-Kernan, and Niara Sudarkasa ("Seeking the Ancestors," 31).

3. A 1997 survey of anthropology PhDs states that during the last twenty years of the twentieth century, cultural anthropology accounted for 50 percent of new PhDs awarded in the United States, while 30 percent were in archaeology, 10 percent in biological/physical anthropology, 3 percent in linguistic anthropology, and 7 percent in applied anthropology or other. For the 1994–95 PhD cohort, 0 percent were in archaeology, 74 percent were in sociocultural anthropology, 4 percent were in linguistic anthropology, and 17 percent were in applied anthropology or other. In the 1996–97 PhD cohort, 16 percent were in archaeology, 71 percent were in sociocultural anthropology, 6 percent were in biological/physical anthropology, 0 percent were in linguistic anthropology, and 6 percent were in applied anthropology or other (see Givens, Evans, and Jablonski, "American Anthropological Association Survey of PhDs").

4. "The American Anthropological Association is the world's largest association for professional anthropologists, with more than 10,000 members. Based in Washington, D.C., the Association was founded in 1902 and covers all four main fields of anthropology (cultural anthropology, biological/physical anthropology, archaeology, and linguistic anthropology)" (www.americananthro.org/ConnectWithAAA/Content.aspx?ItemNumber=1665&navItemNumber=586).

5. Brodkin, Morgen, and Hutchinson point out that organizations like ABA have been the home for developing critical scholarship in anthropology, when anthropology departments have been resistant ("Anthropology as White Public Space?," 546).

6. Ira E. Harrison, email communication, May 2017.

7. It is worth noting other actions the AAA was taking around the same time. In 1969, the AAA established the Committee on Minorities and Anthropology (CMA) in an effort to increase the number of students and faculty from racial-minority backgrounds (Brodkin, Morgen, and Hutchison, "Anthropology as White Public Space?," 546).

8. The signatories were Carlos H. Arce, Paul Arellano, Johnnetta Cole, Herbert G. Ellis, Stephen A. Faustina, Miguel Fernandez, Nancie L. Gonzalez, Ira

E. Harrison, Jean F. Hayes, James Hirabayashi, Joyce A. Hobson, Norman Johnson, Delmos Jones, Jose De La Isla, Mr. and Mrs. Anthony Lauria, Rosario M. Levin, Diane Lewis, Claudia Mitchell, Oliver Osborne, Rafael Ramirez, Octavio Ramario, Belvie Rooks, William A. Shack, Joseph, Spielling, Gobi Stromberg, Council Taylor, and Bettylou Valentine (Harrison "The Association of Black Anthropologists," 17).

9. See aba.americananthro.org/category/pioneers.

10. Zora Neale Hurston, Katherine Dunham, Vera Green, and Irene Diggs were all from working-class backgrounds, and they all won scholarships to pursue their undergraduate degrees and were dependent on grants and prizes to make ends meet (Bolles, "Seeking the Ancestors," 36).

11. This is the university's highest honor.

12. McBroom, "Anthropologist William Shack, Prominent African Scholar and Graduate Dean Emeritus, Dies at 76").

13. This number is current as of June 2018, according to Bianca Williams, a member of the executive board of the ABA (email communication).

14. See http://mappingblackanthropology.com.

15. This special issue featured work from Joy James, Bianca Williams, Christen Smith, Joao Vargas, Aimee Meredith Cox, Matt Richardson, Orisanmi Burton, and others.

16. The working group is cochaired by David Simmons (University of South Carolina) and Marla Frederick (Harvard University). Members include Shalini Shankar (Northwestern University), Dana-Ain Davis (CUNY, Queens College), Bianca Williams (University of Colorado, Boulder), Ruth Gomberg-Munoz (Loyola University), Maurice Magana (UCLA), and A. Lynn Bolles (University of Maryland).

17. See www.americananthro.org/ConnectWithAAA/Content.aspx?Item Number=2583.

18. Panelists on the first included Jemima Pierre, Aisha Beliso-DeJesus, and Faye Harrison. Panelists on the second included Yolanda T. Moses, Lee D. Baker, John L. Jackson Jr., Nicole D. Truesdell, and David S. Simmons. Panelists on the third included Savannah Shange, Alix Chapman, Courtney Desiree Morris, Ashante Reese, Christen Smith, Brittany Webb, and Bianca Williams.

Bibliography

Allen, Jafari Sinclaire, and Ryan Cecil Jobson. 2016. "The Decolonizing Generation: (Race and) Theory in Anthropology Since the Eighties." *Current Anthropology* 57.2 (2016): 129–48.

Bolles, A. Lynn. "Seeking the Ancestors: Forging a Black Feminist Tradition in Anthropology." In *Black Feminist Anthropology: Theory, Politics, Praxis, Poetics*, ed. Irma McClaurin, 24–48. New Brunswick, NJ: Rutgers University Press, 2001.

Brodkin, Karen, Sandra Morgen, and Janis Hutchinson. "Anthropology as White Public Space?" *American Anthropologist* 133.4 (2011): 545–56.

Givens, David B., Patsy Evans, and Timothy Jablonski. "American Anthropological Association Survey of PhDs." American Anthropological Association, 1997. www.americananthro.org/LearnAndTeach/ResourceDetail.aspx?ItemNumber=2637

Harrison, Ira E. "The Association of Black Anthropologists: A Brief History." *Anthropology Today* 3.1 (1987): 17–21.

Harrison, Ira. E., and Faye Harrison, eds. *African-American Pioneers in Anthropology.* Urbana: University of Illinois Press, 1999.

Harrison, Faye V., ed. *Decolonizing Anthropology: Moving Further toward an Anthropology for Liberation.* 2nd edition. Arlington, VA: American Anthropological Association, 1997.

McBroom, Patricia. "Anthropologist William Shack, Prominent African Scholar and Graduate Dean Emeritus, Dies at 76." UC Berkeley Campus News Media Relations Press Release, April 5, 2000. www.berkeley.edu/news/media/releases/2000/04/04-05-2000.html.

THE SECOND GENERATION OF
AFRICAN AMERICAN
PIONEERS IN
ANTHROPOLOGY

1

James Lowell Gibbs Jr.

A Life of Educational Achievement and Service

DALLAS L. BROWNE

Family Background and Early Values

James Lowell Gibbs Jr. was born on June 13, 1931, in Syracuse, New York, to Huldah Dabney, a schoolteacher, and James Lowell Gibbs, executive director of the Paul Laurence Dunbar Community Center in Syracuse. Gibbs was a premature baby who had to fight to enter the world and has repeatedly fought and won since then on matters dear to him.

Gibbs's family ancestry can be traced back to 1814 to his paternal great-grandfather, who was born in Florence, South Carolina. His parents grew up in Richmond, Virginia, where they experienced what a full black community was like, with its own institutions and possibilities. Jim's parents made him aware early in life that the working-class community of Ithaca, New York, where he grew up was not the only kind of black community. Jim made summer visits to Richmond, where he witnessed thriving black institutions. His sister, Huldah, remembers traveling by train to Richmond; the passenger cars were integrated until the train reached Washington, DC, she recalls, but from DC to Richmond they had to travel in segregated Jim Crow passenger cars.

Jim and Huldah's parents subscribed to the *Afro-American* and the *Pittsburgh Courier*, both of which were major African American newspapers; by reading them, his family was able to stay abreast of major issues facing black communities nationwide. As a boy he sold both papers to earn spending money. Throughout his life Jim remained deeply connected with the black community wherever he went.

Jim's father attended Auburn High School in Richmond alongside Jim's mother. Both earned high school diplomas; his mother was valedictorian of her class, while his father was an honor student. His father

James Lowell Gibbs Jr.
Courtesy of Stanford University Libraries, Department of Special Collections and University Archives. Stanford News Service / Leo Holub.

was the first in his family to earn a high school diploma, and his family was very proud of this fact, because at that point in history, earning a high school diploma was considered a great achievement in America. It took considerable determination, courage, and effort to get that far then; thus most African Americans who earned diplomas did so despite considerable resistance. During the slavery and post-slavery era, whites saw education and learning among blacks as a threat to their power, because blacks who could read and write had organized slave revolts.

His father was a pillar of the black community since he served as director of the Ithaca Southside Community Center, which was the pride and focal point of the black community. He was accorded more respect than most social workers because he worked closely with white captains of industry, as well as leaders of the African American community, to place black workers in jobs. He was civic minded, and as head of the local chapter of the NAACP, he sought to peacefully advance the concerns of blacks for justice and equality.

Jim's parents would later take college courses, but neither ever earned a college degree; this was not unusual for African Americans of their generation. Even today, it often takes African Americans who are the first in their family to complete a college degree eight or more years to finish a four-year course because they have to work to support themselves, have to perform military duties, or are forced to drop out to support a family. The same issues plague many white students but in lesser numbers. The huge gains in educational achievement in subsequent generations is staggering and demonstrates how far African Americans have come in a few generations, even though there is much further to go to reach parity with whites.

Jim's mother, Huldah Hortense Gibbs, was an elementary schoolteacher before her marriage. After her family moved to Ithaca, she became very active in the community and in her church. She served as the president of Church Women of Ithaca, ran for the city alderman's office but lost, and was appointed by the governor of New York to the board of visitors of the Elmira State Reformatory. She was very active in the Democratic Party and the local chapter of the NAACP. Both of Jim's parents were excellent community service role models, which would shape his later involvement in civil rights and political activism. Jim was proud of both of his parents for being professionals who led their community; it made him feel special. Huldah says that they always felt themselves to be part of the local African American elite and were well aware of the privileges they enjoyed that few other African Americans did.

Early Education and Goals

Jim attended Henry St. John's Elementary School, skipping second grade. He later attended Boynton Junior High School and Ithaca High School, where he excelled as a student.

Jim and his family lived on the third floor of the Southside Community Center. His family often invited HBCU professors to dinner when they came to visit or study at Cornell. Arthur Teele, then the chair of the Political Science Department at Florida Agricultural and Mechanical University impressed Jim greatly. Throughout his life Jim maintained a friendship with Teele's son. His parents also knew several black graduate students at Cornell and often invited them to Sunday dinners. One of these students was Fenton Sands, who earned a BS and PhD and went on to become one of the Tuskegee Airmen during World War II. Sands enjoyed a distinguished career as an agriculturalist. Later in life, Sands, who was teaching at Cuttington College in Liberia, welcomed Gibbs when he arrived there to do fieldwork for his PhD in anthropology. The environment in which Gibbs was raised made it clear to him even as a boy that black people could become professors who could shape and mold future generations of scholars.

Eslanda Robeson's Influence on James Gibbs

Gibbs initially wanted to become a commercial artist or an architect, and his sister told me that he spent a lot of time making papier-mâché dolls for puppet shows that he performed for classmates. All of this changed when he read a book, written by Eslanda Goode Robeson, titled *African Journey* (1945). Eslanda studied anthropology under Bronislaw Malinowski and participated in his famous seminar at the London School of Economics. Among her seminar mates were colonial officers, as well as Allison Davis and Jomo Kenyatta (the first president of an independent Kenya). This book challenged white colonial rule over black Africa and was among the first voices to call for "Africa for the Africans."

Eslanda Robeson and her husband, Paul, initially aspired to a conventional middle-class status. Paul earned a law degree from Columbia University and wanted a career as a lawyer, but someone discovered that he had a great voice, and this took his life in a direction that he never imagined. Eslanda was a chemist by training who studied anthropology to fill her time while Paul traveled internationally. You might say that she backed into anthropology. She found the views of her seminar mates offensive. These former colonial officials voiced negative views of Africans.

When Eslanda would try to stand up for Africans and argue that their minds were not primitive but rather they had been discriminated against and held back, they would say that she was naïve and had no experience among Africans. Eslanda was wealthy and asked Bronislaw Malinowski and Professor Issac Schapera, who held an appointment at Rhodes University in Grahamstown, South Africa, to introduce her to people throughout Africa so that she could see for herself what Africans were like on the continent. (Gibbs would later make use of Schapera's work on Tswana traditional law when he collaborated with Stanford law professors to produce a book on comparative law.) Eslanda sought empirical knowledge of Africa. She traveled to Africa in 1929 but did not find time to publish her findings until 1945 (Ransby, *Eslanda*). This book was an attempt to defend the honor and innate ability of Africans. Unlike many books of its day, it did not characterize Africans as "savages" who were incapable of self-governance. Given that James Gibbs was brought up to see himself as a defender of the black quest for justice and equality, it is easy to understand the strong influence this book may have exerted on him. Perhaps anthropology would reveal the equality of all humans.

Growing up in the college town of Ithaca, New York, Gibbs came to think of professors as VIPs. He asked, "Why become a doctor when you could become a professor?" Cornell professors made up a large part of the local elite, and this made the idea of becoming a professor attractive to him.

Gibbs states that in the 1940s Ithaca had one junior high school and one high school. This meant that students were exposed to people their own age of all socioeconomic backgrounds and races. He had classmates who modeled good student behavior that classmates could emulate. Good students tend to participate in a wide variety of extracurricular activities. College towns value excellent education, and even though Ithaca did not have its first black teacher until long after Jim graduated from high school, he had many teachers who encouraged him. All successful students need a supportive environment to thrive.

Cornell University

Gibbs graduated from Cornell University, where he was elected senior class president. He was the first African American man from Ithaca to earn a degree from Cornell University. His Cornell BA in sociology and anthropology was awarded in 1952. Jim loved Sociology 101 at Cornell because he learned about social stratification, which fascinated him. He enjoyed reading W. Lloyd Warner's books because he could see evidence of stratification all around him. This course explained why "whoever was up was up and whoever was down was down," in Jim's words. It explained why people behaved the way that they did.

Jim secured research opportunities each summer while still an undergraduate. He worked as a research assistant for Robin Williams, John Dean, and Edward Suchman for their book *Strangers Next Door* (1964), which examines the desegregation of American ethnic enclaves. Robert Johnson, the son of Charles Johnson, who was a sociologist and president of Fisk University, was one of the graduate students who worked with Jim on this project and mentored him in research methodology, as well as the ins and outs of academia.

While an undergraduate at Cornell, Jim participated in many extracurricular activities. He joined Watermargin, the first interracial fraternity at a major American college, and he was invited to join Quill and Dagger, an honor society for outstanding students who have good grades and are active in community service. He also worked part time at various jobs on campus to supplement his scholarship.

The Harvard Years

During his first year at Harvard he enrolled in the new multidisciplinary social relations degree program. In 1946 Harvard College decided to create an experiment in social science education known as the Department of Social Relations. It drew faculty from three departments that continued to exist alongside this interdisciplinary department. The Social Relations Department insisted that first-year graduate students take core courses in anthropology, sociology, and psychology so that their training would be cross-disciplinary; after that, students would major in one of these fields, and that department would award their degrees. Thus, Gibbs took core courses in all fields as well as in the Department of Anthropology. Coursework included tutorials and comprehensive examinations.

Gibbs took a class with Ernest Hooton at the Peabody Museum, and he was surprised when, on the first day of class, Hooton announced, "I have not seen *one of you* since Allison Davis took courses with me!" Gibbs never met Allison Davis, but he was aware of him. He feels that he was a beneficiary of Davis's sterling performance as a student and professor and that people like Davis made it easier for him to pursue his dreams by paving the way for him. Harvard's interdisciplinary approach is reflected in the fact that both Gibbs and Davis dabbled in psychology and published in this area, although neither was a psychologist by training. This eclectic approach is also seen in Gibbs's writing on law, although unlike Sally Falk Moore or John Comaroff, he did not hold a degree in law. Again, this reflects Harvard's interdisciplinary approach to anthropology.

Talcott Parsons taught the sociology course. Parson's daughter Ann sat next to Jim in class, and they became friends. Later that year Ann invited Jim home for dinner, where he got to know the great professor better. During that same year Gibbs was informed that he had been awarded a Rotary Fellowship that he could use anywhere in the world to further his studies. Jim consulted with Parsons about universities, and Parsons suggested that Jim consider Cambridge because Parsons had an invitation from Meyers Fortes, who chaired the Anthropology Department at Cambridge. Fortes convinced Gibbs to spend a year at Cambridge so he could take courses from and become familiar with Great Britain's leading Africanist anthropologists.

Under the Cambridge University system students had to enroll in a particular college. Not being familiar with the college system, Gibbs asked Fortes for advice and Fortes recommended Emmanuel College. Among the many distinguished alumni of this college was John Harvard, after whom Harvard University is named. Affiliating himself with this college was an appropriate way to honor John Harvard.

Gibbs enrolled in Emmanuel College but he had to live off campus because Cambridge had few American students in those days and their housing was off campus. Fortes felt bad about this, so he arranged for

Gibbs to live for the year on campus in the Anthropology Department's guest housing for visiting scholars.

At Harvard, Jim was the first black resident tutor at Adams House, and he also served as a teaching fellow in social relations between 1954 and 1956. Jim believes that his Cambridge experience helped him to secure a tutoring position at Harvard because English universities have residential colleges where students work closely with tutors.

One of the students living at Adams House was Paul Riesman, the son of renowned sociologist David Riesman. David Riesman became a mentor to young James Gibbs. Throughout his life Gibbs has enjoyed phenomenal good luck. It seems that he met many influential social scientists early in his education and career who befriended and mentored him.

While taking graduate classes at Harvard he met his wife, Jewelle Taylor, an undergraduate at Radcliffe College, who was the only African American woman in her class. She barely noticed Jim, so he set up a blind date with her and later took a class in the sociology of law with her. They courted for a year and then married in August 1956. She accompanied Jim while he conducted fieldwork among the Kpelle of Liberia and conducted her own studies of Kpelle women while Jim studied Kpelle men and their legal system. Jewelle Taylor Gibbs is a scholar in her own right; she earned a doctorate in psychology and then joined the faculty of the School of Social Welfare at the University of California at Berkeley. She ultimately became the first African American professor to be appointed to an endowed chair in the ten-campus University of California system. She retired from there in 2000 as the Zellerbach Family Fund Professor of Social Policy, Community Change, and Practice Emeritus. They have two sons; their older son, Geoffrey Taylor Gibbs, is a lawyer who lives in Alameda, California, with his Brazilian wife, Cristina, and their two young children. Their younger son, Lowell Dabney Gibbs, is a financial adviser who lives in Sonoma, California.

Gibbs believes that the Cambridge model of residential education made him a most effective tutor at Harvard and in many ways accounts for his success later as dean of undergraduate education at Stanford University. Leading British Africanists, among them Meyer Fortes, Paul Bohannon, and Max Gluckman, contributed chapters to Gibbs's first book, *Peoples of Africa* (1965), which became the textbook of choice for many courses on African cultures at colleges and universities in the United States for years, although it is now out of print. Gibbs was delighted that senior colleagues agreed to contribute original essays to his book. Securing their contributions for his book gave his career a lift.

The University of Minnesota

Gibbs had a very positive academic experience at the University of Minnesota. He found that his colleagues were congenial and that his students were eager to learn, so he thrived as a teacher and mentor. He soon became involved in several university committees and learned that he was only the third African American faculty member on the campus.

During his six years at Minnesota, he won two teaching awards that attest to his skill in the classroom. In 1961 he received the Distinguished Teacher Award from the College of Science, Literature, and Arts, and in 1970 he was recipient of the C. Harris Harbison Prize for Gifted Teaching from the Danforth Foundation.

E. Adamson Hoebel, the chair of the Anthropology Department, put Gibbs in charge of the department's most popular courses on account of his reputation as a master teacher. Gibbs's teaching record at the University of Minnesota and the fact that Gibbs's textbook on African cultures was selling well led to an invitation in 1966 from D. George Spindler to join the faculty of Stanford University as a tenured associate professor of anthropology.

The Gibbs family flourished in Minneapolis with the birth of their two sons in 1961 and 1963 and the purchase of the family's first home near Lake of the Isles. For James Gibbs it was a time of major professional and personal growth and development.

Stanford University

Gibbs returned to Liberia with his wife and two sons for a year in 1965–66 to conduct further research on the Kpelle tribe. This time the family lived in a brick house in the county seat of Gbargna so their sons could be near a public school and a Peace Corps doctor. Gibbs continued his study of the legal system and kinship patterns in the village of Fokwele during the week and joined his family on weekends. His wife was delighted to have a house with electricity, plumbing, and modern conveniences; eight years earlier they had lived in a traditional mud and thatch house in the village. When they left Liberia at the end of August 1966 they returned briefly to Minneapolis to sell their home and say farewell to all their friends and colleagues before heading to Jim's new position at Stanford University.

From 1968 to 1969, Gibbs served as acting director of the undergraduate program in African and Afro-American studies before St. Clair Drake, who had been hired for this position, moved and settled in. When Stanford's provost decided to expand the university's offerings on African and African American studies in 1967, he turned to Jim for advice. Jim told the provost that Drake was looking for an opportunity to leave Chicago and that since he owned a home in Palo Alto, he was seeking to move to the Stanford area. The provost authorized Gibbs to reach out with a job offer, which Drake accepted immediately. Though many universities attempted to lure Drake away from Stanford, his trust in Gibbs reinforced his decision to stay there until he retired. Drake's daughter, Sandra, also taught English there until her retirement.

Gibbs continued his research on the Kpelle people and their legal system. In 1970 he coproduced the documentary film *The Cows of Dolo Ken Paye* with Marvin Silverman of San Francisco State University, for which he received an award from the Council on International Non-Theatrical Events in 1972. The film depicts the twin roles of reconciliation and restitution in settling disputes among the Kpelle.

From 1970 to1976, Gibbs served as dean of undergraduate studies at Stanford, the first African American dean within the university.

Gibbs's Work with Comparative Law

In 1980 Jim was asked to collaborate with three colleagues at the Stanford School of Law to develop a comparative course on law in different cultures (Barton et. al. 1983). Law professors John Barton, John Merryman, and Victor Li thought that traditional courses in comparative law were too narrow in scope because they examined law only from a Western perspective. Most such courses compared the legal systems of Western Europe, Great Britain, and the United States. Adventurous professors would throw in comparisons of the Soviet Union and Eastern European countries. Burton and his colleagues envisioned a course that would examine law in Western Europe, China, and a traditional African culture. The lawyers felt competent to handle the first cultures but wanted an anthropologist to help them with African legal systems. Since Gibbs had conducted firsthand research on African cultures, they saw him as ideal for this task. They asked him to teach African customary law from an anthropological point of view. The countries that they decided to compare were the United States, China, Egypt, and Botswana. Jim proposed Botswana as the case study of a traditional African legal system.

They decided to examine how each culture handled four common problems. First, inheritance: someone with property, who holds an office and has social status dies. Who gets the property, the office, and the social status, and why? Second, a crime such as embezzlement is committed. What process does the society use to identify and deal with a criminal? Third, when a contract is not kept how does society deal with the "breach of contract? Fourth, how does a legal system deal with population control?

Gibbs recommended Botswana even though his prior fieldwork concentrated on the Kpelle of Liberia. Gibbs reasoned that there was much more literature on law in Botswana than in Liberia and that its history of being a former British protectorate and its proximity to South Africa would make it an especially rich source of information with compelling legal examples. In addition, its unique path to independence and subsequent economic development would make it an exciting choice for Stanford law students to study. In 1967 Botswana had declared itself a nonracial society and adopted a multiparty democracy in which more than one political party contested every election. Presenting itself as a frontline challenge to South Africa's apartheid system, which was remarkably undemocratic, unfair, and racist, it became the darling of the international aid community. The development of the diamond mining industry enabled the country to go from being among the ten poorest on earth to one with the fastest growing economy in the world. Transparency International ranked Botswana the least corrupt country in Africa and one of the best managed (Transparency International Corruption Perceptions Index 2016).

In 1981 Gibbs won a grant from the National Endowment for the Humanities to conduct research on the traditional legal system in Botswana. He spent one month in the capital city, Gaborone, researching documents and sitting in on local hearings about legal disputes among the Tswana people. He also interviewed many legal scholars and indigenous magistrates and procured detailed information on the relationship between the formal and informal traditional legal systems. Gibbs was impressed with the economic development in Botswana, the stability of the political system, and the positive spirit of the people. He discovered interesting contrasts between the vibrant cultures of West Africa and the more placid culture in Botswana. This trip provided Gibbs with a comparative perspective on two African countries as well as their differing approaches to traditional legal systems.

In 1983 Gibbs coauthored *Law in Radically Different Cultures*, which was awarded a certificate of merit from the American Society of International Law in 1984. This book was the textbook for a course that the authors cotaught at Stanford Law School. In it, Gibbs talks at length about *kgotla*, or village council meetings, where the bulk of all legal cases are heard in Botswana, and sheds light on the essential legal mechanisms that make the system function. Gibbs discusses the case of Sir Seretse Goitsebang Maphiri Khama, who had assumed the title of *kgosi*, or king, of the Bamangwato people at the age of four when his father died and who in 1956 brought a white wife, Ruth Williams Khama, back with him when he returned to his country from Great Britain after years of study. Tswana laws of succession dictate that a man who would be their next *kgosi* must hold a "kgotla" and seek permission from all of his people before taking a wife. Part of the ruling elite feared the reaction of South African whites to this marriage, so they called a massive kgotla to discuss it. Seretse explained his great plans to build a modern nation, and he immediately opened health clinics and schools to prove his sincerity. He spoke to his people about connecting them via new roads and other improvements, like extending the vote to everyone. He convinced the majority of people to support him and to accept his wife, Ruth, whom he loved fiercely. Even a very personal matter like whom one loves and marries can be put to a vote in Botswana, demonstrating the value that Botswanans place on consensus. Social context affects how humans interpret behavior. This is one reason why we must strive to understand culture in areas where we intend to live, own property, or work.

We should not allow Gibbs's work on Botswana to remain buried in libraries but retrieve it for new generations to learn from. Gibbs's work has ignited an interest in me to learn more about Botswana, and I plan to visit in the future.

Other Accomplishments of James Gibbs

During his sabbatical year in 1983–84, Gibbs was appointed a senior fellow at the W. E. B. Du Bois Institute for Afro-American Research at Harvard University. While there he continued to study Kpelle culture. Subsequently, Gibbs returned to Stanford to serve as chair of the Stanford/Berkeley Joint Center for African Studies from 1985 to 1987. From 1987 to 1990 Gibbs served as the first African American chairman of Stanford's Department of Anthropology. In 1988 Gibbs was named Martin Luther King Jr. Centennial Professor. After his retirement in 1997, Gibbs was named Martin Luther King Jr. Centennial Professor Emeritus.

The list of Gibbs's professional activities and awards is impressive. He has been a board member of the American Anthropological Association, African Studies Association, and the Society for Visual Anthropology. He served on a number of college trustee and professional panels, including Harvard University visiting committees for the Program in General Education and the Department of Anthropology, the National Research Council's Committee on the Status of Black Americans, and advisory boards for Cornell University, Mills College, and the Carnegie Corporation of New York. In addition, he has served as a grant reviewer for the Social Science Research Council.

The James Lowell Gibbs Jr. Award for outstanding service in anthropology is awarded to a graduating senior annually at Stanford by the Department of Anthropology. The university has also established an endowed research fund in Gibbs's name to fund summer research projects for undergraduates who intend to study issues related to Africa or people of the African diaspora.

Social Justice and Human Rights

Gibbs's striving for social justice, instilled in him by his parents, was enhanced through his participation in Watermargin, the interracial fraternity at Cornell. This provided intense experiences with people different from himself and nurtured a desire to become involved in institutional public service. Becoming good friends with a number of sons of Cornell professors furthered this interest.

He has been active in civil and human rights in Minnesota and in the San Francisco Bay area. In addition to serving as a member of both city and state level antidiscrimination commissions and as a board member of the Minneapolis Urban League while on faculty at the University of Minnesota, he also was a member of the advisory board of the NAACP Legal Defense Fund of Northern California and a member of the Joint Center for Political and Economic Studies think tank in Washington, DC.

Gibbs has also contributed to educational institutions and the arts. He served as the first African American on the board of the Fine Arts Museums of San Francisco, a member of the Cornell University Council, advisor to the Stanford Black Student Union, and president of the Fellowship Forum in Palo Alto.

Among his many honors, Gibbs is most proud of the E. Harris Harbison Prize for Gifted Teaching from the Danforth Foundation he was awarded in 1970, his fellowship at the Center for Advanced Study in the Behavioral Sciences at Stanford in 1969–70, his fellowship at the Woodrow Wilson International Center for Scholars at the Smithsonian in 1976–77, his Dinkelspiel Award from Stanford for service to undergraduate education in 1996, and his Lifetime Achievement Award for contributions to the social sciences from the Institute for Research in the Social Sciences at Stanford University in 2011.

Following his retirement in 1997, Gibbs served as a founder and volunteer consultant for the Museum of the African Diaspora in San

Francisco and as an advisory board member for the Smithsonian National Museum of African Art. He was a tutor for three years for students in the Reading Partners program in East Palo Alto, a low-income minority community in the heart of Silicon Valley. He has also served on the board of trustees of Civic Ventures, a nonprofit organization that encourages and supports the utilization of the experience of older adults in public and community service. Gibbs is a member of Sigma Pi Phi fraternity, a organization of African American business and professional men. He is also a member of the Lakeshore Avenue Baptist Church in Oakland, California. To list all of his consulting jobs, visiting professorships, honors, and awards would take up more space than I am allowed. Those interested in knowing more about Gibbs's accomplishments can watch his biographical video on The History Makers website.

James Lowell Gibbs Jr.'s life has been and continues to be remarkably rich and full of achievements. Young African American anthropologists will be fortunate if they can achieve a fraction of what Jim has in his lifetime, and there is still more to come.

Bibliography

Barton, John, James Gibbs, Victor Lii, and John Merryman. *Law in Radically Different Cultures: Casebook on Law in Botswana, Egypt, Peoples Republic of China, and the United States.* St. Paul, MN: West, 1983.

Bohannan, Paul. *Justice and Judgment among the Tiv.* London: Oxford University Press, 1957.

Comaroff, John, and Simon Roberts. *Rules and Processes: The Cultural Logic of Dispute in an African Court.* Chicago: University of Chicago Press, 1981.

Geertz, Clifford. "Local Knowledge: Fact and Law in Comparative Perspective." In *Local Knowledge: Further Essays in Interpretive Anthropology.* New York: Basic Books, 1983.

Gibbs, James L., Jr. "The Kpelle Moot: A Therapeutic Model for the Informal Settlement of Disputes." *Africa* 33.1 (1963): 1–11.

———. "Law and Personality Signposts for a New Direction." In *Law and Society,* ed. Laura Nader, 176–207. Chicago: Aldine, 1969

———. "Marital Instability among the Kpelle." PhD diss., Harvard University, 1960.

———. "Men of the Machete Carve a Modern World." *University of Minnesota Alumni News* 63.6 (1961): 16–21.

———, ed. *Peoples of Africa.* New York: Holt, Rinehart and Winston, 1965.

———. "Poro Values and Courtroom Procedures in Kpelle Kingdom." *Southwestern Journal of Anthropology* 18.4 (1962): 16–21.

Gibbs, Jewelle Taylor. *Destiny's Child: Memoirs of a Preacher's Daughter.* Charleston, SC: Amazon Create Space, 2014.

14 · DALLAS L. BROWNE

———. "Life in a Liberian Village—Comments of an Anthropologist's Wife." *Radcliffe Quarterly* 6.2 (1958): 20–33.

Gluckman, Max. *The Judicial Process among the Barotse of Northern Rhodesia.* Manchester, UK: University of Manchester Press, 1955.

Hoebel, E. Adamson. *The Cheyenne.* Belmont, MA: Wadsworth, 1978.

———. *The Law of Primitive Man.* Cambridge, MA: Harvard University Press, 1954.

Llewellyn, Karl Nickerson, and E. Adamson Hoebel. *The Cheyenne Way: Conflict and Case Law in Primitive Jurisprudence.* Norman: University of Oklahoma Press, 1941.

Malinowski, Bronislaw. *Crime and Punishment in Savage Society.* London: Routledge and Kegan Paul, 1926.

Rakner, Lisa. "Botswana—30 Years of Economic Growth, Democracy and Aid: Is There a Connection?" *CMI Report* 8 (1996).

Ransby, Barbara. *Eslanda: The Large and Unconventional Life of Mrs. Paul Robeson.* New Haven, CT: Yale University Press, 2013.

Robeson, Eslanda Goode. *African Journey.* New York: John Day, 1945.

2

Charles Preston Warren II

Military Forensic Anthropologist, Scholar, and Applied Scientist

ALICE BALDWIN-JONES

Charles Preston Warren II is best described as a pioneer theoretical and applied forensic anthropologist who also made significant contributions to Philippines studies as well as the National Museum of the Philippines. Throughout this chapter, I refer to Warren as a military forensic anthropologist as well as forensic anthropologist. The larger part of his career was spent identifying the bodies of military personnel, which led to the expansion of forensic anthropology.

Charles Preston Warren II
Courtesy of University of Chicago Library

Warren, the longest-serving military forensic anthropologist, identified America's dead from World War II, the Korean War, and the Vietnam War. Because of the classified nature of his work, he could not always publish his research findings, and when the security clearance was lifted, at least one of his works was published by another forensic anthropologist who did not give him credit. However, Warren did present his work at various academic conferences. Additionally, Warren trained individuals working in the identification laboratories and developed new methodologies for identification. These experiences informed his teaching of forensic anthropology to undergraduate and graduate students working in Chicago's criminal justice system and his own work at the national level as a consultant for the Army Memorial Affairs Agency in Washington, DC, and at the local level as a consultant for the offices of the sheriff and medical examiner of Cook County, Illinois, the coroner's office of Will and Kankakee Counties, Illinois, and in Griffith in Lake County, Indiana. In his work in Philippines studies, Warren argued against the prevailing thinking that the Asian black populations in the Philippines (previously known as Negrito groups) were homogeneous. Warren's work also included cultural anthropology, linguistics, archaeology, African folklore, African and Latin American urban studies, pedagogical issues relating to minority students, and administration. Given the breadth of his work, he is best described as an applied anthropologist. Warren was also one of the first African American faculty members at the University of Illinois, Chicago.

Methodology

Data for this chapter was gleaned from Warren's papers located in the special collections of the University of Illinois, a few forensic anthropology textbooks, and obituaries of Wilhelm G. Solheim II, Henry Otley Beyer, and Robert B. Fox, anthropologists and friends of Warren's in Philippine area studies. My research on Warren's family and colleagues did not yield much information, as his wife, Lastinia Martinez, had died, and I was unable to locate his sons, Joseph and Charles III. I have divided this chapter into three parts: Warren's education, distinctions, and awards, his forensic work, and his work in the academy.

Education, Distinctions, and Awards

Charles Preston Warren II was born in Chicago in 1921. He entered the US Army Air Corps (later known as US Air Force) in 1938 and served until 1946. In the US Army Air Corps, Warren served as a sergeant in the Far East. His career as a scholar and his military service became intertwined when he took up ethnographic study in the Philippines and military forensic identification.

Following his military service, Warren went on to earn a BS in zoology from Northwestern University in 1947. He also played football and was the first black quarterback on a Big Ten team. From there, Warren earned a master of arts in anthropology from Indiana University in 1950, studying African folklore. While pursuing his degree, Warren worked on Native American Indians' remains that had been excavated by a local archaeologist. This work, along with military forensic anthropology to which he had been introduced in the Philippines and Japan, occupied his entire career. Forensic anthropology was in its infancy at the time, and so Warren learned on the job. In a letter dated May 14, 1975, to Bela C. Maday at the National Institute of Mental Health, Warren wrote:

> Neither of the degrees is in physical anthropology, but my teaching and my work experience in the Philippines and Japan have given me the background for this position I presently hold. It is not possible to include such training in any anthropological curricula beyond a familiarity with the literature and the prevailing theoretical approaches. Where can one learn how to put plane crash victims back together, assess their physical characteristics, and match these characteristics with the characteristics of individuals believed to be occupants of the plane?

Warren returned to ethnographic research after he earned his MA. He was awarded a Fulbright fellowship to conduct ethnographic research on the island of Palawan in the Philippines from 1950 to 1951. In addition to conducting research, Warren took anthropology courses at the University of the Philippines with Henry Otley Beyer (doyen of Philippine studies and archaeology) and other Filipino scholars. Warren also visited archaeological sites and sought out scholars studying in the area. While in Manila, Warren met Robert Fox, curator of the Philippine National Museum of Manila and a part-time consultant in physical anthropology for the American Graves Registration Service, Quartermaster Corps, and US Army who furthered his education in military forensic anthropology and museum work. When Robert Fox left the Philippines National Museum to study for his doctorate at the University of Chicago, Warren replaced him. Warren made a significant contribution to the museum in Manila by collecting botanical specimens and other material artifacts from around the Philippines. He was hired part time at the American Graves Registration Service located on Fort McKinley, a job that became full time after his performance in identifying the human remains of a plane crash in Northern Luzon.

He remained in this position until 1952, when Fort McKinley was closed, and then he transferred to Japan, where he remained until the

18 · ALICE BALDWIN-JONES

Korean War ended and the laboratory was closed. Warren then returned to the United States to further his studies in cultural anthropology at the University of Illinois, Chicago. There, he earned a second master of arts in anthropology in 1961, and from 1963 to 1964 he pursued a doctorate at the same university, although he never completed the program. Warren was the recipient of a National Science Foundation grant focusing on anthropology and education, although I was unable to uncover much information on the research he carried out using this grant. In 1957, prior to earning the second MA degree, Warren had begun teaching at the university, then known as the University of Illinois Navy Pier Campus, where he would remain until retirement. The Navy Pier was constructed in 1914 and opened to the public in 1916. After World War II, it served as the Chicago branch of the University of Illinois that was eventually renamed the University of Illinois at Chicago and moved to its current location. Because the military sought his expertise during the Vietnam War, Warren took a leave of absence from the university from 1973 to 1975 to work on the remains of American soldiers who died in battle.

From 1958 to 1960, Warren served as a coinvestigator on a US Public Health Service grant studying the morphology of infants' and children's ears as a means of personal identification at Cook County Hospital and University of Illinois, Chicago. In 1975, Warren was awarded the Meritorious Civilian Service Award by the Department of the Army, USA Central Identification Laboratory, Thailand, for extraordinary service in the "upgrading of the skills and the performance levels of the laboratory personnel by providing university-level classroom experiences and on-the-job training" ("Forensic Anthropology in a Military Setting," 177). In addition to his service to the university and the military, Warren was active in the American Anthropological Association. From 1985 to 1986, he served as president of the Central States Anthropological Society, and in 1987, shortly before his death, he was awarded the Distinguished Service Award by the Association of Black Anthropologists. For his twenty-five years of teaching at the University of Illinois, Warren was presented with a certificate at a recognition dinner in 1982. While he was honored and presented with a certificate, his name was not listed in the program along with other faculty, administrators, and staff also being honored for their years of service. On Warren's death in 1987, the University of Illinois established a Warren Memorial Library Fund.

Pioneer Military Forensic Anthropologist

Thomas Dwight (1843–1911) was the father of forensic anthropology, according to T. Dale Stewart, and its formative period was in the mid-nineteenth century. During this period, forensic anthropologists were engaged in medico-legal work; a good overview can be found in Stewart's *Essentials of Forensic Anthropology* (1979). Prior to World War II, there were no standard procedures for the identification of the dead, but that changed once it became a part of the mission and policy of the US government to identify and return home all its war dead. The work in the military laboratories during World War II and the Korean War created a database and methodology for identifying soldiers. The military employed physical anthropologists and anatomists as laboratory personnel to engage in search and recovery, laboratory processing, and case resolution. The information gathered was used along with soldiers' health records that included age, height, dental records, and illness history taken before they were shipped off to war. Many early physical anthropologists seeking to become forensic anthropologists passed through the military laboratories for on-the-job training then into the academy to create laboratories. Military identification was very dirty, to say the least, and did not have the same kind of prestige as working in a forensic laboratory in the academy. Once in the academy, anthropologists distanced themselves from it and excluded those who remained identified with it. Those ostracized also included minority anthropologists like Warren.

The first laboratory established by the US military was the American Graves Registration Service, which was set up during World War I and expanded through the end of it. Eight other laboratories were set up subsequently. In addition to working in the American Graves Registration Office's Central Identification Unit, Warren worked in Manila, Philippines, from 1951 to 1952; in the 8204th Army Unit at Camp Juno in Kokura, Japan, from 1952 to 1955; in the Central Identification Laboratory at Camp Samae San in Sattahip, Thailand, from 1973 to 1975; and in Honolulu, Hawaii, during 1982.

At various times throughout the Korean War and after, Stewart, McKern, Kerley, and Warren worked as physical anthropologists for the army. The most valuable anthropological result of this work was McKern and Stewart's "Skeletal Age Changes in Young American Males." This important work is still a standard and has led to the development of much additional research into skeletal changes associated with age, sex, and race. Following the Korean War, Stewart returned to his post at the Smithsonian and was active in forensic and archaeological research for the rest of his professional career. McKern returned to teaching. Much later, both Kerley and Warren returned to the academy.

Warren, the only African American forensic anthropologist, was excluded from many forensic anthropology textbooks. A cursory glance at forensic anthropology textbooks reveals that Warren is indexed along with T. Dale Stewart, Tom McKern, Clyde Snow, Mildred Trotter, Tadao

Furue (a Japanese anthropologist), Robert Pickering, Ellis Kerley, and Harry Shapiro in some but absent in others. Both Klepinger (*Fundamentals of Forensic Anthropology*) and Ubelaker (introduction to *Forensic Anthropology and Medicine*) list him but do not elaborate on his contributions. To make up for this exclusion, he published independently. A paper originally titled "Forensic Anthropology in a Military Setting" that he presented at the American Association of Physical Anthropologists in April 1980, in Niagara Falls, New York, was published in 1981 under the title of "Government and Industry" in the journal *Human Organization*. He also published a paper on the effects of tropical plant growth as an agent of decomposition titled "Plants as Decompositional Vectors of Skeletal Human Remains."

In addition to his contributions to forensic anthropology being overlooked, Warren's research was sometimes published without his being acknowledged as the author. For example, Warren and the Japanese forensic anthropologist Tadao Furue conducted research at a US Army hospital using the hospital's ultraviolet light as an aid in the separation of comingled remains. The findings were published in 1955 under the title of "Final Report on Ultraviolet Ray Research." In 1958, McKern published an article titled "The Use of Short Wave Ultra-violet Rays for Segregation of Comingled Skeletal Remains." Warren noted that "after comparing parts of his article with parts of our final report, I am confident that McKern had a copy of our report" (1981, 175). This is another example of Warren's contributions to forensic anthropology going unacknowledged.

In the military laboratories, the civilian staff usually consisted of a physical anthropologist along with a chief of laboratory, a supervisory identification specialist, four identification specialists, and clerical and administrative staff. Individuals engaged in the rescue and recovery were not trained in forensics, and sometimes day laborers were hired as needed. In addition to his identification work, Warren developed a training manual and trained the workers at the level he taught in the academy.

Although the expansion of forensic anthropology was a result of the wars, the Association of American Physical Anthropologists, led by some of the very same anthropologists that spent a short time working in the military laboratories alongside Warren, refused membership to him and other "applied" military forensic anthropologists and did not always allow them to present their work at conferences in the early days. This can be attributed to racism and to the sharp divide between anthropologists in the academy and those who only conducted military forensic work. Furue, another minority forensic anthropologist and longtime friend of Warren, was also excluded from AAPA membership. No forensic anthropologist can be compared to Warren in terms of his contribution to the identification of military service personnel. In addition to the difficulty one faced in identifying unknown remains that had been reinterred from mass graves associated with war camps or remains fragmented by war ammunitions or aircraft explosions, there was also the awkwardness of working in the military laboratory as a civilian, and then later the country's displeasure over the Vietnam War.

Warren viewed his forensic work as being separate from his scholarship in the academy, although they informed each other. Perhaps this was due to the fact that he was employed by the military as a civilian physical anthropologist when he was on leave from the academy. Perhaps he also valued the prestige of forensic anthropologists in the academy versus those who worked for the military. In addition, although his knowledge of forensic anthropology was largely developed on the job, he also learned from each case and developed new methodologies that he later taught to those working in the laboratory and in the academy.

During his time at the US Army Central Identification Laboratory in Sattahip, Thailand, toward the end of the Vietnam War, one difficult and public case on which Warren worked was the crash of a U. S. Air Force C-5A plane. The plane was participating in the controversial Operation Baby Lift, whose mission was to airlift over three thousand orphans from Vietnam to the United States, some of whom were children of American personnel and Vietnamese women and some of whom were not really orphans but children whose parents felt they would have a better life in the United States. The plane, which was filled with military personnel, government employees, dependents, foreign nationals, and orphans, crashed on April 4, 1975, during an emergency landing approach to Tan Son Nhut Air Base, Saigon, in a nearby rice paddy. All total, there were 330 individuals on board, of which 226 were infants and children. Seventy-six of the children and fifty-nine others were killed.

The comingled remains from the recovery were brought to the laboratory in several bags at four different times. The first bag arrived shortly after the crash, while the second bag arrived a day later. Six days later, the third bag arrived, and the fourth, twenty days later. Warren's job was to separate and identify the victims. However, the third and fourth bags of remains were in a state of decomposition prior to arriving at the laboratory. The processing and reprocessing took thirty-five days— working nine hours per day and seven days per week—and resulted in only fifty-eight individuals being positively identified. This case was embarrassing for the United States government at a time when the country was against the Vietnam War. The story was published in the *New Yorker* and the *New York Times*, and various other newspapers also

22 · ALICE BALDWIN-JONES

added fuel to the fire. Warren was interviewed by Susan Sheehan, a reporter from the *New Yorker*. Despite the difficulties he faced in the lab, he answered the reporter very diplomatically, being careful not to inflame the issue. Representatives for some of the remaining orphans sued the US government and Lockheed Corporation, the plane manufacturer. The case dragged on until 1981, by which time some of the records had been destroyed; although the shredding was carried out according to standard operating procedures, the US government was nevertheless accused of covering up the incident. For his part, Warren lamented the inability to positively identify all the remains. He argued, to no avail, that training was necessary for all personnel who were engaged with the search and recovery itself.

Another case Warren worked on was the discovery of remains in a box in the laboratory of a soldier that had been declared absent without leave for over ten years. During this period, the soldier's grief-stricken family members could not receive any military benefits. Thanks to Warren, the soldier's remains were positively identified and returned to the family; his honor was restored and the benefits were paid to his family.

Warren also worked with Clyde Snow identifying the victims of convicted murderer John Wayne Gacy. Gacy was Chicago's most horrific serial killer, responsible for the murder of thirty-three boys and young men over a period of six years. Many of the remains were left in the crawl space or basement of Gacy's home and were in various states of decomposition. As of July 2017, remains from this case are still being identified.

Warren also taught forensic anthropology to undergraduate and graduate students. He drew on his military forensic anthropology experiences, as he believed those experiences could help further the field of forensic anthropology in the classroom and as well as the laboratories. A number of Warren's criminal justice graduates students were also employed professionals who came from "the Chicago Police County of Cook Medical Examiner's staff, the Cook County Sheriff's Department, and the Federal Bureau of Investigation" ("Forensic Anthropology and Military Identification in the Pacific Theaters of Operation," 5).

Researcher and Teacher

At the University of Illinois, Warren taught courses on forensic anthropology, linguistics, ethnography of the Philippines, and ethnography of Southeast Asia, as well an introductory cultural anthropology course and a high-level course on problems in Southeast Asia ethnology. In these courses, he drew heavily from his fieldwork in the region. He also drew on the wide range of topics he incorporated into his teaching in his research and wrote about the impact of his teaching on the minority student body in his "Minority Student Response to the Anthropology of Asian Black Populations," which covered his three Asian studies courses on the Philippine Asian black population (Negrito groups), the Malay, and Thai aboriginal black populations.

Warren began at Navy Pier as a research associate and later was promoted to assistant professor in the Anthropology Department. He also taught in the Philippine studies program at the University of Chicago from 1957 to 1964 (Solheim, "Charles Warren Preston," 183). The first research Warren carried out, funded by a Fulbright fellowship, focused on the Batak of Palawan in the Philippines. This research was for his MA thesis at the University of Illinois. It is this research that provided Warren with the opportunity to engage not only ethnography but archaeology, museum collection, and forensic anthropology. One of his articles on the Batak of the Palawan group focused on their agricultural development. Another demonstrated that the black Asian groups in the Philippines were heterogeneous based on their cultural and linguistic variations, as well as geographic locations. In another article, Warren argued that there was variation in the skin color and hair type of some of the groups. His findings went against the prevailing racist typology of the era. Over the years, Warren continued to study the Batak, including their language, interpretations of dreams, and modernization and changes in their culture, and other black Asian groups. A partial list of Warren's publications on the Asian black groups is as follows: "Anthropology in the Philippines: A Report" (1952), "The Bataka of Palawan: A Culture in Transition" (1961), "Palawan" (1975), "Field Vocabulary of the Batak of Palawan (Philippines)" (1975), "Palawan" (1977), "Agricultural Development of the Batak of Palawan, Philippines: A Case Study" (1984), "Black Asians in the Philippines: The 'Negrito Problem' Revisited" (1985), and "Philippine Anthropology at Mid-Century: 1945–1955" (1986).

In 1973 Warren went to Thailand, South Vietnam, and Kampuchea and combined his twenty-one-month work tour for the American government with an in-country study of additional Asian populations, one being the Semang of southern Thailand. Warren also visited Ban Chiang and other prehistoric archaeological sites in the area. This research broadened his knowledge of the groups. Not only did he argue with the scholars, but he also taught his students about his findings.

> During the introductory lectures of the three courses I discuss the geographic distributions of equatorial black populations of the Eastern Hemisphere as they have been reported in mainland South and Southeast Asia, insular South and Southeast Asia, and in the islands of the Western

Pacific, as contrasted with the Asiatic Mongoloid and other populations of these regions. I do this to establish the heterogeneity of physical types in these regions of the world. Contrary to popular belief, I suggest to my students that there may be some rationale for this distribution other than accidental, and I even go so far as to intimate that the black populations of Asia and the Western Pacific may have some real relationship with earlier black populations of Africa. Of course, this kind of thinking is anthropological heresy, for the geneticists and others have "proven" that black populations in Asia and the Western Pacific are unrelated to their African phenotypic counterparts. However, undergraduate students have formulated no opinions about this kind of theoretical construct, so the concepts can at least be presented to them with minimum or no resistance. ("Minority Student Response to the Anthropology of Asian Black Populations," 213, 216, 217)

In "Philippine Anthropology at Mid-Century," Warren, drawing on his research on the Batak of Palawan, argues that the groups were heterogeneous. He was the only anthropologist who had visited all the groups and examined their culture, agricultural production, language, phenotype and hair type. Warren points out that anthropologists continued to reject the heterogeneity of the black Asian groups, classifying them solely based on the color of their skin despite linguistic and cultural differences and differences in stature. Warren also argues that there was no uniformity in phenotypic appearances. Warren notes that the earliest publications based on the classifications grounded in phenotypic appearances were Beyer's *Population of the Philippine Islands in 1916* and Tangco's *The Christian Population of the Philippines*. Subsequent publications such as Krieger's *Peoples of the Philippines* and Tangco's *Ethnographic Map of the Philippines* followed Beyer's lead. These authors all utilized geographic location as a means of classification, separating the northern groups from the southern groups. Even when scholars found linguistic differences, these were ignored, or attempts were made to classify those differences based on geographic locations. In *The Living Races of Man*, Coon produces a map that "locates ten Negrito groups, including the Batak of Palawan, but no Negritos appear on the island of Panay and Negros." Their absence "must have been a surprise" to Timoteo Oracion, who had documented Negritos on Negros in "Notes on the Social Structure and the Social Change of the Negritos on Negros Island," and Rudolf Rahman and Marcellino Maceda, who had explored Negritos on the island of Panay in "Notes on the Negritos of the Northern Negros." Perhaps, Warren concludes, these ethnographers had "good reasons for ignoring the speculations of the physical anthropologists" ("Black Asians in the Philippines," 17). Warren argues that "the 'Negrito Problem'" was "generated by the anthropologists themselves" and that they "managed to lock themselves into a racist methodology of interpreting Philippines populations, beginning with Beyer, and continuing through the years to the present with the same model, even though new findings have put serious stresses on the model" ("Black Asians in the Philippines," 17).

Another study Warren conducted was an examination of the morphology of the ears of human infants for use in identification in forensic anthropology. The research findings demonstrated that the morphology of the ear changed rapidly during a child's development and therefore the ear was of little value as an identification constant.

Conclusion

Warren pursued his education, studying at three different universities, earning two master of arts degrees but never a doctorate, and conducting fieldwork wherever the opportunity presented itself. He combined his ethnographic studies with his employment with the military, as he did not always have outside funding. His body of work is a testament to his brilliance and stands as an important contribution to the discipline.

Warren contributed to forensic anthropology, linguistics, and the anthropology of Southeast Asia through his insistence that there are distinctions between race, culture and language. His work also contributed to the National Museum of Manila, Philippines. I hope that this essay serves to secure him his rightful place in the history of anthropology.

Bibliography

Beyer, H. Otley. "Christian Population of the Philippines in 1942." In *Christian Population of the Philippines*, ed. Marcelo Tangco, 26–28. Quezon City: University of the Philippines, 1951.

———. *Population of the Philippine Islands in 1916*. Manila: Philippine Educational Company, 1917.

Coon, Carleton S. *The Living Races of Man*. New York: Knopf, 1965.

Klepinger, Linda L. *Fundamentals of Forensic Anthropology*. Hoboken, NJ: John Wiley and Sons, 2006.

Krieger, Herbert. *Peoples of the Philippines*. Washington, DC: Smithsonian Institution, 1942.

McKern, Thomas W. "The Use of Short Wave Ultra-violet Rays for Segregation of Commingled Skeletal Remains." Quartermaster Research and Engineering Center. Technical Report EP-98. Nattick, MA: Environmental Protection Research Division, August 1958.

Oracion, Timoteo S. "Notes on the Social Structure and the Social Change of the Negritos on Negros Islands." *Philippine Sociological Review* 11.1–2 (1962): 57–67.

Rahman, Rudolf, and Marcellino Maceda. "Notes on the Negritos of the Northern Negros." *Anthropos* 50 (1955): 810–36.

Solheim, Wilhelm G., II. "Charles Preston Warren, 1921–1987." *Asian Perspectives* 28.2 (1986–87): 183–84.

Tangco, Marcelo, ed. *Christian Population of the Philippines*. Quezon City: University of the Philippines, 1951.

Ubelaker, Douglas H. Introduction to *Forensic Anthropology and Medicine: Complementary Sciences from Recovery to Cause of Death*, ed. Aurore Schmitt, Eugénia Cunha, and João Pinheiro, 3–12. Totowa, NJ: Humana Press, 2006.

Warren, Charles P. "Black Asians in the Philippines: The 'Negrito Problem' Revisited." *Pilipinas* 5 (1984): 53–67.

———. "Forensic Anthropology and Military Identification in the Pacific Theaters of Operation: 1945–1985." Paper presented at the NIH/MBRS Leadership Program, Herbert H. Lehman College of the City of New York, March 3–4, 1987.

———. "Forensic Anthropology in a Military Setting." *Human Organization* 40.2 (1981): 172–80.

———. "Minority Student Response to the Anthropology of Asian Black Populations." *Philippine Quarterly of Culture and Society* 10.4 (1982): 211–24.

———. "Philippine Anthropology at Mid-Century: 1945–1955." *Journal of Northern Luzon* 12.1- 2 (1982): 52–60.

3

William Alfred Shack

An Unacknowledged Giant

DALLAS L. BROWNE

William Alfred Shack's parents instilled within him a burning desire to become somebody others looked up to, admired, and respected. To achieve this goal, he was willing to bear any burden, make any sacrifice, and forego any pleasure. His story is one of perseverance in the face of obstacles, improvisation as a means of achieving his goals, and calm in the face of danger. He produced books and articles that demonstrated his mastery of anthropological facts, ideas, and concepts. He taught classes to prove that he could transmit these skills from one generation to another, and he developed and administered programs that opened anthropology's doors to people who had once been denied access.

The purpose of this chapter is to provide hope to and instill courage in graduate students of anthropology who may be in departments that are not as supportive or encouraging as they may wish. Determination and perseverance are worth more than easy success. Graduate students should realize that they can make a way where there seems to be no way, and they should keep faith that they can realize their own potential even if everyone around them doubts they have potential. Only they know what they are capable of.

William Shack never received a scholarship, worked full time throughout his graduate career, and ultimately was forced to enroll in school abroad to complete his PhD. Despite all of the obstacles he faced, Shack not only finished his degree but also went on to have a distinguished career as an anthropologist and university administrator. His story teaches us to keep the faith in ourselves even when the whole world may doubt us.

According to the 1930 Chicago census, Shack was born in Chicago, Illinois, on April 19, 1923. He lived with his father, William, his mother,

William Alfred Shack
Courtesy of Hailu Shack

Emma, and his younger sister, Wilma, at 322 East 43rd Street on Chicago's vibrant South Side in the middle of the "Black Belt." Shack's father was listed as a city of Chicago "employee" and described as a "laborer." His steady job enabled him to support his wife and children in a respectable, stable, middle-class life. The African American community depended on such breadwinners to also support churches and social clubs and to contribute to political parties. He watched his father carry out his family responsibilities with dignity and pride and without complaint, unlike some other African American men who never secured employment and who abandoned their families, often drowning their failure in alcohol, drugs, promiscuous sex, and gambling.

Because Shack died of cancer in March 2000, and I began research on him in 2014, I thought that I might never discover much about him other than what was documented in his published work. On a hunch I looked in the telephone directory of Oakland, California, for anyone named Shack, and I came across the name Dorothy Nash Shack. I dialed her telephone number and introduced myself. It turned out that she was his wife. I explained that I wanted to write the story of his life and asked her to tell me about him. Initially, she was shy and very guarded and did not say much, but before hanging up she told me that she would be in St. Louis, where I live, in a week or two and suggested that we meet and talk, to which I agreed. On the scheduled day I called and she suggested that we meet at her brother's home in Olivette, Missouri, in an hour. I rushed to the appointment with excitement. Having called his last known employer, the Department of Anthropology at the University of California, Berkeley, and been told that they knew nothing about Shack, I was desperate for information, and his wife of many decades seemed to be my only hope.

I spoke with Dorothy, her brother Homer Nash, and Homer's daughter in Homer's living room. They asked me about my family, my background, my interests, and myself. I felt like I was interviewing for a prestigious job. After grilling me for about one hour, Dorothy began to tell me how she and her husband met and about his friends, like Father Gerard Savard who had invited Shack to teach at a Catholic school in Ethiopia, which is how he became interested in the Gurage. She was very guarded throughout my first interview and seemed reluctant to reveal intimate or personal details to me. I rushed home, typed up my interview notes, and added my own observations about Shack, the Gurage, and their culture, as well as my experiences traveling often into and out of Ethiopia for many years while I lived and worked in Kenya. The next morning, I took my rough notes and shared them with Dorothy and her family in order to build trust. She promised to read them when she returned to Oakland and let me know what she thought of them.

I waited, and one week later she called me to tell me that she had discovered an interview with Shack that she wanted to share with me. I excitedly told her that I looked forward to reading it. What follows is a paraphrased version of transcriptions of those recordings. Shack shares his views on his own life and time (interested readers can find the verbatim interview in my book *People You Should Know* [2014]). These transcripts are based on a video made in the Shacks' Oakland, California, home. The interview was conducted by James E. Bowman on August 19, 1997. At that time Bowman was dean of students in the Division of Biological Sciences at the University of Chicago, professor emeritus in the Department of Pathology and the Department of Medicine, and a member of the Committee on Genetics and the Committee on African and African American Studies. He was conducting interviews with alumni as a part of an African American alumni history project sponsored by the University of Chicago. Associate director Rosita Ragin, associate dean of students in the Division of Biological Sciences, assisted him. I am eternally grateful to Dorothy Shack for sharing her husband's reflections on his life, his time at the University of Chicago, and his time at the University of California, Berkeley.

30 · DALLAS L. BROWNE

Bowman asked Shack to reflect on his family background and to put himself in context:

Though I had lived in California for many years, I always considered myself a Chicagoan. My mother was from Birmingham, Alabama, and my father was from Richland, Georgia. They both fled from the harsh conditions of the rural south and made their way to Chicago when they were young. My father finished the third or fourth grade of school, and that is all. He was determined to accept whatever job he could find that would support his family. He found a job as a laborer with the city of Chicago. It allowed him to pay the rent, to tithe at church, and to become part of the backbone of the black Chicago middle class.

I was born at 43rd and Indiana in the heart of Chicago's so called Black Belt, and the first school I attended was St. Elizabeth's Catholic school on 4th and Indiana. The nuns and priests enforced discipline by spanking naughty children. I learned to follow instructions and to deliver properly completed assignments on time. I graduated from Catholic grammar school and enrolled at Tilden Technical High School. Tilden was an all-male school; I did not like it so I transferred to Inglewood High School at 53rd and Wentworth. I graduated in 1940. In 1941, the Japanese attacked Pearl Harbor and World War II began.

I had trained as a radio operator when I was fifteen and had learned Morse code and related skills. I was eager to lend my skills to the war effort and help America win. I tried to enlist in several services of the armed forces and was not offered a job that matched my background and training in electronics, so I received a deferment and took a civilian job installing radios in bombers at Wright-Patterson air base in Ohio and Kingman in Arizona. I had a bad experience in Arizona and decided against joining the Air Force. I did see an ad for the Coast Guard showing a black sailor firing a .50-caliber machine gun, so I decided that if they let a black sailor do that, then that was the service for me because at least they were not sweeping floors or cleaning toilets for whites. I joined the Coast Guard and worked my way up to petty officer as a radio technician and a radio technician second class. When I left the service in 1946, I did not go back to school immediately. I tried finding a job in Chicago at Motorola, Philco, Majestic and other firms that advertised "GIs are welcome to apply." But everywhere I applied, I was only offered jobs as a janitor, and I was not interested in this type of work. After searching for an electronics job but failing to find one, I decided to use my GI bill benefits to go to school. I loved drawing and art, so I enrolled at the Art Institute of Chicago, where I took drawing and sculpting classes as well as academic courses. I planned to teach art.

3. WILLIAM ALFRED SHACK · 31

At that time, I worked at the main Chicago Post Office delivering special delivery packages and lived in the middle-class Lake Meadows apartments. After graduating from the Art Institute, I took the teachers' examination for art teachers and passed. Thereafter, I taught at Altgeld Gardens on Chicago's far south side. I had attended a summer social studies program at Harvard where I was exposed to anthropology in 1955, and I fell in love with the subject. Upon returning to Chicago, I enrolled in a master's degree program at the University of Chicago. My thesis was titled "Social Change in an Isolated Negro Community."

I wanted to complete a PhD in anthropology from the University of Chicago. I wanted to study a West African culture, but I could not find funding for this. A fellow master's degree student named Father Gerard Sevard was a Jesuit priest, and he staffed schools in Ethiopia. Sevard offered me a two-year teaching job in Ethiopia, which I accepted. I collected data on the Gurage people who spoke a Semitic language, like the ruling Amhara and Tigray. I immediately liked them because they were despised, looked down on, and discriminated against because they did not farm using plows but digging sticks and because they ate the "false banana," or enstete plant, and did any work made available to them. When I wrote the Anthropology Department at the University of Chicago of my intention to return and complete a PhD, they wrote back saying that they did not think that I was up to the standards of their PhD candidates, sorry. I wrote to Fred Eggan about my dilemma, and he advised me to apply to the London School of Economics PhD program, to which he recommended me. I was accepted and was advised to report to the Department of Anthropology at once, which I did. There I was treated as a valued asset and colleague. I spent two years there, from 1957 to 1959. I wrote up the Gurage research as my dissertation for my PhD and subsequently published it as a book with Oxford University Press. The book was an instant success.

While I was away in Africa and London, Hyde Park underwent "Negro removal," and St. Clair Drake published a groundbreaking book on Chicago titled Black Metropolis, *which he intended to use as his dissertation. The Department of Anthropology would not hear of this, so he went to Cardiff, Wales, to write about a community there. Drake and I both felt that the University of Chicago displayed a pattern of racism toward its black students seeking advanced degrees. This held true for Frank Cherry in history and Charles Warren in anthropology in our opinions. Both Drake and I believed that the University of Chicago's Department of Anthropology underestimated us. After all, less well qualified mainstream candidates were given funding and every conceivable advantage, and few of them completed either a master's or PhD degree, nor could they be found in academia, while both Drake and I were well-published respected academics teaching at prestigious universities. History absolved us! We accomplished what we did without support.*

Upon returning to the United States, Fred Eggan approached me about teaching at the University of Chicago in a college and not in the department. I turned the job down because it is easier to earn tenure if your job is rooted in an established department.

In the meantime, the University of California at Berkeley offered me a professorship in the Department of Anthropology, which I accepted. I offered the French government's award of the National Award of Merit as proof that I had made major contributions to anthropology. The only other anthropologist who had ever won this award was Sir E. E. Evans Pritchard.

I believe that pressure exerted by the civil rights movement, known at Berkeley as the "third world strike," contributed to Berkeley's decision to hire me. The same was true at Stanford University, because black students were demanding that universities hire black faculty. Berkeley's chancellor, Albert Bowker from New York, appointed me as faculty assistant for affirmative action with the support of the vice chancellor, Michael Heyman (who later became the secretary of the Smithsonian Museum system). With the firm backing of these men, I was able to create many programs, such as a postdoctoral fellowship program, which I thought was a good idea because few major universities hired new PhDs unless they had postdoctoral experience. This was especially true for minorities and women. That program was a great success, as was my sabbatical leave program for minorities coming up for tenure that gave candidates time to prepare competitive documents. I also started a graduate professional opportunity program for minorities and women. All of these programs were widely copied across the United States. Unfortunately, proposition 209 and other antiminority programs rolled most of this progress back. I always taught graduate courses even when I was not required to, so when these setbacks occurred, I fell back on my graduate teaching and publishing.

In 1957 Shack met the love of his life, Dorothy Nash, a psychologist from Atlanta, Georgia, and they began a three-year courtship. Dorothy states that while he was teaching in Addis Adaba in 1957, he had noted the plight of the Gurage, who lived and worked in Addis Ababa as a vassal underclass, performing the work other Ethiopians found distasteful or dirty. Being African American, he felt a natural sympathy for this oppressed group. The better off Ethiopians referred to them as "coolies" and showed little or no outward sympathy for them. Shack's research revealed why the Amharic and Tigray despised the Gurage, even though all three groups speak Semitic languages. First, the Gurage did not use plows to cultivate their farms but instead used simple digging sticks. Second, they did not cultivate or center their diet on wheat and tef like the northern Semites; rather their survival depended on cultivating the "ensete" or "false banana," which protected them from drought and crop failure but whose taste the Amhara and Tigrey did not like (*The Gurage*; *The Central Ethiopians*).

With enthusiastic recommendations from Fred Eggan, Shack applied to earn a PhD from the London School of Economics. His dedication to hard work and diplomatic demeanor won over the anthropology faculty, who strongly supported him. By 1960 he had completed several study tours of Gurageland and collected an impressive array of data on their culture. He wrote his dissertation and submitted it to his PhD committee and returned to Chicago to teach at Northeastern Teachers College of Chicago, on Chicago's North side, which is now known as Northeastern Illinois University. In the summer of 1960 he married Dorothy in Chicago, and when he returned to London to accept his PhD from the London School of Economics, his wife went with him, confident of his success. This power couple had one son, Hailu, in 1963, who is a professional photographer and lives in Oakland, California, near his mother. With his PhD in hand Shack returned to Chicago and taught for a while. By this time Father Savard was affiliated with a Jesuit school in Addis Ababa, and he offered Shack an opportunity to teach there. Later, Savard arranged for Shack to return with his wife to organize and chair the first Department of Anthropology at the Haile Selassie I University. While teaching in Addis Ababa between 1962 and 1965, Shack conducted a total of twelve months of empirical research among the Gurage. Soon after this, in 1966, he published his first book on Gurage culture.

An offer to join the faculty of the University of California's Department of Anthropology at the rank of full professor followed quickly. He and his wife moved to Berkeley, where he taught anthropology for three years then was called on to help the chancellor's office develop affirmative action programs. He carried out this job with distinction for three years, but then the pull of teaching drew him back in to the classroom. He taught for several more years and then was drafted by the chancellor to serve as graduate dean. Close colleagues at Berkeley included Elizabeth Colson and Burton Benedict, as well as Chancellor Michael Hartman.

Writing about Gurage agriculture, Shack notes that the ensete plant is involved in all aspects of the lives of the people from nutrition to religion to self-government. He argues that they lived within an "ensete culture complex." The ensete he describes had massive stems that grew underground. Gurage wrap corpses with ensete fronds and use it to tie babies' umbilical cords after birth. They wrap trade goods with it and use it to fireproof thatch roofs. They use it as compensation for service rendered. They grow it along with coffee and qat and sell it, and they raise longhorn cattle so that they can use the manure to fertilize this plant. They eat it with cabbage, cheese, butter, and grains. Meat is seldom consumed; normally, they eat it only after a ritual sacrifice. Gurage pound the root of the ensete to derive edible food, which they place in deep pits, where it can be stored for several years if necessary. They maintain large surpluses of ensete as a hedge against famine. They use this buried paste to make porridge and bread. Gurage seldom drink milk; rather they churn it to make butter. They store spiced butter in clay pots that hang from the walls of their homes. They believe that butter is a medicine, and they use it in lotions and poultices. A Gurage proverb states, "A sickness that has the upper hand over butter is destined to death." Certain types of ensete, according to Shack, are also eaten to relieve illness.

The Gurage have an abundance of food and a cultural obligation to share it freely, but they may hoard extra food and eat it secretly to avoid sharing, which causes anxiety. The Gurage see gluttony and overeating as coarse and vulgar. Guests should never eat all of the food a Gurage offers them. Shack tells his readers that the Gurage love to eat "kocho," which is made by shaping the ensete paste into a thick circle, wrapping it in a thin layer of leaves, and baking it in pits over coals.

Shack's research revealed spirit possession among the Gurage. Some spirits possess men, others possess women, and other still can possess either men or women. Affected individuals lose their appetite, experience nausea, stomach pains, and in severe cases paralysis of their extremities. "Sagwara," or traditional healers, are called to treat victims. They use divination and call out many names to determine which spirit is inhabiting the victim. Such cures are temporary and often need to be repeated. The traditional healer prepares a nice dish of ensete for the victim, with butter and peppers. During the ritual, a blanket covers the victim's head, and he is urged to eat while the onlookers chant ritual verses. The ritual ends when the possessing spirit announces that its hunger is satisfied. Shack discovered that most men who were possessed were poor. Due to ritual food distribution and consumption, they felt they seldom got enough to eat. This ritual allowed them to become the center of social attention and to gain prestige while eating to their heart's content in public without shame or guilt. Shack's descriptions of Gurage rituals and culture are truly a treasure trove of skilled observation and deft analysis. I offer these short descriptions of his research results to provide a glimpse of this man's brilliance.

Shack began studying urbanization, kinship, religion, and political organization of the Gurage, whose culture is centered in southwestern Ethiopia about 125 miles south of Addis Ababa. Gurageland is bounded by the Awash River in the north, which is only four inches deep and twenty feet across during the drought season but is sixty feet deep and several miles across during the rainy season, effectively isolating Gurageland from the rest of the world. The Gobe River forms its western border, and Lake Zway is on its eastern border. Shack wrote that there are few or no cities within their home territory, but one-third of all Gurage migrate to and live in cities like Addis Ababa. About one million live in cities, while another two million farm and live off of the land. Their language is not written, so when they attend school most study the Amharic language or English. Shack claims that the Gurage love to trade and do business, which the Amharic elite feel is vulgar and beneath them. Gurage whom I met in Addis Ababa and Dire Dawa while I was conducting research on the Amhara told me that many started making money shining shoes or recycling bottles and cans. From such humble beginnings a few became big businessmen and are proud to be self-made men. Shack writes that many crafts people are Gurage. There was a gold merchant who made jewelry for the emperor long ago. He lamented the gradual loss of Gurage culture and showed me a copy of Shack's book on his culture, which modern Gurage businesspeople use to enlighten their children about their own culture, as many of these children have been assimilated into either Oromo or Amhara culture.

Shack notes that when Menelik II invaded the Gurage, they opposed him fiercely because he tried to convert the Gurage Muslims to Christianity. At the time the Gurage were 51 percent Muslim, 41 percent Ethiopian Orthodox Christian, 6 percent Protestant, and 1 percent Catholic. However, the Gurage liked conquest and plunder, so "Fitwarfi" Habte Giyorgis rose to the position of minister of war for Menelik II and also served as war minister for Haile Selassie, which brought fame and fortune to the Gurage. He tells us "Abba" Francoise Markos ascended the ranks within the Catholic Church as a priest, social worker, and famous Gurage educator, and that Mahmoud Ahmed became a famous and beloved Gurage singer and musician, as Gurage music is energetic and lively and thus is played in many bars and restaurants all over Ethiopia.

Conducting research on the Gurage converted Shack into an Africanist, and he decided to complete his PhD at the London School of Economics. Shack wrote the first ethnographic monograph about this interesting group of Ethiopians. At the London School of Economics, he became steeped in structural functionalism, since Bronislaw Malinowski

36 · DALLAS L. BROWNE

and his students dominated the department, and they were the leading proponents of this theoretical approach within anthropology.

Throughout his career, Shack maintained the rigorous standards of research and descriptions of cultures that he learned from Lucy Mair and Isaac Shapera at the London School of Economics and Fred Eggan and his professors at the University of Chicago. Shack returned to the London School of Economics as a visiting professor of anthropology in 1974–75. He considered it his intellectual home.

A fuller assessment of Shack's contributions to anthropology would require at least two biographical books, and even two books could not cover everything. He was a giant. Now we know part of his inspiring story; another generation will have to finish this tale of accomplishment.

Bibliography

Browne, Dallas. *People You Should Know: Biographies of William Shack and James Gibbs*. Amazon.com. 2014.

Dyja, Thomas. *The Third Coast: When Chicago Built the American Dream*. New York: Penguin, 2013.

Feinberg, Richard, and Karen Ann Watson-Greeo, eds. *Leadership and Change in the Western Pacific: Essays Presented to Sir Raymond Firth on the Occasion of His Ninetieth Birthday*. London: Athlone Press, 1996.

Gabreyesus, Hailemaryam. *The Gurage and Their Culture*. New York: Vintage, 1991.

Kingsley, G. Thomas, and Margery Austin Turner, eds. *Housing Markets and Residential Mobility*. Washington, DC: Urban Institute Press, 1993.

Shack, Dorothy. "Nutritional Processes and Personality Development among the Gurage of Ethiopia." In *Food and Culture: A Reader*, ed. Carole Counihan and Penny van Estrerik, 118–23. New York: Routledge, 1997.

Shack, William A. *The Central Ethiopians: Amhara, Tigrina and Related Peoples*. London: International African Institute, 1974.

———. *The Gurage: A People of the Ensete Culture*. London: Oxford University Press, 1966.

———. *Harlem in Montmartre: A Paris Jazz Story Between the Great Wars*. Berkeley: University of California Press, 2001.

———. *The Kula: A Bronislaw Malinowski Centennial Exhibition*. Berkeley: University of California Press, 1985.

Shack, William A., and Percy S. Cohen. *Politics In Leadership: A Comparative Perspective*. London: Oxford University Press, 1979.

Shack, William A., and Elliott P. Skinner, eds. *Strangers in African Societies*. Berkeley: University of California Press, 1979.

Wilkerson, Isabel. *The Warmth of Other Suns: The Epic Story of America's Great Migration*. New York: Random House, 2010.

4

Diane K. Lewis and the Transformation of Anthropology

An Ideology of Radical Change

CHERYL R. RODRIGUEZ

In his 1976 article "Anthropology: For Whom and What?," Anselme Remy briefly refers to Diane Lewis, Leith Mullings, Johnnetta Cole, and William Willis as progressive Afro-American anthropologists who were "assuming their responsibility to the colonized peoples" (15). Based on a talk he had presented to the Anthropology Club at Howard University in 1975, Remy's essay critiques anthropology's collusion with colonialist and imperialist ventures and argues that numerous anthropologists received and accepted funding from individuals, organizations, and corporations that benefited from colonial or imperialist policies. Inspired by the revolutionary social movements of the 1960s and 1970s, Remy contends that black anthropologists and a "small number of Euro-American anthropologists" (15) were "aware of the need for anthropology to divorce itself from its imperialistic roots" (15). He concludes by encouraging progressive anthropologists to study both imperialist penetration of marginalized peoples and imperialist responses to liberation struggles.

Remy's reference to Diane Lewis as a progressive anthropologist could have been informed by the short but powerful record of publications she had generated by 1976, in which she addressed a series of critical social, political, intellectual, and methodological issues. Her passionate, perceptive writings analyzed such diverse subjects as the paradoxical relationship of anthropologists to colonialism ("Anthropology and Colonialism"), the impact of culture, class, and racism on sex role socialization in black families ("The Black Family"), and the relevance of multiculturalism to addressing minorities' educational problems ("The Multi-Cultural Education Model and Minorities"). Lewis had also been

Diane K. Lewis
Courtesy of Christian Havens and Raven Chaney

an active member of the American Anthropological Association's Committee on Minorities, which published a report on the personal and professional experiences of minority anthropologists in 1973 (Hsu et al., *The Minority Experience in Anthropology*). Hence, there was much evidence that Lewis was aware of the need for transformation in anthropology and that she was using her knowledge of anthropology's history to influence theoretical and methodological changes in the discipline. Yet after retiring from an accomplished and stimulating career as a teacher, intellectual, scholar, and applied anthropologist, she commented that in retrospect, she did not think of herself as "progressive." Rather, her teaching and writing were responses to the tumultuous events of the late 1960s at San Francisco State College, where black students spoke truth to power through demonstrations and protests. Shortly after earning her doctorate at Cornell University, Lewis arrived at the University of California as an experienced Southeast Asianist who had conducted a year of fieldwork in Malaysia after extensive training in Cornell's Southeast Asia program. She taught courses in her area of expertise but also took seriously the challenges being mounted by students who were demanding social responsibility, relevancy, and truth from institutions of higher learning. Lewis recalled that "one day a group of black student activists came to my class, overturning desks and chairs and demanding to know the relevance of my course on 'Peoples and Cultures of Malaysia' to their lives and their struggle. They were demanding a college curriculum that included their history and that mirrored their reality. They wanted to know how my discipline and my courses could help them in their struggle for self-awareness and equality. Their discontent resonated with me. As an undergraduate at UCLA in the 1950s I had experienced a similar frustration and joined other black students in picketing the history department to protest what we considered a one-sided and biased representation of American history. The black students' demand for change led me to reexamine my discipline and helped me to crystallize my growing disillusionment with traditional anthropology. Considerable soul searching ensued about what I wanted to do in my personal life and as a teacher and researcher."[1] She would devote her entire career to examining issues that affected black people in America.

Lewis was a courageous, self-determined intellectual activist. She studied anthropology at predominantly white institutions during the years when apartheid policies and practices were firmly in place in the United States. Racial and sexual discrimination were engrained in the American psyche, including the worldviews of social scientists and other scholars. Institutions of higher learning—some of which had been built by slave labor—remained inaccessible to African Americans. Yet she became an anthropologist despite the barriers erected by both academia and the discipline of anthropology. Moreover, she had the courage to critique the discipline even as she worked to influence, change, and transform the perspectives and methodologies of its scholars and practitioners. Through an examination of some of her most important publications during the 1970s and 1980s, this chapter considers Lewis's role in addressing racism and colonialism in anthropology as well as her unacknowledged role in creating a foundation for black feminist anthropology.

A Black Woman Negotiating White Anthropology

Because African Americans were prevented from acquiring basic literacy and educational skills for centuries and because institutions of higher learning upheld discriminatory practices that prohibited black men and women from attaining college degrees, it has been crucial to document and explore African Americans' extraordinary efforts to become formally educated citizens. The work of an interdisciplinary body of feminist scholars has been invaluable in identifying black women's quests for learning and the intellectual traditions black women have created.[2] This interdisciplinary body of scholarship has also been important in revealing how

40 · CHERYL R. RODRIGUEZ

black women have been affected by their experiences in academia (as students and as scholars), how they have sought to change the politics of the academic landscape, and the multiple implications of their academic experiences for the larger black community.[3] Detailed historical, biographical, and ethnographic accounts of black women as students, faculty, and administrators in higher education reveal an intellectual tradition that disrupts long-held notions about black women's capabilities as learners, knowers, creators of knowledge, and academic leaders. Historian Stephanie Evans argues in *Black Women in the Ivory Tower* that "black women's educational history complicates ideas of what an academic should do or be" (2). This suggests that black women scholars have brought skills to the academic environment that may be different from but no less valuable than those of white men, black men, and white women.

In 1989, anthropologist Yolanda Moses published a report on the experiences of black women students, faculty, and administrators in institutions of higher learning entitled *Black Women in Academe: Issues and Strategies* in which she enumerated the "subtle and not so subtle ways in which race and gender stereotypes can combine to create double obstacles for black women" (1). One of Moses's conclusions was that black women experience isolation and invisibility as college students in predominantly white colleges and universities. This report was written forty years after Lewis matriculated at a historically white university. Lewis's experiences mirror those documented in Moses's report. As an undergraduate at UCLA in 1949, she found that she was often the only black student in her classes. "Nevertheless, I had a strong social support system because I lived at Stevens House, an ecumenical and multiracial undergraduate girls' co-op located a few blocks from campus."[4]

Black women's unique experiences in the discipline of anthropology beg the question of why, if given the opportunity to study in an institution of higher learning (and earn a terminal degree), a black woman would choose to study anthropology. This is a particularly compelling question when exploring the academic and professional lives of those few black women who became anthropologists in the decades of the 1940s through the 1960s. According to black feminist anthropologist A. Lynn Bolles, there were only eight women in that group by 1967 ("Seeking the Ancestors," 31).[5] Undaunted by rigid social barriers, these women matriculated at predominantly white institutions of higher learning and pursued their intellectual goals. They stared down racist and sexist cynicism about their intellectual capabilities and conducted fieldwork in places around the globe. Bolles discusses the discriminatory and exclusionary practices that were common and acceptable in the academy during the early to mid-twentieth century. Notions about black intellectual inferiority were embedded in anthropological thought as well. "Anthropology itself, although a liberal discipline, was not ready for 'the natives' to study themselves or anyone else" ("Seeking the Ancestors," 31). Nevertheless, Bolles and others suggest that despite its racist and colonialist roots, anthropology could provide answers and solutions to social inequality. St. Clair Drake, for example, disclosed that he and a few others chose careers in anthropology because "we believed the discipline had relevance to the liberation of black people from the devastating consequences of over four centuries of white racism" ("Reflections on Anthropology and the Black Experience," 86). Indeed, it was Lewis's experiences with social inequality and blatant discrimination as an undergraduate that led her to the study of anthropology. When she graduated from high school, Lewis had planned to major in Spanish. She had been inspired by the career of UN diplomat and Nobel Peace laureate Ralph Bunche, and her dream was to become a Spanish translator and work for the United Nations.[6] Consequently, she declared herself a Spanish major when she arrived at UCLA in 1949. Having studied Spanish for six years by the time she was a college freshman, Lewis was confident in her ability to speak the language. Yet she faced a challenge that no white student of her time would encounter. "At UCLA, freshman Spanish majors had to take Spanish 3, the gateway course to all upper-division Spanish. It was taught by a southern white woman. The first day of class she took me aside and informed me that Negroes could not learn foreign languages and therefore no matter what I did in class I would not receive above a C. Discouraged, I decided to change my major. By chance, I stumbled into a class in physical anthropology taught by Professor Joseph Birdsell. His lecture was on the anthropological evidence for 'equality of the races.' After learning more about the discipline, I chose anthropology as my new major."[7]

Lewis remained at UCLA to pursue a master's degree in anthropology. "Graduate school seminars brought me into close contact with anthropology faculty. This was not an altogether positive experience. In fact, my interactions with two members of the department convinced me I needed to leave UCLA if I ever hoped to earn my doctorate. One well-known white scholar of anthropology gave the keynote address at the Phi Beta Kappa banquet honoring new inductees in 1952. His presentation included a disparaging joke about his 'Negro washerwoman in Texas.' When I confronted him privately, he claimed the joke was harmless and that he harbored no ill will toward Negroes. This same professor called me to his office after I completed the MA degree. He wanted me to know that in his opinion I had too many strikes against me to earn a PhD and become a professional anthropologist. Those 'strikes' included being a Negro and a woman."

The other disturbing encounter was with a white faculty member who took a small group of first-year graduate students on a short field study to a Native American reservation. He had established a cordial relationship with one of the families on the reservation. The students were served a traditional meal prepared by members of that family. "Later that evening, back at our camp site, and while discussing the day's events, the advisor made what I considered a prejudiced observation about Native Americans. I verbally objected to his remark in front of the other students and this angered him. He warned me that I had better watch myself. If I wasn't careful and didn't change my attitude I could be kicked out of the program!" Although her academic record in the UCLA graduate program was excellent, Lewis decided that the odds for her ultimate success were not good, and she decided to leave.[8]

Lewis left California for New York, where she began a doctoral program at Cornell. Cornell appealed to her because it offered courses in applied anthropology and had two highly regarded area programs in Southeast Asia and India. "When I got to Cornell I discovered that the Southeast Asia program not only had an exciting multidisciplinary faculty but also a large number of students from every country in Southeast Asia. The courses were innovative and helped expand my understanding of cultural processes and cultural change. Most importantly, I was able to interact daily with representatives of the people I was learning about. The faculties in the Southeast Asia program and the Anthropology Department, unlike UCLA at the time, were very supportive of their graduate students. They treated not only their students with respect but also the people they collaborated with and studied in the field."

Lewis completed the anthropological rite of passage by conducting fieldwork from 1957 to 1958 in Inas, a small Malaysian village. Supported by a Ford Foundation fellowship and a Cornell Southeast Asia fellowship, she conducted interviews with several male leaders, from whom she learned about the origins, traditional practices, social organization, and political structures of Inas. She used this local knowledge to construct a history of a village that had no written documentation. Upon returning to the United States she published an article, "Inas: A Study of Local History," based on her fieldwork. In 1962, she completed her PhD at Cornell and returned to California, where her education in anthropology had begun. She was a lecturer at UC Santa Barbara and UC Riverside for a year and in 1963 assumed a permanent position at San Francisco State College, the site of the first black studies department in the United States.

Lewis notes that the blatant racism and sexism she faced as a student was not unusual for black women seeking higher education in the 1950s.

Reflecting on a long and successful career in academia, she concludes that "anthropology was a stepping stone that helped me to do satisfying research and teaching in the end, and I am grateful for the opportunities it provided, even while I am critical of its history and of some of its practitioners."[9]

Beyond Examination to an Active Commitment to Change: A Challenge to Anthropology

Lewis's first publication in an influential American journal of anthropology was a brief but bold commentary responding to an excerpt from Charles Valentine's book *Black Studies and Anthropology: Scholarly and Political Interests in Afro-American Culture* that was published in *Human Organization* in 1972. Lewis was among six scholars invited to comment on the article, entitled "Racism and Recent Anthropological Studies of U.S. Blacks." In this provocative essay, Valentine examines the influence of institutionalized racism on social science research, critiques anthropological studies of black life in the United States, and supports the development of black studies by black scholars.[10] Valentine argues that in order for white researchers to free themselves of "ethnic biases" they should "recognize, renounce and repudiate their own present culture as racist through and through in its systemic exploitiveness and oppression" (96). He further asserts that American anthropologists working outside of the United States feel very little connection to or responsibility for colonization and the oppression of people they study in other countries. These anthropologists simply study village or rural life "as though it were isolated from the rest of the world" (96). Valentine makes the case that it is more difficult for white scholars to renounce racial discrimination in the United States, since a realistic assessment of the scholar's social and economic position "would require admitting that the very institutions, professions, and systems of knowledge which are the basis for his career . . . exist in part through the exploitation of Afro-Americans" (96). Valentine's most severe criticism of anthropological studies of US blacks is that they all promote the simplistic idea that troubled race relations are just a matter of misinformation and a lack of understanding about group differences between blacks and whites. He is particularly cynical about social science knowledge production, which he views as grounded in race and class privilege (97). In her powerful response to Valentine's article, Lewis supports his assertions and encourages him to push his ideas even further. Arguing that most anthropologists had been reluctant to look at the "structure of oppression" when studying nonwhite people, Lewis makes three critical points. First, she contends that white anthropologists cannot see the world from the perspective of poor black people and may never be able to do so. Second, she questions the ability of white researchers to "free themselves of ethnic biases." Finally, she reiterates the idea that black scholars must not only conduct research in black communities but also "move beyond examination to active commitment to change" ("Comment," 345–46).

Lewis expands on these thoughts in "Anthropology and Colonialism," which was published in 1973. This article is a brilliantly conceptualized and meticulously researched analysis of the historical relationship between anthropologists and the nonwhite people they study. Lewis ponders the impact of this relationship on the discipline and questions the relevance and usefulness of anthropology to historically oppressed and dominated peoples. A call for change or transformation of the discipline is a recurring theme in her analysis. Lewis begins by identifying a "crisis" in anthropology characterized by a very clear estrangement between anthropologists and their nonwhite subjects. The disillusionment both within and outside of the discipline results from anthropologists' failure "to come to terms with and accept responsibility for the political implications of their work" (581).

Lewis first examines the colonial context of fieldwork from a historic perspective. She argues that the role of the detached outsider was one that the anthropologist consciously assumed in the name of science. The outsider could also assume the role of an applied anthropologist, who served as a liaison between the dominant European group and the nonwhite subject group. However, all roles chosen by anthropologists were significantly affected by their membership in the dominant group. Hence, anthropologists were no different from any other Europeans in a colony—they all "occupied a position of economic, political, and psychological superiority vis-à-vis the subject people" (582). Lewis concedes that while most anthropologists may have been appalled by colonialism, they found it almost impossible to work outside of the colonial system because it is difficult to reform a system from which one derives definite benefits.

Lewis then considers the ideological bases of both colonialism and racism, as well as anthropologists' relationships to these ideologies. First, anthropologists' recording of *difference* between Western and non-Western cultures invariably acquires a racist connotation in the context of colonialism. Hence, this documentation of difference is interpreted as evidence of the need for continued subjugation of the groups studied by anthropologists. Second, anthropologists benefit personally and professionally from the exploitation of these differences. Just as colonial powers assumed the right to exploit human and natural resources of non-Western people, anthropologists have assumed they have the right to unlimited access to different cultural beliefs and practices. Third, once difference is defined, described, and documented by the anthropologist, this becomes the definitive word about that culture. Hence, Lewis contends that the anthropologist's reification of culture parallels the racist's use of biological determinism "to explain social and historical differences" (584).

Lewis concludes that the social sciences are in need of radical transformation. She not only challenges the notion of objectivity but also asserts that the assumption of objectivity reinforces anthropological and colonial privilege. The idea of a detached, objective, outsider blinds both the colonizer and the anthropologist to "the validity of other than a single view of reality" (585). Lewis suggests that objective knowledge be replaced with "perspectivistic knowledge," which is multidimensional and "views reality from the particular existential position occupied by the observer" (586). This means that the possible ways of understanding life in any cultural context are not just multiple but infinite. More importantly, perspectivistic knowledge includes views of both outsider anthropologists and insider anthropologists. Lewis concludes that if anthropology is to adjust and adapt to a changing world, "it will be necessary to approach the study of all men through a multiplicity of perspectives. . . . The views of both insider and outsider must be accepted as legitimate attempts to understand the nature of culture" (590). Citing the scholarship of numerous influential anthropologists, Lewis wrote this article as a detached observer, using the pronoun "he" in reference to the ubiquitous white male anthropologist. Although she did not refer to her own research experiences, Lewis had conducted fieldwork in Malaysia in the late 1950s. In the mid-1960s, she turned her attention to African American life in San Francisco. Hence, as an anthropologist, she had experienced both insider and outsider status. As her career progressed, she understood that she could play an important role in transforming anthropology by engaging with black communities on some of the most critical issues of the day. Some of these issues centered directly on black women's lives.

A Foundation for Black Feminist Anthropology

Published at the dawn of the contemporary black feminist movement in 1977, Lewis's article "A Response to Inequality: Black Women, Racism and Sexism" analyzes black women's relationship to "women's liberation," which—before the 1970s—was viewed primarily as a movement created by white, middle-class women to address their personal and political concerns. Decidedly feminist in its goals and conclusions, "A Response to Inequality" was among the first publications in the social sciences to declare, discuss, and describe black women's feminist consciousness. In the early 1970s, publications on the intersection of racism and sexism in black women's lives were generally limited to brief newspaper or magazine articles.[11] Exceptions include Toni Cade Bambara's anthology *The Black Woman* (1970) and Shirley Chisholm's unabashedly black feminist autobiography *Unbought and Unbossed* (1970). These publications contributed to the popular literature on black women and feminism, but Lewis's work broke new ground in social science scholarship. Lewis begins by noting the emergence of several organizations formed by black women with the specific aim of combatting sexism and racism. For Lewis, these organizations and their rising memberships were evidence of black women's increasing interest in feminist issues. In fact, she argues that the severe poverty many black women live in makes feminist-identified issues such as childcare and health care of greater concern to black women than white women (340). In order to explain black women's "initial rejection and then more favorable reaction" to feminism (340), Lewis proposes a model of inequality that problematizes theories regarding universal female subordination developed by white feminist anthropologists. Lewis cites Michelle Rosaldo's theory that women were subordinate to men because men participated in the public sphere while women were largely consigned to the domestic sphere. She questions the validity of Rosaldo's theory in a society in which black men and black women are racially oppressed. In the United States, black men and black women were rendered powerless by centuries of slavery, racial discrimination, and segregation. Further, Lewis argues that rape and the sexual exploitation of black women intensified black men's powerlessness. Because of this history of racial oppression, the public-private dichotomy cannot fully explain the differential participation of black women and men in the public sphere. Certainly for black people, differential participation in the public sphere is an indication of a society grounded in structural inequality, but Lewis contends that this is not a useful explanation. However, Lewis argues that even though they have primarily fought against racism, black women are members of two subordinate groups and are in structural opposition to a dominant racial group as well as a dominant sexual group.

In the final section of "Response to Inequality," Lewis argues that while it was critical to identify racism as a historic and pervasively oppressive force affecting an international community of black people, black women increasingly began to note the complex ways in which their lives were affected by sexism as well as racism. Black women witnessed male domination within the civil rights and black power movements. Structural changes influenced by these movements privileged black men, giving them more educational and employment opportunities and enabling them to participate more in the political process.

Lewis uses census data to show very dramatic shifts in access to opportunities for black men in the immediate post–civil rights era. In the mid-1960s, for example, more black women than black men had earned college degrees (6.1 and 5.2 percent, respectively). However, by 1974 "8.8 percent of the men and 7.6 percent of the women had achieved that level of education" (350). Lewis cites data that illuminates the increasing opportunities for black men in graduate and professional schools, increasing access to better jobs and higher pay for black men, and an increasing presence of black men as faculty in institutions of higher learning. Lewis concludes that "if, as an aftermath of the 1960s, a number of black men were recruited into higher-paying, more authoritative, and prestigious positions, black women generally moved into the lower-status and lower-paying jobs traditionally reserved for women in the dominant society" (357). Ultimately, Lewis asserts that social conditions in the immediate post–civil rights era compelled black women to think about sexual discrimination while also continuing their struggles against racism.

"A Response to Inequality" was one of the first scholarly articles in the early post–civil rights period to examine black women's awareness of what Deborah King would later name "multiple jeopardy." It speaks to the reality of sexism in black women's lives and documents their resistance and agency, which they demonstrated through the creation of black feminist organizations. While Lewis does not discuss black women's historical tradition of organizing to fight against sexual violence and racist images of black womanhood, she does make the case that black women were aware of their complex social, economic, and political positionality in the United States and that they were capable of addressing these issues. Lewis's use of data to show the impact of 1970s–era social policies on black women's lives and her focus on black women as agents of change brought new perspectives to the discipline of anthropology, which had been focused on either exoticizing black culture or ignoring it. Moreover, black women were completely invisible or brutally mischaracterized in anthropology. Hence, Lewis's work laid a foundation for the development of an anthropology that could acknowledge black women's visions and voices. Beyond its contribution to anthropology, "A Response to Inequality" also laid the foundation for the development of a complex, nuanced, and interdisciplinary body of literature that—by the early 1980s—would be known as black women's studies. Originally published in *Signs*, a leading journal of feminist scholarship, the article was reprinted in other feminist publications including *Issues in Feminism*, *The Signs Reader*, *Women and the Politics of Culture*, and *Black Women in America: Social Science Perspectives*.

Lewis's decision to write about black women in a feminist context reflected her own core beliefs that racism and sexism in anthropology must be challenged, that issues relevant to people of the black community must be made visible in anthropology, and that black scholars must not only generate research on black communities but also "develop an explicit ideology of radical change to replace the covert ideology of racism and exploitation" ("Comment," 346). In order to move toward achieving those goals and toward developing scholarship on black women's experiences in America, Lewis conducted research on women and the criminal justice system in San Francisco from 1979 through 1982. Her work in this context focused on the social, educational, vocational and health needs of women inmates as well as the barriers to satisfying these needs when women are released from jail.[12] Lewis also studied the role and implications of family ties in black and white women's incarceration and recidivism rates.[13]

Lewis also made a substantive contribution to the scholarship on minority women's health. In 1987 she earned a master of public health in epidemiology, which offered her new research tools and new ways to approach her anthropological work. Lewis renewed her commitment to the relevant, applied, and activist research she had argued for earlier in her career. She embraced this new direction with enthusiasm: "I first heard about HIV and AIDS when I was studying for the MPH at the UCB School of Public Health during a sabbatical in 1986. The CDC researcher informed us that the then so-called gay epidemic was in fact a disease that affected heterosexuals as well, and that the fastest growing incidence was among people of color. In fact, recent data were beginning to suggest that black women were particularly vulnerable. Stunned, I demanded to know why the general public had not been informed. When I learned about this conspiracy of silence, I decided to devote my research to women and HIV-AIDS."[14] Lewis would spend the rest of her career working in black communities and writing about the impact of HIV/AIDS on black women.[15]

Diane K. Lewis and the Transformation of Anthropology

More than just a progressive thinker, Diane Lewis was an activist intellectual who found her voice in the 1970s through publications grounded in anthropological theory, black social thought, and feminism. Formally educated during the civil rights and women's rights eras and informed by her personal experiences as a black woman living in a racist and sexist country, she was persistent in her efforts to dismantle all forms of social inequality. Lewis's critical analyses of anthropology derived from what she and other anthropologists saw as a growing disillusionment with the discipline by its scholars and practitioners, who were increasingly aware of a "marked estrangement between anthropologists and the nonwhite people" they traditionally studied ("Anthropology and Colonialism," 581). In addition to providing insightful, incisive, and important analyses of racism in academia and the larger society, Lewis also made a profound contribution to the development of what would later be known as black feminist anthropology.

Most importantly, Lewis advocated the insider or native perspective in anthropology and viewed this methodology as critical to decolonizing the discipline. Although trained as an Asianist and committed to global perspectives in her research and teaching, she began to consider the importance of the insider perspective in anthropology and turned her attention to local African American communities in San Francisco. And, as Anselme Remy suggested in his talk to the Anthropology Club at Howard University, it was to these communities that Diane Lewis was most deeply and enduringly committed.

Notes

1. Diane K. Lewis, email communication to Cheryl R. Rodriguez, November 12, 2014.

2. See Bay, Griffin, Jones, and Savage, eds., *Toward an Intellectual History of Black Women*, and Waters and Conway, eds., *Black Women's Intellectual Traditions: Speaking Their Minds*.

3. See James and Farmer, eds., *Spirit, Space and Survival: African-American Women in (White) Academe*.

4. Diane K. Lewis, email communication to Cheryl R. Rodriguez, November 30, 2014.

5. According to Bolles, this group included Irene Diggs (1944, Havana), Manet Fowler (1954, Cornell), Diane Lewis (1962, Cornell), Audrey Smedley (1965, Victoria University of Manchester, England), Vera Green (1967, Arizona), Johnnetta Betsch Cole (1967, Northwestern), Claudia Mitchell-Kernan (1967, UC Berkeley), and Niara Sudarkasa (1967, Columbia).

6. Lewis explained that Ralph Bunche had been a classmate of one of her relatives. Her family followed his career with pride. He became an inspiration and role model.

7. Diane K. Lewis, email communication to Cheryl R. Rodriguez, November 30, 2014.

8. Diane K. Lewis, email communication to Cheryl R. Rodriguez, November 30, 2014.

9. Diane K. Lewis, email communication to Cheryl R. Rodriguez, November 30, 2014.

10. Valentine was both a scholar and an activist. During his tenure as a faculty member at the University of Washington he was very involved with the Seattle chapter of the Congress of Racial Equality, a historic civil rights organization.

11. Examples include Renee Ferguson's editorial "Women's Liberation Has Different Meaning for Blacks," published in the *Washington Post* on October 3, 1970, and a brief essay by Margaret Wright titled "I Want the Right to Be Black and Me," published in *West Magazine, Los Angeles Times*, June 7, 1970.

12. See Lewis, "Black Women Offenders and Criminal Justice," Lewis and Bresler, *Is There a Way Out?*, and Lewis, "Female Exoffenders and Community Programs."

13. See Bresler and Lewis, "Black and White Women Prisoners."

14. Diane K. Lewis, email communication to Cheryl R. Rodriguez, November 12, 2014.

15. See Lewis and Watters, "Human Immunodeficiency Virus Seroprevalence in Female Intravenous Drug Users," Lewis and Watters, "Sexual Risk Behavior among Heterosexual Intravenous Drug Users," and Lewis, "African-American Women at Risk."

Bibliography

Bambara, Toni Cade, ed. *The Black Woman*. New York: Penguin, 1970.

Bay, Mia E., Farah J. Griffin, Martha S. Jones, and Barbara D. Savage, eds. *Toward an Intellectual History of Black Women*. Chapel Hill: University of North Carolina Press, 2015.

Bolles, A. Lynn. "Seeking the Ancestors: Forging a Black Feminist Tradition in Anthropology." In *Black Feminist Anthropology: Theory, Politics, Praxis, and Poetics*, ed. Irma McClaurin, 24–48. New Brunswick, NJ: Rutgers University Press, 2001.

Bresler, Laura, and Diane K. Lewis. "Black and White Women Prisoners: Differences in Family Ties and Their Programmatic Implications." *Prison Journal* 63.2 (1984): 116–23.

Chisholm, Shirley. *Unbought and Unbossed*. Boston: Houghton Mifflin, 1970.

Drake, St. Clair. "Reflections on Anthropology and the Black Experience." *Anthropology and Education Quarterly* 9.2 (1978): 85–109.

Evans, Stephanie. *Black Women in the Ivory Tower, 1850–1954*. Gainesville: University Press of Florida, 2007.

Hsu, Francis L., Delmos Jones, Diane Lewis, Beatrice Medicine, James L. Gibbs, and Thomas Weaver. *The Minority Experience in Anthropology: Report of the Committee on Minorities and Anthropology*. Washington, DC: American Anthropological Association, 1973.

James, Joy, and Ruth Farmer, eds. *Spirit, Space, and Survival: African-American Women in (White) Academe*. New York: Routledge, 1993.

King, Deborah K. "Multiple Jeopardy, Multiple Consciousness: The Context of a Black Feminist Ideology." *Signs* 14.1 (1988): 42–72.

Lewis, Diane. "African-American Women at Risk: Notes on the Sociocultural Context of HIV Infection." In *Women Resisting AIDS: Feminist Strategies of*

Empowerment, ed. Beth E. Schneider and Nancy E. Stoller, 57–73. Philadelphia: Temple University Press, 1995.

———. "Anthropology and Colonialism." *Current Anthropology* 14.5 (1973): 581–602.

———. "The Black Family: Socialization and Sex Roles." *Phylon* 36.3 (1975): 221–337.

———. "Black Women Offenders and Criminal Justice: Some Theoretical Considerations." In *Comparing Female and Male Offenders*, ed. Marguerite Warren, 89–105. Beverly Hills, CA: Sage, 1981.

———. "Comment on 'Racism and Recent Anthropological Studies of U.S. Blacks.'" *Human Organization* 31.3 (1972): 345–46.

———. "Female Exoffenders and Community Programs: Barriers to Service." *Crime and Delinquency* 28.1 (1982): 40–51.

———. "Inas: A Study of Local History." *Journal Malaysian Branch Royal Asiatic Society* 33.1 (1960): 65–94.

———. "The Multi-Cultural Education Model and Minorities: Some Reservations." *Anthropology and Education Quarterly* 7.4 (1976): 32–37.

———. "A Response to Inequality: Black Women, Racism, and Sexism." *Signs* 3.2 (1977): 339–61.

Lewis, Diane K., and Laura Bresler. *Is There a Way Out? A Community Study of Women in the San Francisco County Jail*. San Francisco: Unitarian Universalist Service Committee, 1981.

Lewis, Diane K., and John Watters. "Human Immunodeficiency Virus Seroprevalence in Female Intravenous Drug Users: The Puzzle of Black Women's Risk." *Social Science and Medicine* 29.9 (1989): 1071–76.

———. "Sexual Risk Behavior among Heterosexual Intravenous Drug Users: Ethnic and Gender Variations." *AIDS* 5.1 (1991): 77–83.

Moses, Yolanda. *Black Women in Academe: Issues and Strategies*. Washington, DC: Association of American Colleges and Universities, 1989.

Remy, Anselme. "Anthropology: For Whom and What?" *Black Scholar* 7.7 (1976): 12–16.

Valentine, Charles A. "Commentary: Racism and Recent Anthropological Studies of U.S. Blacks." *Human Organization* 31.1 (1972): 95–98.

Waters, Kristin, and Carol B. Conway, eds. *Black Women's Intellectual Traditions: Speaking Their Minds*. Lebanon, NH: University Press of New England, 2007.

5

Delmos Jones and the End of Neutrality

ELGIN L. KLUGH

Delmos Jehu Jones (1936–1999) was an anthropologist primarily concerned with social justice and equality. He sought to replace theoretical paradigms, praxis, and outcomes of anthropological work that he regarded as supportive of, or neutral to, oppressive ends with constructs that would be useful for realizing the goals of justice and equality for oppressed populations. An active contributor to efforts to "'decolonize' anthropology," Jones is most remembered for his work on the ethics of basic research and his theoretical arguments concerning native anthropology.[1]

Delmos Jones
Courtesy of Adrian Jones

Early Years

Delmos Jones was the fourth of five children born to a sharecropping family in the small community of Browns, Alabama, twenty miles to the west of Selma, Alabama. The family lived a modest, rural life and would relocate as needed to find work. Additionally, his father took various off-season jobs to "fill the gaps."

As a poor black boy in the Jim Crow South, Jones's access to learning opportunities and materials was limited. In order to pursue his education beyond the segregated Dallas County Training School in Beloit, Alabama, he traveled to live with an older sister who had settled in Oakland, California; however, his experiences in the South laid an important foundation for who he was to become and how he would interpret the conditions and struggles of distant peoples and cultures that he would eventually encounter.

Jones arrived in California at the age of fifteen. Oakland, a booming blue-collar town, allowed him to experience life outside of the South's strict codes of racial segregation. In the midst of new experiences, like sitting on the front seat of a bus, Jones encountered diverse individuals with even more diverse sets of ideas. His sister, a secretary for the local communist party, likely facilitated these entrées.

This first experience of living in an urban setting, surrounded by those working a mix of blue and white-collar jobs, likely impacted Jones's notion of the range of possibilities for his own life. After graduating from Oakland Technical High School in 1954, the first possibility that Jones chose to pursue was college. He enrolled in what is now San Francisco State University, and although his initial intent was to become a writer, there his intellectual curiosities led him to the field of anthropology.

During his time at San Francisco State, Jones was greatly influenced by the founder of the university's Anthropology Department, Adán Treganza. Treganza was an adventurous outdoorsman who, in spite of a shoestring budget, took students into the field for archaeological training.[2] Under his tutelage, Jones gained his first hands-on experiences in anthropology. Duly inspired, Jones earned a BA in anthropology from San Francisco State University in 1959 and went on to pursue graduate studies in the discipline.

Becoming an Anthropologist

During the time that Delmos Jones was working to become an anthropologist, the discipline, like academia and society in general, was undergoing significant changes. Within academia, the era of McCarthyism was coming to an end, precipitating an era of antiestablishment thought and action among university students that would quickly lead to a proliferation of campus movements. Within anthropology, marginalized minority and female voices were gravitating toward center stage within a discipline increasingly focused on human rights and a rejection of biological race.[3]

Jones left college instilled with ideas concerning social inequality and a desire to work for social justice from within the disciplinary perspective of anthropology. However, practical life considerations compelled him to first move in a different direction. Now married and with a young child, Jones sought to enlist in the military to secure the stabilizing foundation he thought a military life would provide. To his chagrin but eventual good fortune, his application was refused. In spite of his openly admitting the extent of his earlier associations with leftist groups, on the basis of those connections Jones was denied as a potential security risk.[4] He had only been marginally involved in these groups, which included the Junior Youth League, the San Francisco Writers Workshop, and the Youth Recorder, and had not participated in any subversive activities. However, the hysteria surrounding McCarthyism meant that the armed forces would not tolerate anyone in its ranks having even the slightest connections to left-leaning ideas or individuals.

THE UNIVERSITY OF ARIZONA

Jones's second option was to move his family and enroll in the University of Arizona, where he had been accepted into the master's program in anthropology. There, his anthropological curiosities were nurtured under the tutelage and mentorship of Robert Hackenberg. At the time, Hackenberg was completing his dissertation, entitled, "Indian Administration and Cultural Change," for his doctorate at Cornell University (which he completed in 1961). Jones arrived in Arizona to find Hackenberg engaged in work, under the auspices of the University of Arizona's Bureau of Ethnic Research, focusing on a Southwest Native American tribe, then known as the Papago (now the Tohono O'Odham Indians).[5] Through his work with Hackenberg, Jones was able to acquire substantial skills and experience in the large-scale collection of ethnographic data.

Jones compiled thorough descriptions of existing Papago settlements. While still a master's student, he published an article entitled "A Description of Settlement Pattern and Population Movement on the Papago Reservation." In this article, he focuses on the linkage between economic changes and residential patterns as the Papago became less involved in "subsistence activities" and increasingly reliant on a cash-based economy (1).

5. DELMOS JONES · 55

While exhaustively collecting and reporting information on characteristics and settlement patterns of the Papago, Jones reflected on similarities between his earlier life experiences and the lives of those whom he encountered:

> As a graduate student, whenever I read descriptions of other people's way of life, I could never quite escape the notion that the writer could just as well be talking about me, and the way I lived as a Black youth in the rural South in the 1940s. We lived a peasant life style, under very oppressive conditions, yet the idea of the "happy darkey," was a common theme applied to our way of life by many writers. . . . Here I am referring to those who write about the poor as if they were just another cultural form or exemplars of some kind of non-capitalistic life rather than in terms of the brutal, destructive, and, yes pathological situation that it is. . . . I saw the Papago more as poor people than as "Indians". . . . What I saw were people, who lived very similar to the rural Black and White people of my childhood in rural Alabama. (Epilogue, 193)

This ability to relate to the lived experiences and struggles of his "subjects" caused Jones to question basic ethnographic descriptions that neglected a critical discussion of the impacts of poverty and racism.

Jones completed his master's in anthropology in 1962 with the penning of his thesis "Human Ecology of the Papago Indians." Encouraged by his mentor, he left Arizona and moved to Ithaca, New York, to begin his doctoral work.

CORNELL UNIVERSITY

Scholars associated with the Anthropology Department at Cornell University have had a long-standing impact on the development of the discipline. As research associates, faculty, and/or students, individuals such as Frank Hamilton Cushing, Lauriston Sharp, G. William Skinner, Allan Holmberg, and Victor Turner contributed to the expertise and perspectives that came to characterize the department.[6] At Cornell, Jones minored in Asian studies and archaeology. Taking advantage of the program's strong Asian studies focus, Jones chose Southeast Asia as his site for dissertation research.

Initially, Jones prepared to do research among ethnic minorities in Burma. However, a fragile political stability in the country degenerated into violent conflict, barring it as a possible research site. Given his investment in language training, Jones chose to do research among a linguistically similar ethnic minority, the Lahu, in neighboring Thailand.[7] He eventually completed a dissertation titled "Cultural Variation among Six Lahu Villages, Northern Thailand." According to Spielmann in "A

Note on the Literature on the Lahu Shehlen and Lahu Na of Northern Thailand," Jones's dissertation was among the first publications to offer "useful information on the Lahu in Thailand" (2–3).

In choosing Cornell at this time, Jones unwittingly positioned himself in an academic community influenced by CIA-sponsored intelligence-gathering activities. Cornell's medical school had recently become a center of operations for the Human Ecology Fund, an arm of the CIA used to fund research on mind control. The CIA had established an effective academic cover, and so researchers were oblivious to the true source of their funding. Concerning the Human Ecology Fund, David Price writes:

> Unwitting participation by reputable scholars channeled what appeared as innocuous academic research into covert unethical programmes. Through this practice the CIA helped build up the careers of some academics, influenced social science and behavioral research, and generally attempted to create informal networks they could tap for information to provide input into their covert goals. By their own admission, CIA money-laundering was at its most cost effective when funds flowed through seemingly innocent private foundations like the Human Ecology Fund. Few participants had any inkling that what they were doing served any goals other than their own. ("Buying a Piece of Anthropology," 13)

Although Jones's research was unrelated to ideas concerning mind control, he would eventually have to deal with his own ethical dilemma regarding the confluence of his research goals and counterinsurgency agendas.[8]

In 1964–65, Jones was a PhD student focused on doing good research and completing his dissertation. For fourteen months he explored cultural variation among the Lahu. During this time, his research was guided by John Roberts, the chairman of his dissertation committee, Lauriston Sharp, the member of his committee from the Asian Studies program, and Judith Triestman, the member of his committee from the Archaeology Department (Jones, "Cultural Variation among Six Lahu Villages, Northern Thailand," iii).

Jones traveled to Thailand with his wife and children. While he conducted ethnography in Lahu villages, his family stayed in the nearby city of Chiang Mai. Thus, while conducting research, Jones also had eyes and ears in Chiang Mai. Over time, the Jones family came to see that there was a significant American presence in Thailand associated with unspoken activities, and it soon became apparent to Jones that covert operations were taking place in the region (Price, "Counterinsurgency, Vietnam, Thailand, and the Political Uses of Militarized Anthropology," 68).

5. DELMOS JONES · 57

Although aware of these covert activities, Jones was not cognizant of any connections between his data and those operations. Thus, he focused on his work with the Lahu and, in his usual way, was able to relate to them in their experiences of prejudice and discrimination suffered from the majority lowland Thai population. Jones completed his research and went on to finish his dissertation, earning his doctoral degree in 1967. From there, he once again found Hackenberg at the University of Colorado, where he accepted his first professorship.

The Thailand Affair

In 1970, with the support of a Fulbright fellowship, Jones was again among the Lahu in Thailand. His plan was to study the "relationship between agriculture and urbanization" (Susser, "Delmos Jones," 582) and to "expand upon the village-based research studies that he'd undertaken five years earlier" (Price, "Counterinsurgency, Vietnam, Thailand, and the Political Uses of Militarized Anthropology," 68). Again, the whole family came, settling down for a second time in Chiang Mai.

By this time, the war in Vietnam was under way and the use of social science research to analyze and direct anticommunist interventions was routine (Price, "Counterinsurgency, Vietnam, Thailand, and the Political Uses of Militarized Anthropology," 69). Given this context, Jones had more impetus to think about the uses of the data he collected and how individuals with whom he built rapport could possibly be affected. Additionally, Jones was likely aware of accusations recently leveled against anthropologists working in the region, which included Lauriston Sharp, his former professor, who was one of four scholars implicated in March and April 1970 when the Student Mobilizing Committee to End the War in Vietnam publicized documents "detailing extensive contacts between distinguished American academics and the U.S. Defense Department" (Wakin, *Anthropology Goes to War*, 1).

The Lahu lived in largely "scattered, semi-isolated, semi-autonomous hill villages" (Jones, "Social Responsibility and the Belief in Basic Research," 347). Their geographic location and the prejudice they faced and general neglect they suffered from at the hands of the majority population and government exposed them as "easy targets for communist subversion" (347). Available data on these populations aided in targeting key individuals and networks and in identifying which villages warranted relocation out of the hill region in order to sever communist influences (Price, "Counterinsurgency, Vietnam, Thailand, and the Political Uses of Militarized Anthropology," 69).

Perhaps due to his earlier associations with leftist-leaning individuals and organizations, Jones did not immediately see communism as an evil that needed to be eradicated. In fact, he thought about the social reality of the Lahu from their perspective. Given the discrimination that they experienced, Jones saw the forcible integration of the Lahu as oppressed minorities within the Thai political system as disadvantageous. Unless positive social and structural safeguards were to be put in place to prevent maltreatment, Jones suspected that in the long run, the hill tribes "would be better off with the Communists" (Jones, "Social Responsibility and the Belief in Basic Research," 347). In these internal deliberations, Jones demonstrated that the well-being of his subjects was his first priority.

If Jones still thought it was possible there was no outside interest in his research, he was quickly disabused of that idea on this second trip to Thailand. In Chiang Mai, Jones and his wife were told that he was to share his research with government officials. Concerning this dictum, Linda Jones remembered:

> We were both appalled and disgusted. When we got to Chiengmai, we found that we were to report to the head of USAID (commonly known to be CIA). It became evident that even if Del did not cooperate, the results of his current and earlier research, along with that of other anthropologists and linguists would be assembled into a picture of the hill tribes. Anthropologists typically recorded the names of the important individuals in a tribe and gave location information. When we decided to leave in the middle of the Fulbright, we were told that our airfare home would not be paid. Del threatened to go public with all he knew and they relented.[9]

Jones and his wife came to the conclusion that the best way to protect the individuals and communities that he was working with was to simply stop collecting data and to discontinue publishing about them. What Jones wrote instead is a thoughtful exploration of the purpose and potential uses of anthropological research in a publication that he entitled "Social Responsibility and the Belief in Basic Research: An Example from Thailand."

In his analysis of the situation in Thailand, Jones implores anthropologists to be more politically savvy concerning the context and consequences of what otherwise may seem to be harmless efforts to gather descriptive data for the objective advancement of knowledge: "There is no longer any excuse for any of us to pretend that the results of our research are not being used to help bring about the oppression of groups" (350). Jones felt that the individual scholar should be free to choose his or her own research agenda. However, he strongly urged that the discipline develop a broader conception of ethical responsibility and political awareness and pushed for anthropologists to proceed with unambiguous conviction in whatever their choice.

Although Jones made no efforts to draw attention to himself, his research experience in Thailand and his subsequent writings about the ethics of conducting basic research landed him squarely in the middle of current debates about ethics within the discipline. The initial uproar caused by the Student Mobilizing Committee's revelations concerning anthropologists and counterinsurgency activities in Thailand only persisted as further events unfolded. Many anthropologists were alarmed by what they considered to be unethical uses of disciplinary knowledge and tools. Conversely, individuals in defense of the accused were concerned about what they considered to be the mishandling of controversial documents, rash judgments, and overstepped boundaries on the part of Eric Wolf, chair of the Ethics Committee of the American Anthropological Association (AAA), and committee member Joseph Jorgensen.

AAA executive board members were initially less judgmental of those accused of misconduct and critical of actions taken by Ethics Committee members. Disappointed by what they viewed as a misdirected focus on their actions, both Wolf and Jorgensen resigned from the Ethics Committee.[10] Shortly thereafter, they submitted their now widely cited article "Anthropology on the Warpath in Thailand" to the *New York Review of Books*. It was in this article that the first reference to Delmos Jones was made (although he was unnamed at this time and only referred to as a "lone dissenter"):

> At least one person who was engaged in ethnographic research among hill people of northeastern Thailand is not present in these documents. He appears to have understood that the request for "raw data" and the eagerness of unnamed persons to "use the processed data" are politically and professionally intolerable. He has, therefore, refused to make available his field research data, and has asked other anthropologists to do the same. Furthermore, this lone dissenter has called on anthropologists to help create radical political alternatives for the people among whom they work, people whose social integrity is already—and whose physical existence may soon be—at stake. (16)

They later revealed (in an April 8, 1971, letter to the *New York Review of Books*) this "lone dissenter" to be Delmos Jones, who at this time, was just beginning what would prove to be a long and productive tenure at the Graduate Center of the City University of New York.

In an effort to resolve the ethical questions presented by the work of anthropologists in Southeast Asia, the AAA executive board appointed the most well-known anthropologist of that time, Margaret Mead, to

60 · ELGIN L. KLUGH

chair a committee to investigate the controversy (McNamara and Rubinstein, "Scholars, Security, Citizenship," xvii–xviii). The result of the Mead investigation was the fomenting of more rancor when, at the November 1971 AAA meetings, Mead read the findings of the committee, which exonerated the anthropologists implicated by the Student Mobilizing Committee and criticized members of the AAA Ethics Committee that had been pivotal in bringing the accusations to the attention of anthropologists. This report was met unfavorably by a gathering of as many as seven hundred anthropologists (Wakin, *Anthropology Goes to War*, 206–9). Subsequently, Mead acknowledged that this was one of only two occasions in her career when she was "publically hissed" (Shenker, "Anthropologists Clash Over Their Colleagues' Ethics in Thailand," 1).

For his part, Jones expressed discomfort over the way Jorgensen and Wolf characterized him in "Anthropology on the Warpath in Thailand." Specifically, he described his portrayal as an overstatement of his political and professional positions and actions as a young scholar in Thailand. He explained:

> But if there is any implication that I have not published on the tribal group that I studied or that such publications are not in the hands of various governmental agencies, then the record should be set straight. I wish now that I had the insight then that I have now. But hindsight is the cheapest commodity on the market. . . . I have no basis to divorce myself from most of the other anthropologists who worked in Thailand. At one point I stated that to the extent that the Thai government has used anthropological data to develop techniques of dealing with particular tribes they have been aided by all of us who have done research on hill culture. ("Anthropology on the Warpath: An Exchange")

Jones did not see himself as a hero and did not think he should be singled out as an exemplar of anthropological ethics. However, as Wolf and Jorgenson point out (although conceding that he did indeed publish and report at least some of his work in Thailand), Jones's statements in his article "Social Responsibility and the Belief in Basic Research" are not incongruent with their overall interpretation of them ("Anthropology on the Warpath: An Exchange").

In recognition of his personal sacrifice (giving up his fellowship and potential publications) and his genuine concern for the well-being of those whom he studied, Jones was commended by the AAA Ethics Committee (Susser, "Delmos Jones," 582). Although he had abruptly stopped data collection on the Lahu, he did not cut off his ties with the people or stop taking an interest in their concerns. In spite of eventual research projects that took him to Australian Aboriginal communities and African American communities in NewYork City, Jones maintained his relationships in Thailand and visited when he was able. Additionally, he financially assisted some of the Lahu with whom he worked so that they could acquire land.[11]

The extent to which Jones was predisposed to question a paradigm wherein anthropological work was an extension of oppressive systems is attributable to his ability to relate to the personal experiences and struggles of his subjects. No matter how distant or culturally different, Jones could recognize and readily relate to politically marginalized and oppressed people dealing with circumstances of poverty. This, after all, characterized his beginnings. This same social positioning drove his perspectives regarding native anthropology.

A Native Anthropology

Perhaps Jones's most influential contribution to theoretical approaches within the discipline is his now classic 1970 article "Towards a Native Anthropology." In this article, Jones reflected on his fieldwork experiences, the critical issues confronted by those whom he studied, and how his own identity impacted his interpretations of and insights regarding research populations. Beyond methodological approaches, he was genuinely concerned about the political context of anthropological research and aimed to disrupt a paradigm wherein anthropologists could disregard the consequences of their research by hiding behind a screen of scientific objectivity.

Jones was more predisposed to identify with the social conditions of his study populations than many of his fellow anthropologists, but although his background provided a basis for his views on native anthropology, for Jones, being a native anthropologist went beyond membership in a minority group that had traditionally been the subject of anthropological study. He was troubled by an overly simplistic native anthropology characterized by little more than the deployment of minority ethnographers into ethnically similar venues where they presumably had an easier time establishing rapport and therefore gaining access to more in-depth and/or different data. Jones lamented that minority and female anthropologists were viewed more as "potential tools to be used to provide information to the 'real,' white male anthropologists" than as professionals expected to "conduct research and develop theories and generalizations" (252).

Jones envisioned native anthropology as a transformative theoretical model, as opposed to a tool to supplement dominant paradigms. In

62 · ELGIN L. KLUGH

defining his conception of native anthropology, he explained, "I mean a set of theories based on non-Western precepts and assumptions in the same sense that modern anthropology is based on and has supported Western beliefs and values" (251). From this perspective, native anthropology presented an alternative to existing models that allowed anthropologists to work so seamlessly with and for hegemonic forces.

Jones conducted research in foreign communities and in communities where he was viewed as an "insider." In the context of his research among African American community organizations in Denver, Colorado, Jones stated that his similarities with his community of study "involved intuition, experience, and self-interest (or more properly speaking, group interest)" (253) to a degree not considered in communities where he was an outsider. Additionally, these same feelings of connectedness complicated decisions concerning what to write and report about the community.

For Jones, these reported biases did not discount the value or validity of the research. In comparing outsider and insider perspectives, he notes:

> One vantage point cannot be said to be better than the other. There are logical dangers inherent in both approaches. The outsider may enter the social situation armed with a battery of assumptions which he does not question and which guide him to certain types of conclusions; and the insider may depend too much on his own background, his own sentiments, his desires for what is good for his people. [. . .] The problem at this point is that there are native anthropologists, but there is no native anthropology. [. . .] Thus, the whole value of the inside research is not that his data or insights into the social situation are better—but that they are different. (256)

Jones considered the advancement of native anthropology as essential for the decolonization of a discipline historically dominated by the unquestioned authority of outsider voices and perspectives. Consequently, he submitted that a more developed and better-defined, insider-based epistemological approach would lead to a better and more ethical discipline.

A CRITICAL NATIVE ANTHROPOLOGY

Twenty-five years later, Jones revisited his earlier ideas in his article "Anthropology and the Oppressed: A Reflection on Native Anthropology." Still disturbed with racial and social-class biases within the discipline, Jones explains, "What concerned me then, as now, is that anthropology is essentially a discipline that studies oppressed peoples, but the concepts and theories used to describe the lives of these groups do not adequately deal with the realities of their oppression" (58).

In this extension of his discussion, Jones criticizes what he calls the "cohesive model" (60). He explains that this model errs in viewing the native population as a homogeneous entity and in its assumption that the native anthropologist is seamlessly aligned with the values and perspectives of the native population. To the contrary, Jones states, "the anthropologist who is a member of an oppressed population may or may not be an advocate of an anthropology of the oppressed." Thus, the "central question is whether a native anthropology advances the goals of social justice and social equality, or whether it merely mirrors mainstream anthropology" (58).

Jones identifies the cohesive model as an underestimation of political, social, and economic diversity within a group. The danger of this underestimation, he writes, is that the "failure to acknowledge political and cultural divisions within a group can become an aspect of domination" (60). Noting that within a group, there are likely to exist "indigenous elites" that "benefit from the inequality that exists within [the] group" (61), Jones is clear in his concern that the fact that there are anthropologists from the native population carrying out research does not necessarily mean that the critical work is being done. Additionally, he warns against an uncritical native anthropology that is more oppositional than transformative (67). The danger with an oppositional stance, he argues, is the unquestioned embrace of the same theoretical constructs and perspectives that have dominated the discipline.

An aspect of domination of concern to Jones was what he saw as mainstream anthropology's tendency to elevate analyses of "authentic" practices traceable "to a pre-contact period" over the analyses of "contemporary socio-structural and economic realities" (Epilogue, 194): "This idea that all ethnic cultures are relative leads to the conclusion that each culture has a permanent value and must be preserved for as long as possible in its 'pure' form. The result, however well intended, is the perpetuation of the existing inequality within groups and between groups" ("Anthropology and the Oppressed," 68). Describing his work with the Kouries of Australia, Jones expounds: "On my first encounter with the Aborigines I was struck most by the racism that dominated their lives. As I read the anthropological reports, I was struck by the almost complete absence of any reference to racism, but lots of material on social organization, kinship system, and religion. However, racism was the most common topic that the people themselves wanted to talk about" (Epilogue, 194). Jones was discomforted by scholarly work that emphasized a reductionist type of essentialism instead of engaging in a critical interrogation of the contemporary realities of socioeconomic injustice and political marginalization.

In advancing a critical native anthropology, Jones envisioned a theoretical paradigm shift within the discipline wherein research and scholarship would deconstruct—rather than reinforce—hegemony. His contributions to the discourse of transformation made a substantial impact, as noted by Louise Lamphere:

> It set the stage for a reanalysis of field research in the 1980s. Along with Black and Latino feminists, Jones viewed the role of "anthropologist" as always socially positioned in terms of his or her class, race, gender, nationality and sexual orientation, and the practice of anthropological knowledge as always partial and fragmentary. Furthermore, Jones was acutely aware of how often anthropologists are in a position of power in relation to their subjects. Yet his vision of a native anthropology opened the way for establishing more collaborative relations between anthropologists (both insiders and outsiders) and communities. ("Unofficial Histories," 106)

Indeed, the generation of disciplinary transformers to which Jones belonged did much to advance the relevance, appeal, effectiveness, and integrity of anthropological research.

Conclusions

Delmos Jones identified with the political marginality and socioeconomic struggles of his subjects and sought ways to push anthropological research toward the dismantling of hegemony, oppression, and inequality. He advocated a critical interrogation of the uses of anthropological research, the subject matter anthropologists chose to research, and the biases laden within the mind of the ethnographer.

In northern Thailand, Jones came face-to-face with the fact that his work was being used toward ends that he was neither in full agreement with or able to control. His response was to stop his data collection and to call on all anthropologists to be more mindful of the ways that data and publications can be used. His actions took on greater significance in a time when the political and military uses of anthropological research had emerged as a prominent ethical preoccupation within the discipline. Jones did not see himself as an exemplar of anthropological ethics; however, when careers are in the balance, it is not clear how many researchers would go to the lengths that he did to protect his research population.

Jones questioned monolithic assumptions concerning political interests and views within study populations, as well as the idea that a native anthropologist would naturally share these perspectives. He also

5. DELMOS JONES · 65

questioned the extent to which anthropological descriptions avoided dealing with the socioeconomic realities of oppression and the degree of emphasis placed on a cultural authenticity marginal to present-day circumstances. In conjunction with writings from other anthropologists (many female and many from minority communities), his writings on the subject of native anthropology "set the stage for a reanalysis of field research in the 1980s" (Lamphere, "Unofficial Histories," 106).

As a second-generation African American pioneer in anthropology, Delmos Jones was among the initial gathering of anthropologists at the 1968 AAA annual meetings in Seattle, Washington, that united to form a Minority Caucus. He continued his service with this group, which subsequently became the Caucus of Black Anthropologists, serving for a time as its chair. He also served on the steering committee that drafted a constitution when the caucus became the Association of Black Anthropologists (Harrison, "The Association of Black Anthropologists," 17–20). For a time, he was a member of the editorial board for *Transforming Anthropology*. He was well respected among his peers.

Jones continued to achieve and earn recognition right up until the very end of his life and beyond. In addition to undertaking work among the Papago in Arizona, the Lahu in northern Thailand, and the Kouries of Australia, Jones researched issues affecting urban African American communities in the United States. As an urban anthropologist, he was a prolific writer who contributed much to the field, and he was also an active member of the AAA Task Force on Poverty and Homelessness.[12]

Throughout his career, Jones maintained a critical focus that is reflected in his legacy of scholarly contributions and that lives on in the work of students and colleagues he inspired. As a researcher, Jones was awarded major grants from organizations such as the National Institutes of Health, the National Institute of Mental Health, and the Social Science Research Council. In recognition of his work, he was honored with the Lifetime Achievement Award from the Society for the Anthropology of North America and with the rank of professor emeritus from the City University of New York Graduate Center. His posthumous awards include the Graduate Center Delmos Jones Visiting Scholar Program, the Society for the Anthropology of North America Delmos Jones and Jagna Sharff Memorial Book Prize for the Critical Study of North America, and the Del Jones Memorial Travel Award from the Society for Applied Anthropology.

Notes

1. See Jones, Epilogue.
2. Linda Jones, personal communication to Elgin Klugh, August 17, 2013.

3. See Lamphere "Unofficial Histories."

4. See www.nomadnewyork.com/dad-gets-turned-down-by-the-u-s-army.

5. See http://www.tonation-nsn.gov/history-culture for background on the Tohono O'Odham Indians.

6. See http://anthropology.cornell.edu/about/history.cfm.

7. Linda Jones, personal communication to Elgin Klugh, August 17, 2013.

8. Jones's dissertation research in Thailand was funded by the Foreign Area Fellowship Program, which was sponsored by the Social Science Research Council and the American Council of Learned Societies (Jones, "Towards a Native Anthropology," 251).

9. Linda Jones, personal communication to Elgin Klugh, August 17, 2013.

10. See Wolf and Jorgensen, letter to the editor.

11. Adrian Jones, personal communication to Elgin Klugh, August 17, 2013.

12. See Jones, "The Culture of Achievement among the Urban Poor," Jones, "The Community and Organizations within the Community," Jones, "Applied Anthropology and the Application of Anthropological Knowledge," Jones, Turner, and Montbach, "Declining Social Services and the Threat to Social Reproduction," and Kadushin and Jones, "Social Networks and Urban Neighborhoods in New York City."

Bibliography

Fluehr-Lobban, Carolyn. "Ethical Challenges, New and Old in National Security and the Global War on Terror." *Anthropology News* 47.3 (2006): 5.

Hackenberg, Robert A. "Indian Administration and Social Change." PhD diss., Cornell University, 1961.

Harrison, Ira E. "The Association of Black Anthropologists: A Brief History." *Anthropology Today* 3.1 (1987): 17–21.

Jones, Delmos. "Anthropology and the Oppressed: A Reflection on 'Native' Anthropology." *NAPA Bulletin* 16.1 (1995): 58–70.

———. "Anthropology on the Warpath: An Exchange." *New York Review of Books*, July 22, 1971.

———. "Applied Anthropology and the Application of Anthropological Knowledge." *Human Organization* 35.3 (1976): 221–30.

———. "The Community and Organizations within the Community." In *Cities in the United States*, ed. Leith Mullings, 99–122. New York: Columbia University Press, 1987.

———. "Cultural Variation among Six Lahu Villages, Northern Thailand." PhD diss., Cornell University, 1967.

———. "The Culture of Achievement among the Urban Poor: The Case of Mothers and Children in a Head Start Program." *Critique of Anthropology* 13.3 (1993): 247–66.

———. "A Description of Settlement Pattern and Population Movement on the Papago Reservation." *Kiva* 27.4 (1962): 1–9.

———. Epilogue to *Decolonizing Anthropology: Moving Forward toward an Anthropology for Liberation*, 2nd ed., ed. Faye V. Harrison, 192–200. Washington, DC: American Anthropological Association, 1997.

————. "Human Ecology of the Papago Indians." MA thesis, University of Arizona, 1962.

————. "Social Responsibility and the Belief in Basic Research: An Example from Thailand." *Current Anthropology* 12.3 (1971): 347–50.

————. "Towards a Native Anthropology." *Human Organization* 29.4 (1970): 251–59.

————. "The Tribe, the Village and Over-generalization: Example of Black Lahu." Unpublished report.

Jones, Delmos, Joan Turner, and Joan Montbach. "Declining Social Services and the Threat to Social Reproduction: An Urban Dilemma." *City and Society* 6.2 (1992): 99–114.

Jorgensen, Joseph G., and Eric R. Wolf. "Anthropology on the Warpath in Thailand." *New York Review of Books*, November 19, 1970, 43–46.

Kadushin, Charles, and Delmos Jones. "Social Networks and Urban Neighborhoods in New York City." *City and Society* 6.1 (1992): 58–75.

King, William S., and Delmos J. Jones. *Papago Population Studies*. New York: Garland, 1974.

Lamphere, Louise. "Unofficial Histories: A Vision of Anthropology from the Margins." *American Anthropologist* 106.1 (2004): 126–39.

McNamara, Laura A., and Robert A. Rubinstein. "Scholars, Security, Citizenship: Anthropology and the State of War." In *Dangerous Liaisons: Anthropologists and the National Security State*, ed. Laura McNamara and Robert Rubinstein, xiii–xxxiv. Santa Fe, NM: School of Advanced Research Press, 2011.

Price, David. "Buying a Piece of Anthropology," pt. 1: "Human Ecology and Unwitting Anthropological Research for the CIA." *Anthropology Today* 23.3 (2007): 8–13.

————. "Counterinsurgency, Vietnam, Thailand, and the Political Uses of Militarized Anthropology." In *Dangerous Liaisons: Anthropologists and the National Security State*, ed. Laura McNamara and Robert Rubinstein, 51–76. Santa Fe, NM: School of Advanced Research Press, 2011.

Shenker, Israel. "Anthropologists Clash Over Their Colleagues' Ethics in Thailand." *New York Times*, November 21, 1971.

Spielmann, Hans J. "A Note on the Literature on the Lahu Shehlen and Lahu Na of Northern Thailand." *Journal of the Siam Society* 57.2 (1969): 321–33.

Susser, Ida S. "Delmos Jones (1936–1999)." *American Anthropologist* 102.3 (2000): 581–83.

Wakin, Eric. *Anthropology Goes to War: Professional Ethics and Counterinsurgency in Thailand*. Madison: University of Wisconsin Press, 1992.

Wolf, Eric R., and Joseph G. Jorgensen. Letter to the Editor. *Newsletter of the Anthropology Association of America* 11.7 (1970): 2, 19.

6

Niara Sudarkasa

Inspiring Black Women's Leadership

ERICA LORRAINE WILLIAMS

Pioneering cultural anthropologist Niara Sudarkasa has traveled to twenty-seven African countries and conducted research in West Africa, the Caribbean, and the United States. Her research interests have included West African trade and migration, anthropology and development, the roles of African women, African and Caribbean immigration to the United States, African and African American family organization, race and ethnicity, and diversity, equity, and excellence in higher education. Born in 1938 as Gloria Marshall in Ft. Lauderdale, Florida, she adopted the name Niara—an adaptation of a Swahili word meaning "woman of high purpose."[1] Her choice of this name is fitting, considering how she has earned nearly twenty fellowships, grants, and awards, more than seventy-five civic and professional awards, and honorary degrees from a dozen colleges and universities.[2]

Sudarkasa has long been recognized for her many "firsts." She was the first black woman to teach at New York University and the first African American woman to teach anthropology at the University of Michigan. In her twenty years at the University of Michigan, she was the first African American woman to earn tenure in the arts and sciences, become full professor, head an academic center, and become the associate vice president for academic affairs. In 1972, at the age of thirty-four, she became one of the youngest people to be elected to the executive board of the American Anthropological Association (AAA).[3] From 1987 to 1998, Sudarkasa served as the president of historically black Lincoln University. This chapter explores Sudarkasa's trajectory as a scholar, advocate, and higher education administrator, and describes her contributions to scholarship on feminist anthropology, gender and migration, black women's leadership, and extended families in the African diaspora.

Niara Sudarkasa
Courtesy of Pauline Walter's photo album. Call #HS5690. Bentley Historical Library, University of Michigan.

Personal and Educational Background

Niara Sudarkasa was born to seventeen-year-old Rowena Marshall and raised by her maternal grandparents, who had migrated to Florida from the Bahamas. Her mother "picked beans, scrubbed floors and worked in a dry-cleaners most of her life to send her four children to college" (Sudarkasa, "Don't Write Off Thomas"). Her grandfather was a farmer and her grandmother was a housewife. Sudarkasa's upbringing in an extended family, where financial responsibility and decision making was shared between her mother and grandparents, most likely fueled her later research interest in extended families in the African diaspora.

Sudarkasa started school at the age of five and skipped the sixth grade. She reflected, "My mother assumed that we were all going to go to college. She was very keen on our going. So were my grandparents and my teachers at Dillard High School, which was the only school that black children could attend in Ft. Lauderdale."[4] In 1953, at age fifteen, Sudarkasa entered Fisk University on a Ford Foundation early entrant scholarship. Sudarkasa majored in English at Fisk, but transferred to Oberlin College in 1956 after participating in a domestic exchange program. Sudarkasa's time at Oberlin introduced her to the anthropology of Africa and the African diaspora. In a course with George E. Simpson, she was amazed to discover that the *esus* (practice of pooling money together) that she witnessed in the Bahamian community in South Florida were cultural legacies from the Yoruba people.[5] Another course introduced her to topics such as polygyny, polyandry, patriarchy, and matriarchy. She reflects on the impact Simpson had on her career trajectory: "I was really fascinated by the courses that I had with George Simpson, who had been a student of Herskovits and had done his research in the Caribbean—that's when I learned a lot about the African cultures that had survived in the New World."[6] In 1957, she graduated from Oberlin College at the age of eighteen in the top 10 percent of her class.

Sudarkasa pursued her master's and doctoral degrees in anthropology at Columbia University. Her decision to apply to Columbia was largely motivated by the fact that her mother had moved to New York a few years earlier. Interestingly, she described the process of applying to graduate school as one that was shrouded in mystery: "I didn't know a lot about getting into graduate school. When I decided I wanted to go, nobody at Oberlin gave me any advice about it. I thought if I go to Columbia, I could always stay with my mother if I didn't get a scholarship."[7]

She was awarded a scholarship for tuition, lived with her mother, and worked part time in the registrar's office. Influenced by the work of Melville Herskovits, Sudarkasa's master's thesis focused on the historical influences of African and European mutual aid associations on benefit societies in the West Indies.[8] Although Herskovits has been criticized for engaging in gatekeeping practices by discouraging African American scholars from conducting research in Africa and the African diaspora, Sudarkasa benefited from having Eliott Skinner as her research supervisor. She says, "I didn't feel discouraged from studying Africa, because Elliott Skinner was at Columbia. . . . He encouraged me to do research in Africa as opposed to the Caribbean."[9] Skinner pointed out that before she could study the diaspora, she must first know the continent.

Sudarkasa's doctoral research consisted of twenty-one months of fieldwork in Nigeria on the impact of Yoruba women's economic activities on their gender roles within the family.[10] On her first journey to the African continent, she traveled by ship from Liverpool to Lagos.[11] Although she had spent six months studying the Yoruba language at the School of Oriental and African Studies in London, she was disappointed to learn that her Yoruba comprehension was limited. Despite this linguistic setback, she was struck by the familiarity of what she saw in Nigeria—Lagos reminded her of the South Florida towns of her childhood.

At the beginning of her fieldwork, Sudarkasa was based at the University of Ibadan, but she later moved to Awe, a small rural town of five thousand inhabitants. She rented a bungalow from an Awe businessman and was quickly adopted as the town's guest and "daughter." Because the community was concerned for her safety as a young unmarried woman, the chairman of the town council provided her with a night watchman, a live-in interpreter, and a steward who lived in the quarters behind her bungalow. Town residents would often visit her bearing food gifts, and they would send their children to do chores for her. Reflecting on the gendered implications of her fieldwork experience, Sudarkasa notes that "one of the first decisions I had to make in Awe was whether I would make an attempt to act in accordance with the general rules governing subordinate/superordinate relationships or whether, as an outsider, I would for the most part ignore them" ("In a World of Women," 203). This is a dilemma that many women anthropologists face in doing fieldwork, as Paulla Ebron suggests in *Performing Africa*. Ultimately, Sudarkasa chose to "behave like a Yoruba" by curtsying, bowing, and sometimes kneeling to show respect toward her elders, to the surprise and approval of the people of Awe.

In 1964 at the age of twenty-five, Niara Sudarkasa had completed her PhD in anthropology from Columbia University. Her first academic job was as assistant professor of anthropology at New York University. In 1967, she moved on to become assistant professor in the Anthropology Department at the University of Michigan. After a year-long sabbatical to study Yoruba traders in Ghana, she returned to the University of Michigan in 1969, at a time when black students were fighting for increased minority enrollment. At the request of black students, she readily agreed to speak on behalf of faculty who supported the Black Action Movement (BAM) at the university, and she was one of thirty-one faculty members to sign a statement backing the demands of the organization ("BAM Ends Class Strike!"). In April 1970, BAM launched an eight-day class strike to pressure the administration to act on their demands for more black students, more financial aid for disadvantaged students, a black community center, and a community-oriented black studies program.[12] Reflecting on this period, Sudarkasa stated,

> There were other blacks at Michigan but most of them were older and not as involved. . . . Most of my friends were graduate students—they were about the same age as I was. They were very active in the BAM and I just went along with it. I didn't think about the implications for my career because I was doing well. . . . Maybe I just wasn't smart enough to think about it! [laughs] At that time of course, activism was very much expected among the people with whom I associated.[13]

This shows how many of Sudarkasa's experiences were structured not only by race and gender but also by age. She often had to negotiate various spaces of power as "the youngest" person in the room.

Interestingly, despite the fact that Sudarkasa came of age during the civil rights and black power movements, this was the first time she had taken an active role in these movements. She was a senior at Oberlin when Martin Luther King Jr. came to speak after the bus boycott, and in the early 1960s, she went to London and Nigeria for research. She says, "When I came back from fieldwork in 1962, my mom and brothers had to bring me up to date on what had been going on."[14] When the Regents rejected several of BAM's demands, Sudarkasa was quoted in the newspaper as saying, "We say there can be no total victory until the racist malignancy either consumes this country or we cut it out. . . . [W]e will fight on, because like all mankind we hope, and because we're arrogant enough to know we'll win" ("BAM Ends Class Strike!"). The day after the assassination of Martin Luther King Jr., Sudarkasa went before her Introduction to Anthropology class and stated,

> If I were just another professor, on this day, perhaps I could deliver this lecture as planned. But I am not just another professor, I am not just another anthropologist, I am not just another American; I am a black professor, a black anthropologist, and a black American, who, like all other black Americans, can never for a single day in my life forget this fact. Today I am enraged; I am insulted; I am bewildered and perplexed and I am profoundly sad.[15]

Her commitment and dedication to this cause at an early stage of her career is instructive and inspiring, particularly in light of the common refrain circulating within academia about the risk of pretenured faculty involving themselves in activism.

Another example of her outspoken and courageous personality can be seen in her struggle to be promoted to full professor at the University of Michigan. Initially, the Anthropology Department's Ad Hoc Committee of Full Professors did not recommend her for full professor. She formally appealed the department's decision by writing the dean to request an independent review of the Anthropology Department's tenure procedure.[16] In a letter dated August 25, 1975, Roy Rappaport, then chair of the department, denied that racism or sexism was a factor in the decision. He mentioned that her teaching was peripheral to the department, since not many students enrolled her classes. In fact, he cited one (white) student who was unable to take Sudarkasa's class because Sudarkasa allegedly said that black students would be given first priority for available spaces.[17] In her response letter dated August 26, 1975, Sudarkasa denied the student's claim, adding that

> as for my "peripheral position" in the department, I can only state that I regard myself as providing a service to the department by presenting

what was for a long time the only on-going critique of the racist themes and perspectives that pervade the field of anthropology. . . . The very fact that you would assume that it is my "fault" that white students do not flock to my courses confirms my impression that you need to do a lot more serious reflection on the subject of racism.[18]

Despite these setbacks, she stayed at the University of Michigan until 1987, serving as the associate director of the Center for Afro-American and African studies from 1970 to 1973, earning full professor in 1976 and serving as director of the center from 1981 to 1984.

The Lincoln University Years

In 1987, at the age of forty-nine, Sudarkasa was sworn in as president of Lincoln University, where she served for eleven years. At the time there was a growing network of black women presidents of HBCUs, including Johnnetta B. Cole at Spelman College and Gloria Scott at Bennett College. Sudarkasa felt that her appointment as president was the "perfect meeting of scholar and institution" because of the university's important historical connections to African and African American leaders such as Kwame Nkrumah, Nnamdi Azikiwe, Thurgood Marshall, and Langston Hughes (McKinney, "Sister Presidents"). In an *Essence* article, Sudarkasa was described as a tough yet caring administrator with a dynamic personality, keen intelligence, and a strong sense of self ("Niara Sudarkasa," 1989). Her goals were to increase Lincoln University's competitiveness in the fields of science, math, and engineering, as well as to ensure that the student body became more aware of the connections with Africa. A Lincoln University newsletter stated, "under Dr. Sudarkasa's bold and visionary leadership, Lincoln University . . . has become a model for internationalizing the curriculum and providing a twenty-first century education with a global perspective."

Unfortunately, the end of Sudarkasa's presidency was shrouded in a scandal. Richard Glanton, Lincoln's former chief counsel, accused her of mismanaging funds. Sudarkasa called these allegations "false and malicious," and she highlighted the great strides that the university made under her leadership: an increase in enrollment; a 400 percent increase in endowment; two new buildings (including the $17.1 million Thurgood Marshall Living Learning Center); a strong faculty, 75 percent of whom held doctorate degrees; a successful honors program; a ranking of ninth in the nation in awarding bachelor degrees to African Americans in the physical sciences; and so forth (Sudarkasa, "Lincoln President Responds to Allegations"). Noted economist Julianne Malveaux came to Sudarkasa's defense by pointing out that the charges may have been the result of "men resistant to female leadership" ("Why Can't Black Folks Stand Success?").

After Sudarkasa left Lincoln, she moved to Silver Spring, Maryland. She and her husband were planning to move to Ft. Lauderdale to build a house on property she had inherited from her grandparents, but he died in 1999. She lost interest in academia after he died. She turned down an invitation to apply for a job at the University of Pretoria, despite the fact that her son had recently moved his family to South Africa. She decided to move home to Ft. Lauderdale, where she served as scholar in residence at the African American Research Library and Cultural Center and distinguished visiting scholar at Florida Atlantic University, Davie/Ft. Lauderdale campus. In the remainder of the chapter, I analyze the themes of Sudarkasa's publications and highlight her contributions to anthropology, African and African diaspora studies, and women's and gender studies.

Doctoral Research: Yoruba Women Traders

In *Where Women Work: A Study of Yoruba Women in the Marketplace and in the Home* (1973), a book based on her dissertation, Sudarkasa points out that virtually all Yoruba women were engaged in some type of trade activity long before the twentieth century. Arguing that Yoruba women saw trade "as a necessary component of their role as women," she describes the impact of trading on the marital relationship and on the socialization of children in Yoruba society (117). She argues that Yoruba women did not see work as a distraction from home and the family. Rather, they saw it as something that *enabled* them to fulfill their roles within the family (117). This argument is still relevant today in the ongoing debate as to whether professional women can "have it all." Ultimately, Yoruba women's involvement in trade meant that responsibility for childcare could not be the sole obligation of mothers. Instead, they relied on other women to help with childcare and taught their children to be self-sufficient at an early age. Mothers were not perceived as "neglectful" on this account; rather this was part and parcel of what being a "good mother" meant in Yoruba society (132).

Sudarkasa's research explores seniority, polygyny, and gendered economic activities in West Africa. Long before Oyeronke Oyewumi's groundbreaking book *The Invention of Women: Making an African Sense of Western Gender Discourses* (1997), Sudarkasa emphasized the importance of seniority in the structuring of interpersonal relations. She also demystified polygyny by describing its structure and organization in a nonjudgmental way. For instance, a first wife might suggest that her husband take another wife to help with household duties so she could devote more time to trade activities (*Where Women Work*, 129). Sudarkasa describes Yoruba women's trading as an autonomous space where women worked with little interference from their husbands. Husbands, who often worked as farmers, did not offer advice concerning their wives' trade or contribute to their trading capital, and women's income was kept separate from their husbands' income. Trading fostered mobility for Yoruba women, who were "virtually free to go wherever" their work led them (132). This certainly disrupts the domestic/public paradigm that was commonplace in feminist anthropology in the 1970s, which posited that the subordination of women could be explained by the fact that they had been relegated to the less valued domestic domain, while men enjoyed the privileges of the public domain.[19]

Extended Families in Africa and the African Diaspora

In 1970, after she returned from conducting research in Ghana, Sudarkasa found herself increasingly drawn into debates around the black family. Consequently, she began to lecture and write about the African origins of African American family structure. Two motivating factors for this shift in her research interests were the publication of the Moynihan report in 1965 and her continuing fieldwork in West Africa. From the late 1960s to the early 1980s, her research on Nigerians trading in Ghana and the growing number of female-headed households in Benin revealed patterns of separate domiciles for wives and husbands. For women traders in Benin, living separately offered independence from husbands who wanted to control their activities.

In *The Strength of Our Mothers: African and African American Women and Families* (1996), Sudarkasa makes several interesting arguments about families that are still relevant today. First, she argues that the dissolution of a marriage does not necessarily entail the dissolution of the family (xxi). In other words, marital stability should be distinguished from family stability. Second, she urges people not to pathologize black family structures and single mothers for not following the nuclear ideal. She claims that the flexibility of black family structures was the key to African Americans' survival. Finally, she disrupts the assumption that in single mother–headed households, the mothers are usually teenage mothers by providing data that shows they are most often older, adult, mature mothers. Thus, she argues that the idea that female-headed households are inherently "unstable" is a fallacy by emphasizing that they often consist of "multigenerational units clustered around a core" of adult blood relatives (xxi). Furthermore, in the chapter entitled "Dispelling the Myths about Black Families," she blames the rise of teenage mother–headed households on welfare and public housing policies that prohibit multigenerational families from living together in one household.

In *Extended Families in Africa and the African Diaspora*, coeditors Aborampah and Sudarkasa assert that the extended family is important in African societies for social and economic reasons, including that it makes shared labor possible and helps with the "socialization of children" and the "education and placement of relatives" and also provides "support for the elderly" (introduction, 2). They critique studies that see black families in the United States as "aberrant forms of the nuclear family rather than as re-adaptions of the African extended families out of which they evolved" (introduction, 7). In her essay "Value Premises Underlying Black Family Studies and Black Families" (from her book *The Strength of Our Mothers*), Sudarkasa criticizes European scholars for assuming that the nuclear family is universal and that it is the building block of extended families. She argues rather that extended families in Africa were built around blood ties rather than conjugal ties and claims that the Western nuclear family ideal promotes "individualism, competition, and accumulation," while African extended families emphasize "communalism, cooperation, and sharing" ("The Changing Roles of Women in Changing Family Structures in West Africa," 186). Sudarkasa outlines five fundamental myths about black families: that black families are inherently unstable, that most black men do not contribute to their families, that the black family is always hostile, that black families do not value education, and that the deplorable conditions in inner cities are a byproduct of black family structures. Furthermore, she argues that the high value placed on children in African and African American culture provided a context in which African Americans could have children out of wedlock without stigma, which made female-headed households acceptable ("Female-Headed African American Households," 27).

Sudarkasa also revisits the classic Frazier-Herskovits debate to analyze the black family. As she notes in "The Changing Roles of Women in Changing Family Structures in West Africa," while Frazier traced the origin of female-headed households to the breakdown of institutions and morals caused by slavery, Herskovits claimed that those features were New World variants of African family practices. Sudarkasa critiques the Frazier-Herskovits dichotomy for juxtaposing "the experience of slavery and the heritage of Africa as if only one could be the explanation of the emergence of the patterns in question" ("Roots of the Black Family," 86). While she suggests that Herskovits was generally right and Frazier generally wrong about the origins of African American family structure, she argues that both had overlooked "important features of female-headed households that could be traced back to African kinship patterns" (*The Strength of Our Mothers*, xx). She moves beyond this debate by presenting a more nuanced argument: while we cannot definitively say that female-headed households grew directly out of African traditions, understanding the importance of consanguinity in African kinship can help explain why these types of households persisted among African Americans. In other words, "we cannot explain African American families *only* by reference to their West African cultural antecedents, but we cannot understand African American families *without* taking into account the West African family structures out of which they evolved" ("African American Families and Family Values," 43).

Contributions to Feminist Anthropology

Sudarkasa's scholarship both challenges and contributes to feminist anthropology by showing that African women are not the "docile, submissive, downtrodden, powerless creatures they have often been portrayed to be" (*The Strength of Our Mothers*, xxiii). For instance, in an article for *Feminist Studies*, she critiques Western feminist scholars' concern with the "status of women" in African societies, arguing that this concept implies "that women and men were everywhere related to each other in a hierarchical fashion" ("The Status of Women in Indigenous African Societies," 92). She also critiques scholars' tendency to assess the "status of women" only in relation to the conjugal roles of wife instead of also considering women's roles within their natal families.

As a graduate student, I read "Woman, Culture, and Society: A Theoretical Overview" by Michelle Rosaldo (1974), which discusses the universal subordination of women. Rosaldo describes Yoruba women as wives who "must feign ignorance and obedience, kneeling to serve the men as they sit" (20). Having studied Yoruba language and spent time in Nigeria, I remember being shocked at how she decontextualized and misinterpreted the practice of kneeling, taking it as evidence of Yoruba women's subordination when in fact in Yoruba culture, both women *and men* prostrate as a sign of respect for the elderly. Sudarkasa takes issue with Rosaldo's characterization of gender relations in West Africa, rejecting her claim that "public and domestic spheres and male and female roles are 'firmly differentiated" in West Africa and arguing instead that the "public domain" in West Africa is not seen as "the world of men" but rather as an arena in which both sexes are "recognized as having important roles to play" ("Female Employment and Family Organization in West Africa," 223). She points out that women in West Africa are consulted in internal political and governmental affairs and

78 · ERICA LORRAINE WILLIAMS

that their economic roles are both "public" and "private." Ultimately, she argues that "rather than being subordinate, women's activities" are "complementary to those of men (227).

Sudarkasa's research on migration in West Africa explores the gendered differences in migration and the effects of migration on the marital relationship. For example, she found that men usually embarked on their first migration in their twenties when they were still unmarried, while Yoruba women who migrated to Ghana were usually first wives accompanying their husbands ("Women and Migration in Contemporary West Africa," 184). While Yoruba women usually carried on their trade independently of their husbands in Nigeria, they often engaged in joint trading ventures with their husbands in Ghana. Because they lived in closer proximity with their spouses in rented rooms in Ghana as opposed to compounds in Nigeria, the couples often relied on each other more and made domestic and business decisions together.

Sudarkasa's scholarship has also explored issues of gender, education, and development in West Africa. In one essay, she describes how African women's economic status deteriorated under colonial regimes, as the spread of Western education increased the economic gap between genders. She urged state governments and schools to increase their efforts to recruit and retain girls ("Sex Roles, Education, and Development in Africa," 286). Elsewhere, in "Male/Female Disparities in Education and Occupations in Nigeria," she discusses the gendered disparities in the educational system in Nigeria; the higher up one goes on the educational ladder, the fewer women there are. Finally, in "Planning for the Family versus Family Planning," she criticizes development policies for failing to emphasize the role that the institution of the family should play in the development process.

African American Women's Leadership: Skirting the Borders of Feminism

Sudarkasa has had an interesting and complicated relationship with feminism. On the one hand, she has made major contributions to feminist anthropology by challenging Western assumptions about gender relations in West African societies. She has offered an astute critique of the universality of the domestic/public binary and problematized the ideological origins of the concern with women's "status." In "African American Women: A Legacy of Leadership" and "African American Women: A Case of Strength without Power?," she discusses the important positions that women historically held in Africa in their capacity as queen mothers, chiefs, and traders. She calls for an end to male domination and discrimination against women and argues that African American women's leadership tradition is rooted in West African heritage.

On the other hand, she has also made statements that challenge the black feminist concept of intersectionality. In "Reflections on the Positions and Problems of Black Women in America," she denies the existence of the "double jeopardy" of racism and sexism by claiming that "the mere fact that we are female and black does not mean that our plight has been any worse than that of Black males" (315). Furthermore, she argues that "the treatment of women of African descent in America derives fundamentally from the fact of our blackness, not from the fact of our being women" (320). In another essay, she claims that women occupational roles in indigenous African societies were not considered "inferior" to those of men, so "if one were to apply the 'beast of burden' stereotype to women, one should also apply it to men" ("Sex Roles, Education, and Development in Africa," 280).

Another controversial aspect of Sudarkasa's legacy is her support in 1991 of the nomination of Clarence Thomas to the Supreme Court. On September 17, 1991, she testified before the Senate Judiciary Committee, making her the only black college president (out of 117) to do so ("Lincoln President Says Link between Her Pro-Thomas Testimony and Promise of $10 Million is 'Far-Fetched,'" 18). She supported Thomas's nomination because of his education, experience, intelligence, integrity and "high ideals" and defended him as an "open-minded and independent thinker" who was unfairly criticized for being "insensitive to the concerns of African Americans" ("Testimony"). She claimed that "In the era of a conservative Supreme Court, Clarence Thomas is a known quantity. He is a bird in the hand. We do not know who might emerge from the bush" ("Thomas Should Be Approved"). Sudarkasa was widely criticized for this position. A 1992 *Black Issues in Higher Education* article stated that "many who have watched Sudarkasa closely since her appointment as president in 1987 said they were stunned to learn that she, a self-described 'Democrat, radical and liberal,' had presented such an impassioned case for Thomas, an outspoken opponent of affirmative action." Lincoln University students launched a demonstration and threatened to walk out in response to Sudarkasa's position. Her response was that "I have always been an independent thinker. I thought that it was a very unusual stance for African Americans to take to say that they would prefer any white over Clarence Thomas. I looked at the record and made my own judgment" ("Lincoln President Says Link between Her Pro-Thomas Testimony and Promise of $10 Million Is 'Far-Fetched,'" 18).

Conclusion

Sudarkasa always pushed the boundaries and limitations of the discipline of anthropology. In a plenary session titled "Confronting Racism: A Challenge to the Anthropological Profession" at the AAA meetings in November 1989, Sudarkasa spoke alongside other prominent scholars including panelists Derrick Bell and Johnnetta B. Cole. She stated, "If there is one discipline that should make racism the object of serious study, it is anthropology" because anthropologists have a "special responsibility" and "the requisite skills, to help America see itself, confront itself, understand itself, and change itself" ("Confronting Racism," 1989). She critiques black studies scholarship on Africa and the diaspora on the grounds that it lacks an activist framework. Her passion for African studies was captured in her comments at a 1995 roundtable on Africa in Washington, DC, when she stated, "I have been in and out of Africa for almost 35 years. I am not only an observer and an analyst of events on the continent, but one for whom the sense of kinship with Africa is very personal and profound. Therefore, I cannot view developments in Africa with dispassion."[20]

Sudarkasa's lifetime of achievements and accomplishments cannot be overestimated. As a fellow of the AAA, a member of the Council on Foreign Relations, and a senior Fulbright research fellow, Sudarkasa has been nationally recognized for her expertise on Africa. President George Bush appointed her to the Peace Corps National Advisory Council, and President Bill Clinton appointed her to the White House Commission on Presidential Scholars. She is a lifetime member of the National Council of Negro Women and the National Association for the Advancement of Colored People. In May 2001, she received the chieftancy title of Yeye Olokun Igbadero ("Mother from Across the Seas Who Brings a Time of Peace") from the Ife Kingdom in Nigeria. Sudarkasa's accomplishments as a scholar, leader, and politically engaged citizen are part of the legacy of African American anthropologists to the field of anthropology in general and to African and African American studies and women's studies in particular.

Notes

I would like to thank Niara Sudarkasa for participating in a telephone interview with me, as well as archivist Kala Luzia of the African American Research and Cultural Center in Ft. Lauderdale, who gave me access to Sudarkasa's personal papers and provided me with support.

1. Her birth name was listed on official documents and publications until 1970. She began using Niara after 1973. She acquired her last name through her

first marriage to Delmar Sudarkasa. She married her second husband, John L. Clark, in 1977. Her son, Michael Sudarkasa, is a Harvard-trained lawyer who has worked for many years throughout Africa (Washington, "Niara Sudarkasa").

2. Sudarkasa received honorary degrees from Fisk University, Oberlin College, Radcliffe College, Seton Hill University, Lehigh University, Franklin and Marshall College, Susquehanna University, SUNY Binghamton, Hobart and William Smith College, the University of Louisville, the University of Nigeria-Nsukka, and Fort Hare University in South Africa. She is a member of Delta Sigma Theta sorority and was an inaugural member of the Dillard High School Academic Hall of Fame in 1989. She also received the Award for Visionary Leadership from the Center for Afro-American and African Studies at the University of Michigan (1991), the National YWCA Career Women of Achievement Award (1993), the 100 Black Men of America President's Award for Excellence in Education, the Delta Sigma Theta Civil Rights Award, the Distinguished Friends of Nigeria Award, and the Philadelphia Martin Luther King Jr. Association for Nonviolence Drum Major for Human Rights Award.

3. Letter from Elliott Skinner supporting Sudarkasa's promotion to full professor at the University of Michigan, series 4, box 25, Niara Sudarkasa Papers, 1934–2006, African American Research Library and Cultural Center, Ft. Lauderdale.

4. Niara Sudarkasa, telephone interview with Erica Williams, August 2012.

5. Fall 1956–57, Oberlin, series 1, box 41, folder 9 Niara Sudarkasa Papers, 1934–2006, African American Research Library and Cultural Center, Ft. Lauderdale.

6. Niara Sudarkasa, telephone interview with Erica Williams, August 2012.

7. Niara Sudarkasa, telephone interview with Erica Williams, August 2012.

8. She completed her master's degree in 1959.

9. Niara Sudarkasa, telephone interview with Erica Williams, August 2012.

10. She received funding from the Ford Foundation Foreign Area Training Fellowship program.

11. See "In a World of Women."

12. Black Action Movement files, series 4, box 25, Niara Sudarkasa Papers, 1934–2006, African American Research Library and Cultural Center, Ft. Lauderdale.

13. Niara Sudarkasa, telephone interview with Erica Williams, August 2012.

14. Niara Sudarkasa, telephone interview with Erica Williams, August 2012.

15. Introduction to Anthropology lecture, April 5, 1968, University of Michigan, series 2, box 28, file 15, Niara Sudarkasa Papers, 1934–2006, African American Research Library and Cultural Center, Ft. Lauderdale.

16. Michigan tenure file, series 4, box, 25, Niara Sudarkasa Papers, 1934–2006, African American Research Library and Cultural Center, Ft. Lauderdale.

17. Her courses included Introduction to Anthropology, Precolonial Africa, Cultures of Africa, African Women, Seminar on Problems in African Ethnology, Seminar on Contemporary Africa, Social Organization in Contemporary Africa; African People in the Americas, and Issues in Afro-American Development.

82 · ERICA LORRAINE WILLIAMS

18. Michigan tenure file, series 4, box 25, Niara Sudarkasa Papers, 1934–2006, African American Research Library and Cultural Center, Ft. Lauderdale.

19. See Lewin, ed., *Feminist Anthropology*, and Rosaldo and Lamphere, eds., *Women, Culture and Society*.

20. See series 2, box 30, file 25, Niara Sudarkasa Papers, 1934–2006, African American Research Library and Cultural Center, Ft. Lauderdale, for a copy of these remarks.

Bibliography

Aborampah, Osei-Mensah, and Niara Sudarkasa. Introduction to *Extended Families in Africa and the African Diaspora*, ed. Osei-Mensah Aborampah and Niara Sudarkasa, 00–00. Trenton, NJ: Africa World Press, 2011.

"BAM Ends Class Strike!" *Michigan Daily*, April 2, 1970.

Ebron, Paulla. *Performing Africa*. Princeton: Princeton University Press, 2002.

Lewin, Ellen, ed. *Feminist Anthropology: A Reader*. Malden, MA: Blackwell, 2006.

"Lincoln President Says Link between Her Pro-Thomas Testimony and Promise of $10 Million is 'Far-Fetched.'" *Black Issues in Higher Education* 9.8 (July 1992): 18–19.

Malveaux, Julianne. "Why Can't Black Folks Stand Success? Unjust Accusations against Lincoln President Niara Sudarkasa." *Black Issues in Higher Education* 15.13 (1998): 51.

McKinney, Rhoda. "Sister Presidents." *Ebony*, February 1988, 84–88.

Oyewumi, Oyeronke. *The Invention of Women: Making an African Sense of Western Gender Discourses*. Minneapolis: University of Minnesota Press, 1997.

Rosaldo, Michelle Z. "Woman, Culture, and Society: A Theoretical Overview." In *Women, Culture, and Society*, ed. Michelle Z. and Louise Lamphere, 17–42. Stanford, CA: Stanford University Press, 1974.

Rosaldo, Michelle Z., and Louise Lamphere, eds. *Women, Culture and Society*. Stanford, CA: Stanford University Press, 1974.

Sudarkasa, Niara. "African American Families and Family Values." In *The Strength of Our Mothers*, 41–76.

———. "African American Women: A Case of Strength without Power?" In *The Strength of Our Mothers*, 295–302.

———. "African American Women: A Legacy of Leadership." In *The Strength of Our Mothers*, 291–94.

———. "The Changing Roles of Women in Changing Family Structures in West Africa: Some Preliminary Observations." In *The Strength of Our Mothers*, 181–90.

———. "Confronting Racism: A Challenge to the Anthropological Profession." Paper presented at the American Anthropological Association Meeting, Washington, DC, November 1989.

———. "Dispelling the Myths about Black Families." In *The Strength of Our Mothers*, 13–22.

———. "Don't Write Off Thomas." *Newsweek*, August 19, 1991, 10.

6. NIARA SUDARKASA · 83

———. "Female Employment and Family Organization in West Africa." In *The Strength of Our Mothers*, 221–36.

———. "Female-Headed African American Households: Some Neglected Dimensions." In *The Strength of Our Mothers*, 23–33.

———. "In a World of Women: Fieldwork in a Yoruba Community." In *The Strength of Our Mothers*, 191–220.

———. "Lincoln President Responds to Allegations." *Philadelphia Tribune*, June 23, 1998.

———. "Male/Female Disparities in Education and Occupations in Nigeria: Implications for Technological Development." In *The Strength of Our Mothers*, 281–90.

———. "Planning for the Family versus Family Planning—The Case for National Action in Nigeria." In *The Strength of Our Mothers*, 149–64.

———. "Reflections on the Positions and Problems of Black Women in America." In *The Strength of Our Mothers*, 313–22.

———. "Roots of the Black Family: Observations on the Frazier-Herskovits Debate." In *The Strength of Our Mothers*, 77–89.

———. "Sex Roles, Education, and Development in Africa." *Anthropology and Education Quarterly* 13.3 (1982): 279–89.

———. "The Status of Women in Indigenous African Societies." *Feminist Studies* 12.1 (1986): 91–103.

———. *The Strength of Our Mothers: African and African American Women and Families.* Trenton, NJ: Africa World Press, 1996.

———. "Testimony." *Black Scholar* 22, nos. 1–2 (Winter 1991–Spring 1992), 100–102.

———. "Thomas Should Be Approved." *Philadelphia Inquirer*, July 28, 1991, 9-C.

———. "Value Premises Underlying Black Family Studies and Black Families." In *The Strength of Our Mothers*, 3–12.

———. "Women and Migration in Contemporary West Africa." *Signs* 3.1 (1977): 178–89.

———. *Where Women Work: A Study of Yoruba Women in the Marketplace and in the Home.* Anthropological Papers No. 53. Ann Arbor: University of Michigan, Museum of Anthropology, 1973.

Washington, E. B. "Niara Sudarkasa: Educator for the 1990s." *Essence*, May 1989, 106.

7

Johnnetta Betsch Cole

Eradicating Multiple Systems of Oppression

RICHÉ J. DANIEL BARNES

There is a well-worn story that has been passed down throughout the years about a senior administrator at a prestigious university who says to the incoming class, "Look to your left, look to your right, one of you will not make it to graduation." Many of us who aspired to go to college heard this story. It was our elders' way of telling us that college was difficult and that we would have to work to get there and stay there. It was also their way of ensuring we were clear that making it to graduation was our responsibility.

Johnnetta B. Cole
Courtesy of Jessica Suwarof, Eliot Elisofon Archives, Smithsonian's National Museum of African Art

As I sat with the entering class of 1995 at Spelman College in the fall of 1991, and Johnnetta Betsch Cole, the first African American woman to take the helm of that historic institution for the higher education of Black women, began delivering her remarks to the "freshwomen" class, I expected to hear this familiar story again and to take it as my marching orders as I always had. But although our "sister president" began with the familiar words that asked each of us to turn our attention to the young Black woman sitting on either side of us, she then went on to alter the saying in a small but significant way: "It is your responsibility to make sure all three of you make it to graduation."

This one statement sets the scene for a review of Cole's anthropological contributions. First, it grounds her commitment to education in general and to the education, specifically, of people of African descent, and Black women in particular. Second, it reveals her commitment to equity in all its various forms. Cole, who grew up the child of elite African Americans in the Jim Crow South, has made race, class, and gender equity the hallmarks of her research, philanthropy, and service. And finally, the simple turning of this well-known statement from one that highlights a hypercompetitive and individualistic perspective to one that emphasizes a communal perspective most associated with descendants of African and Native American peoples reveals her commitment to eradicating multiple systems of oppression in all their many forms.

But Cole, who received her master's and PhD in anthropology at Northwestern University as a student of Melville Herskovits and Paul Bohannon, famous early scholars of the African diaspora in the American School of Anthropology, is rarely noted for her contributions to the discipline of anthropology in the mainstream public.[1] As the president of the only two historically Black colleges for women—Spelman College (1987–97) and Bennett College for Women (2002–7); a member of president-elect Bill Clinton's transition team for education, labor, and the arts and humanities (1992); an inductee into the American Academy of Arts and Sciences; and the recipient of over sixty honorary degrees and several awards, including the 2015 BET Honors Award for Education, Cole is primarily seen as a consummate educator and mentor.[2] While that she most certainly is, she should also, and maybe even more importantly, be acknowledged within the discipline of anthropology for being one of the founders of the subfield of Black/African diaspora studies and insisting on its gendered analysis. She should also be credited with bringing a racialized analysis to feminist anthropology, including the ways in which feminism and gender equity operate differently within Black communities than in White communities. Additionally, having been brought up as the great-granddaughter of the first African American millionaire in Florida and as a member of one of few wealthy, upper-class Black families in the

Jim Crow South, she always turned a critical eye in her anthropological scholarship toward the ways in which socioeconomic class and privilege affect multiple identities. Her analysis of the inequitable distribution of wealth, often closely associated with race, gender, and sexuality, demonstrates how people are locked into impoverished conditions without access to resources or power over their own lives. And while making these multiple contributions to the discipline, Cole also brought anthropology into the public view, and more specifically into the Black American public view.

Anthropology, Africa, and Its Diaspora

Cole was introduced to what she later learned was sociocultural anthropology as a young girl growing up in Jacksonville, Florida. Cole recounts not learning until she took an undergraduate course at Oberlin University that her great-grandfather's life insurance company, which was founded "as a reliable alternative to passing the plate on Sunday mornings every time a member of the congregation stood up (and asked) could we help?," was built in the spirit of the "West African economic cooperative arrangements such as the Sou Sou, where each member makes a weekly or monthly contribution to the communal pot and then, when he or she is in need, receives the whole pot" (*Conversations*, 6). Similarly, Cole watched her parents reach out to people in need in her community and learned about the variations in Black family life both as practiced by her parents when they took in people in need, and by the family lives of those who needed their assistance. As a student, Cole learned that what she saw as her "family circle," "just being family," "just being neighborly," or "just doing the right thing," sociologists called "extended family," which was not usually viewed as part of the "normal" realm of family life (*Conversations*, 9–10). Cole also remembers being taught by her "family," which included educators in her community and at Fisk University, that she was somebody, that she should pursue her education as far as it can take her, and that she should have strong affirmation of self. As a child of the Jim Crow South, she also learned that regardless of these attributes and her belief in herself, racism persisted in institutional and individual forms. Her aim was to eradicate it.

It was with all of these experiences in tow that young Johnnetta, still planning to be a pediatrician, entered her first Introduction to Cultural Anthropology class taught by George Eaton Simpson at Oberlin College, where she had transferred from Fisk after her father passed away. She writes in her book *Conversations:*

On the first day of class, Professor George Eaton Simpson stood before us and began to stimulate hyperventilation, moving his body to Jamaican revivalist cult music. Between breaths he talked about this music, Jamaican religious cults, and much of the culture that is in the Caribbean and throughout the Americas as expressions of African culture in the New World. This, he said, is what anthropologists study. For me, it was an immediate, passionate reaction: Goodbye pediatrics! (18)

Cole says she took that hundred-dollar word, "anthropology," that no one she knew had ever heard of and decided to make something of it. She later realized that although people in her community were unfamiliar with the word and had no formal training, "there were many folks . . . who were keen observers of human behavior" (Heyward-Rotimi, "Perspectives of Black Feminist Anthropology," 2). Simpson's class had ignited a curiosity about her people that spurred her to pursue anthropology in graduate school. She explains, "I had some serious questions about being Black in America, and anthropology was at least speaking to, if not answering these questions. . . . [It] did not come with a set agenda, . . . but it did give me the tools to better understand and gain some perspective on my experiences" (*Conversations*, 20).

Cole's focus on the African diaspora and systems of oppression has cast her, like many African American anthropologists of her generation, to the margins of the discipline.[3] Beginning with her earliest anthropological research question under the direction of Melville Herskovits, Cole has faced what many young scholars of anthropology who choose to conduct research on their own societies have faced, the question of whether or not they can be objective. Cole often recounts the interaction she had with Herskovits when she petitioned to complete her master's research on the historically Black Greater Harvest Baptist Church in Chicago.[4] In an interview conducted by anthropologist Kevin A. Yelvington, Cole remembers that after being rebuffed several times when trying to get Herskovits to approve her proposal, she finally decided, taking advice from her fellow Black classmates, to ask Herskovits again and not leave his office until he had signed off on her proposal (279). When she approached him again, she finally learned that Herskovits was concerned that as a young Black person studying a Black space, she could not be objective. Cole says she explained to her esteemed mentor that she could do it. She understood objectivity as well as anyone could understand and practice it, and she knew she wanted to do "native anthropology." While Cole admits that the church had an extraordinary hypnotic affect, being Black wasn't what made it difficult for her to do the study, as White graduate students too were subject to such hypnosis. If Herskovits "really understood the nature of human empathy and ability to really do fieldwork," she adds, "then why would he think I wouldn't be able to do that study? The question should have been whether anybody could do that study" (279). Cole has pursued Herskovits's concern with objectivity throughout most of her career by calling into question whether or not anyone can be objective in the study of human cultures and behaviors and by making it clear that the study of Black culture and history should not be marginal to that of Whites; instead, human history and culture should be balanced and accurate and include studies of all people.

Cole went on to complete her study at Greater Harvest Baptist Church, which became the basis of her master's thesis, and then pursued her doctorate. After earning her PhD, she took a teaching position at Washington State University. At this time, she became more involved in the civil rights movement and, with several other faculty, founded the Black studies department at Washington State University, one of the first in the country. Cole's training as an Africanist anthropologist gave her the tools necessary to legitimate Black studies as an interdisciplinary field that not only explored African diasporic history and culture but also viewed it as the intellectual wing of a political movement (*Conversations*, 26; Yelvington, "An Interview with Johnnetta Betsch Cole," 281). "My decision to study anthropology and pioneer in founding one of the first Black studies programs in a U.S. university," she notes, "spoke to my ongoing struggle against racism as an entrenched system of inequality" ("Audre Lorde," 236).

While developing the program at Washington State, Cole, along with other Black anthropologists, was also challenging mainstream anthropology and the visible lack of diversity within the discipline. According to Ira Harrison, the Association of Black Anthropologists (ABA) began as a minority caucus organized during the 1968 annual meetings in Seattle, Washington. Following a panel discussion on the black curriculum in anthropological studies, with panelists Council Taylor, Delmos Jones, Diane Lewis, Johnnetta Cole, and Oliver Osborne, a meeting was held to determine what persons might be interested in forming a group. It was agreed that a caucus should be formed "to continue to discuss the issues and problems concerning the lack of minorities and their contributions in anthropology and the social sciences" (Harrison, "The Association of Black Anthropologists," 17). Johnnetta Cole was one of twenty-eight anthropologists who signed the agreement that would lead to the creation of the Minority Caucus in the American Anthropological Association (AAA) (17). The group grew in numbers and stature and became the ABA in 1975. Cole was the president of the organization from 1979 to 1980 (20).

Cole continued her studies and activism around issues of race and the diaspora through fieldwork and scholarship. After joining the faculty of the W. E. B. Du Bois Department of Afro-American Studies and the Anthropology Department at the University of Massachusetts at Amherst in 1970, Cole traveled to Cuba as part of a delegation sponsored by *The Black Scholar* to conduct research on the effect of the Cuban revolution on racism (Yelvington, "An Interview with Johnnetta Betsch Cole," 282). This was one of many trips to Cuba during which she explored race, racism, and sexism. She writes, "Intellectually that trip was the first step in closing the Pan-African circle that I began to draw as a graduate student" (*Conversations*, 30). Cole went on to carry out studies in many parts of the Caribbean, including Haiti, the Dominican Republic, St. Croix, and Grenada. In 1982, Cole left the University of Massachusetts and took a visiting professor position at Hunter College, where she eventually became director of the Latin American and Caribbean studies program and had the most creative teaching experiences of her career, teaching students about the variation in human experiences in the city of New York and publishing two texts instrumental to documenting the shifts in anthropology at the time, *Anthropology for the Eighties* (1982) and a revised and expanded edition, *Anthropology for the Nineties* (1988).

Black Feminist Anthropology

Cole admits that her attention to gender and sexuality came later in her research and teaching.

> So entangled was I in the web of racism that my consciousness about sexism . . . did not receive my serious attention until the 1970s, when I began to explore the arena of inquiry called Women's Studies. . . . It was not long after those explorations that I began to ask the fundamental questions: Where are the women in Black Studies, and where are the Black folks in Women's Studies? Because I continued to raise those questions at Hunter College, I was ripe for reading about and hearing about Audre Lorde's notions about the intersection of race, class, gender, and sexuality—and the importance of not privileging one form of oppression over another. . . . Oppression does not prevent one from oppressing someone else. ("Audre Lorde," 236)

Cole recounts coming to understand more deeply the oppression experienced by the LGBTQ community, particularly within Black communities, through Audre Lorde. It was through their friendship that Cole came to know, understand, interrogate, and speak about her own struggles with homophobia and heterosexism. She credits Lorde with teaching her two very important lessons: that there are various ways multiple identities can intersect, which she learned from how Lorde introduced herself as "a black woman, lesbian, feminist, poet, professor, mother," and that "what is destroying us" is "not our differences, but our silences about our differences."[5]

This understanding of human variation, and more specifically the diversity among women, is underscored most prominently in Cole's anthology *All American Women: Lines That Divide, Ties That Bind* (1986). At that time, Cole was among the early voices emphasizing the diversity of women's experiences within the discipline of anthropology. She drew analytical attention to Black feminism's need for a deeper inquiry into the human condition that probed the impact of race and gender and was a proponent of a Black feminist anthropology that combined scholarship and activism and that encouraged participation in the struggle against racism, sexism, and all other systems of inequality.[6] In *All American Women*, still cited heavily by women's studies and feminist anthropology scholars, Cole describes her impetus for writing the book and her intentions as they relate to women's studies:

> My own experiences as an Afro-American woman and my knowledge as an anthropologist led me to question the homogenizing of women's diverse cultures, languages, sexualities, classes, and ethnicities in the interest of paying homage to a mythical uniformity called sisterhood. . . . The oppression of women cuts across lines of class, race, ethnicity, age, religion, sexual orientation, region, and physical abilities. Yet, these same realities create the specific content of the oppression. (xiv)

As with her introduction to anthropology, Cole credits her introduction to "feminism" to her childhood. She calls her parents "race proud" and "protofeminist," concerned with issues of gender equality without thought to the terminology (*Conversations*, 7). But it was the women's movement and her position within the academy at the time that brought issues of gender into clear focus for her as a unit of analysis. As feminist anthropology began to gain greater traction within the discipline in the 1970s, Cole's work with race and gender helped establish the area of specialization now known as black feminist anthropology. She writes,

> Black studies in the 1960s and women's studies in the 1970s challenged the field of anthropology with respect to who was traditionally studied, by whom, in what ways, and toward what end. . . . As anthropology reinvented itself in response to such criticisms, the number of women and people of color who engaged in fieldwork increased. In what has come to be called native anthropology, more people from marginalized communities began to do anthropology "on them," and the very notion

of applied anthropology earned greater acceptability. These substantial changes laid the foundation for feminist anthropology, Black anthropology, and . . . Black feminist anthropology. (foreword, x)

According to Cole, Black feminist anthropologists, particularly those who are Black women conducting research on Black women, have an openness to disciplines outside anthropology because they are aware that any discipline can offer insights into the lives of the folks they are studying. They are also willing to use multiple tools to address the issues the Black women they work with confront because they feel a particular kinship and closeness, usually because they or the people they know and love face many of the same issues. They are engaged in research that is at once personal and political, and they "move through the world with a commitment to the kind of praxis that addresses changing the condition of their people, their discipline of anthropology, and indeed, themselves" (xi).

Cole speaks for herself as well as she articulates the tenets under which Black feminist anthropologists attempt to change their people, the discipline, and themselves. In *Gender Talk*, Cole and Beverly Guy-Sheftall take on some of the toughest subjects in African American communities. For too long, they maintain, race and racism have taken precedent over sexism and heterosexism, which has left African American women vulnerable to abuse within Black spaces in addition to outside. Cole and Guy-Sheftall's work boldly critiques those who blame Black women for the ills that plague Black communities, including patriarchal oppression. And as great Black feminist scholarship so often does, their book concludes with a chapter suggesting how Black men and women might work together to undermine the power of patriarchy.

Similarly, Cole and Guy-Sheftall refuse to ignore the different perspectives of White women, Black women, and other women of color in *Who Should Be First?* While many White women backed Hillary Clinton over Barack Obama in the 2008 presidential election, many Black women were excited by the possibility that Michelle Obama and her two daughters would get the respect of the nation previously reserved only for White women.[7]

Cole masterfully incorporates the tensions inherent in the intersections of identity into each of her authored and coauthored texts. She repeatedly stresses that "each of us has some form of power and privilege" and that the fact that this is the case "is not simply an important theoretical point. This reality requires each of us to confront the basis or bases from which we have the potential to harm others" ("Audre Lorde," 237).

Race, Class, and Power

It was when she was doing her dissertation research in Liberia that Cole says she was introduced to the idea that "no particular people has got a monopoly on oppressing other folks (Yelvington, "An Interview with Johnnetta Betsch Cole," 281). "For the first time in my life I began to seriously consider the issue of oppression along class lines. It was an important discovery, particularly in the 1960s, when in America there was such a focus on oppression along racial lines" (*Conversations*, 23). Along with her research in Liberia, both her research in Cuba and her tenure as president of Spelman and Bennett solidified her focus on socioeconomic class. For Cole, the accumulation of wealth and educational attainment or the lack thereof has had profound effects on the opportunities for advancement among Black people in the United States.

As president of Spelman and Bennett Colleges and board member of various organizations and corporations, moving throughout the country and traveling in multiple, often disparate circles, Cole learned of the hope as well as the despair that are sewn into the fabric of our nation. Cole has addressed socioeconomic issues not only through her scholarship and board memberships but also through her involvement in community service and her urging Spelman women, Bennett women, and all young people she has come into contact with to give back to the community. Aware that individual actions will not solve all that ails our world, at one of the many commencement addresses she has been asked to give, she said to the graduating class of Mount Holyoke College,

> Of course volunteerism or community service can never be a substitute for the responsibility of our government to do its part to help fix that which is broken in our communities, to help heal that which hurts—especially what hurts the most vulnerable: our children, our elders, womenfolks and people of color. But there is so much that we—you and I—can do to help transform American communities into safer, more vibrant and more just places for all of us. . . . If we are to genuinely engage in community building, not simply "do goodism," then we must go into communities as partners in transformation not missionaries of salvation. We must assume that such communities have many assets, not just a string of liabilities. And more than anything else, we must park at the local dump any signs of arrogance and attitudes of "I know it all."[8]

The Teachable Life: Raced and Gendered Contours of Marriage and Family

As a scholar of Black marriage, motherhood, and family life, I would be remiss if I did not address the ways in which Cole organized and led her extraordinary life with a husband and children in tow.[9] In many ways it is equally as instructive as her scholarship, as she admits managing a marriage can be a conundrum for women, particularly African American career women. Her most frequent advice to young women (which included me at one time) who are curious about how to combine career and family, is to make sure they have a partner who is invested in being a full participant in raising children. If not, be sure to have sister-friends and other-mothers available.

Johnnetta Betsch married a partner in scholarship, activism, parenting, and life when she married Robert Cole, an economics student from Iowa whom she met while completing her doctoral studies at Northwestern University. Cole happened to be White. According to Johnnetta, this was a sticking point for both sets of parents, as the two fell in love and decided to marry when the civil rights and black nationalist movements were just getting under way, a time when interracial marriages, especially in the South, were illegal (*Conversations*, 23).

The two married and then went to Liberia to conduct their fieldwork, both working on their dissertations. When they returned in 1962 they had their first son, David. Johnnetta remembers their marriage operating as a partnership and the two having a mutually beneficial intellectual exchange. Robert Cole got a job at Washington State University, and Johnnetta finished her dissertation, taught a few classes, and had another son, Aaron. In 1967, Johnnetta finished her dissertation and continued teaching at Washington State. The couple then moved to the University of Massachusetts, Amherst, and had their third son, Ethan Ché, shortly thereafter. It was in Amherst that things took a turn for the worst for the Coles. Johnnetta's career was taking off while it seemed Robert's had stalled. Johnnetta became an associate provost while at the University of Massachusetts, while Robert was only able to get a visiting professor position in the Economics Department at Amherst College and could not find a permanent position. This put him in an increasingly asymmetrical and culturally incongruous situation. "Underlying a marriage of equality on certain levels," Johnnetta explains, "was a tension created by my success as an African American and a woman in a society where it is assumed that greater success is practically a birthright for White people and for men" (*Conversations*, 24).

In Cole's assessment, many things have shifted in Black male-female relationships over the last few decades. Men and women are engaging in a range of lifestyles that are not new but that are now gaining more acceptance and acknowledgment. Nevertheless, the challenges she and Robert experienced, regardless of cross-race difficulties persist. She writes,

Today, African American women must think about what they want in terms of intimate relationships in ways they never have before. . . . In the past women entered marriage to varying degrees for economic security, social acceptability, and to have "legitimate" children. . . . If you are a feminist . . . you have to imagine the development of new ways of being woman and man whereby identity and esteem are not bound up in a paycheck or professional title. (*Conversations*, 99–101)

When she was the president of Spelman, Cole married a childhood sweetheart, Arthur Robinson, and came to understand firsthand the tall order she was asking. They had a marriage that actualized the partnership she imagined, but due to an "unforgiveable act" he committed, the marriage ended in divorce. Shortly thereafter Cole accepted the invitation made by Bennett College for Women to become the school's fourteenth president. It was while she was in North Carolina that she met James Stanton. The two married and maintained a commuter marriage until both careers could be relocated to Washington, DC.

Cole describes herself as having four sons and thousands of daughters, and she has seemingly raised them all similarly.[10] She is visibly proud but quite private about her sons' lives, only acknowledging a few things about them. She tells stories of taking them with her when she engaged in activist and service initiatives and notes that one of her sons' names was inspired by the Cuban revolutionary Che Guevara. Because of her focus on their full development, each of her sons pursued their many interests with zeal. Among them, one is a jazz musician, one is a hockey coach, and one is a connoisseur of Japanese language and culture. She talks about her "daughters" from Spelman and Bennett and her Delta Sigma Theta sisters and underscores the overwhelming honor and responsibility that comes with educating Black women, often quoting the African adage "When you educate a man, you educate a man. When you educate a woman, you educate a nation."[11] It is admittedly an adage that appears paradoxical on its face, particularly for a scholar-activist who believes in equality of the sexes. In response Cole states,

Women all over the world are the primary socializers of the next generation. Those of us who work for gender equity would like men to participate a little more in this process, but until we have that happen, it is we, as women who have the greatest influence on that next generation. . . . And so, when we educate girls and women, they then have an unusually powerful role in educating the next generation, but something else happens, let's look at a continent like Africa. When girls and women are educated it means that they will think a little more about family planning. It means that they will understand more the centrality of clean water and certain foods for not only their health but the health of their family. It gives us a possibility at least that they will be more active in fighting against gender violence. Education is such a powerful tool and in the hands of a girl and a woman, it's an extraordinarily powerful tool.[12]

Public Engagement and Leadership

When people learn that Cole has a doctorate in anthropology their understanding of the field is broadened. Additionally, considering the array of careers she has had as an anthropologist, she provides multiple answers to the popular question "What can you do with anthropology?" She does not see herself as the typical anthropologist but rather defines herself as a public anthropologist and an educator. Coming out of her third retirement, Cole became the director of the Smithsonian Museum of African Art, and set herself the goal of using "the stories told through art by African and African-American artists to contribute to our understanding of not only why and how race and other differences continue to divide us, but also of how we might move closer to the day when around the world, there is widespread respect for our common humanity."[13]

Cole's approach has been focused on making the critical tools of analysis most often linked to anthropologists accessible to the public and on teaching the world how to use those tools to break down and eradicate all systems of oppression and inequality. Her accomplishments on several corporate and philanthropic boards have been justly praised, but it is clear that as she continues to transform each and every space in which she takes the helm, she is teaching the world to be the consummate sociocultural anthropologist.

For Cole, "liberation is not a sudden event, but a process—a process I firmly believe will largely depend on another process called 'education'" (*Conversations*, 161). According to Cole, education does not simply mean formal schooling. It requires knowledge of oneself, knowledge of others and about the world that prepares us to live purposefully in the world, knowledge of and respect for diversity, and a participatory education that engenders a true understanding of the diversity in the human condition along with an insatiable desire for lifelong learning. And in this process, she concludes, there must also be the need and desire to teach others. This is the "stuff" of anthropology according to Cole. And while she has received most of her accolades within anthropology from the relatively small ABA and has had the most scholarly influence in the often marginalized disciplines of African diasporic studies, and women's studies, it is in these marginalized communities that Cole

96 · RICHÉ J. DANIEL BARNES

found the resources and the strength to develop her understanding of anthropological theories and methods and apply them to our world as an agent of change. She has made that work her life's work, but it was through the little-known field of anthropology that she found, and in many cases developed, a means by which to understand and also fight for African-descended communities, communities of women, and multiplicatively oppressed groups in general.

Notes

1. Melville Herskovits is renowned as a founding scholar of African and African American studies. He founded the first major interdisciplinary African studies department in the United States at Northwestern University. His most well-known book is *Myth of the Negro Past* (1941). Paul Bohannan is known for his extensive research on the Tiv people of Nigeria. He also wrote some of the most seminal textbooks in anthropology, including *High Points in Anthropology* (1973) and *How Culture Works* (1995).

2. Cole was nominated as secretary of education. However, when conservative groups learned of her research and activism in Cuba (in the 1970s and 1980s) on behalf of marginalized groups, a fact she has always been vocal about, Clinton rescinded his nomination.

3. Cole has received two of the AAA's most prestigious awards. She received the Distinguished Service Award in 1994 and was chosen to give the biennial distinguished lecture at the 107th annual meeting in 2008. Cole has also received several awards from various sections of the AAA, including the ABA, the Society for the Study of North America, and the Association for Feminist Anthropology.

4. Cole completed her master's degree at Northwestern University under Herskovits's direction in 1959. She completed her PhD in 1967 under the direction of Paul Bohannon.

5. "The Power of Diversity," keynote address, Third Annual Women and Power Conference, organized by Omega Institute and V-Day, September 2004, www.feminist.com/resources/artspeech/genwom/powerofdivers.html.

6. See Heyward-Rotimi, "Perspectives of Black Feminist Anthropology."

7. See Coleman, "Michelle Obama on My Mind," and Walker, "Lest We Forget."

8. One hundred sixty-first commencement address at Mount Holyoke College, June 9, 1998, www.mtholyoke.edu/media/dr-johnnetta-cole-speaks -mhcs-161st-commencement .

9. I am the author of several articles and a book entitled *Raising the Race: Black Career Women Redefine Marriage, Motherhood, and Community* that consider work and family policy as they relate to Black women. I also developed the concept of Black strategic mothering that draws heavily on Cole's work on African American women's work and family decisions.

10. Cole has three biological sons with her first husband, Robert Cole, and one stepson through her union with James Stanton.

11. C-Span question and answer with Johnnetta Cole, August 13, 2014, www.c-span.org/video/?320982-1/qa-johnnetta-cole.

12. C-Span question and answer with Johnnetta Cole, August 13, 2014, www.c-span.org/video/?320982-1/qa-johnnetta-cole.

13. "Why I Kept Open an Exhibit Featuring Art Owned by Bill Cosby," *The Root*, www.theroot.com/articles/culture/2015/08/exhibit_featuring_art_owned _by_bill_cosby_why_i_kept_it_open.html. Cole retired from Spelman College, Emory University, and Bennett College before taking the helm of the Smithsonian Museum of African Art in 2009. She retired from the Smithsonian in March 2017 to become, as she describes it, "a part-time consultant."

Bibliography

Barnes, Riché J. Daniel. *Raising the Race: Black Career Women Redefine Marriage, Motherhood, and Community*. New Brunswick, NJ: Rutgers University Press, 2016.

Bohannan, Paul. *How Culture Works*. New York: Free Press, 1995.

Bohannan, Paul, and Mark Glazer, eds. *High Points in Anthropology*. New York: Knopf, 1973.

Cole, Johnnetta Betsch, ed. *All American Women: Lines That Divide, Ties That Bind*. New York: Free Press, 1986.

———, ed. *Anthropology for the Eighties: Introductory Readings*. New York: Free Press, 1982.

———, ed. *Anthropology for the Nineties: Introductory Readings*. New York: Free Press, 1988.

———. "Audre Lorde: My Shero, My Teacher, My Sister Friend." In *I Am Your Sister: Collected and Unpublished Writings of Audre Lorde*, ed. Rudolph Byrd, Johnnetta B. Cole, and Beverly Guy-Sheftall, 231–37. New York: Oxford University Press, 2009.

———. "*The Black Scholar* Interviews Dr. Johnnetta B. Cole." *Black Scholar* 19.6 (1988): 60–64.

———. *Conversations: Straight Talk with America's Sister President*. New York: Doubleday, 1993.

———. Epilogue to *Words of Fire: An Anthology of African-American Feminist Thought*, ed. Beverly Guy-Sheftall, 549–51. New York: New Press, 1995.

———. *Dream the Boldest Dreams, and Other Lessons of Life*. Atlanta, GA: Longstreet, 1997.

———. Foreword to *Black Feminist Anthropology: Theory, Politics, Praxis and Poetics*, ed. Irma McClaurin, ix–xii. New Brunswick, NJ: Rutgers University Press, 2001.

———. "Theorizing Black Studies in Liberal Arts Education." In *The Black Studies Reader*, ed. Jacqueline Bobo, Cynthia Hudley, and Claudine Michel, 21–40. New York: Routledge, 2004.

Cole, Johnnetta B., and Beverly Guy-Sheftall. *Gender Talk: The Struggle for Women's Equality in African American Communities*. New York: One World/Ballantine, 2003.

98 · RICHÉ J. DANIEL BARNES

———, eds. *Who Should Be First? Feminists Speak Out on the 2008 Presidential Campaign.* Albany: State University of New York Press, 2010.

Coleman, Arica. "Michelle Obama on My Mind." In *Who Should Be First: Feminists Speak Out on the 2008 Presidential Campaign,* ed. Johnnetta B. Cole and Beverly Guy-Sheftall, 215–30. Albany: State University of New York Press, 2010.

Harrison, Ira. E. "The Association of Black Anthropologists: A Brief History." *Anthropology Today* 3.1 (1987): 17–21.

Herskovits, Melville J. *The Myth of the Negro Past.* New York: Harper, 1941.

Heyward-Rotimi, Kamela. "Perspectives of Black Feminist Anthropology: An Interview with Dr. Johnnetta B. Cole." *Voices* 2.2 (1998): 1–5.

Walker, Alice. "Lest We Forget: An Open Letter to My Sisters Who Are Brave." In *Who Should Be First? Feminists Speak Out on the 2008 Presidential Campaign,* ed. Johnnetta B. Cole and Beverly Guy-Sheftall, 47–52. Albany: State University of New York Press, 2010.

Yelvington, Kevin A. "An Interview with Johnnetta Betsch Cole." *Current Anthropology* 44.2 (2003): 275–88.

8

John Langston Gwaltney

The Development of a Core Black Ethnography and Museology

DEBORAH JOHNSON-SIMON

Most of us live our lives by challenging ourselves or being challenged by others to strive for success in the areas of our endeavors. We may create lists of benchmarks for ourselves and share our thoughts about our goals with friends, family, or colleagues to keep us on point and then mark each thing off the list once we've accomplished. Even as children we are encouraged to construct lists of career possibilities. The reality is that anthropology is rarely a consideration for career checklists among African American children or young adults.

In an article entitled "Choosing Anthropology as a Career," John Langston Gwaltney explains what led him to pursue this field. He starts by sharing that anthropology is the primary scientific discipline that touches on everything concerning humanity. Anthropologists investigate everything from fossilized human and animal excrement to the invention of religions and races. He points to his personal disability (visual impairment) as one that was shared by three other professional anthropologists known to him. Therefore, he could also make his mark as the first visually impaired African American to conduct fieldwork independently. "It is a rare career for a blind person," he notes, "but not an impractical one." He goes on to say that his "own career in anthropology alternates between teaching and field research" ("Choosing Anthropology as a Career," 70).

Gwaltney entered the world on September 25, 1928, in Orange, New Jersey, and became a scholar, teacher, writer, artist, and mentor. By the age of two months John Langston was blind. The cause of his blindness is never mentioned in any of his writings or by those who have written about him. His parents, siblings, and extended family enriched his life

John Langston Gwaltney
Courtesy of Judy Gwaltney

by allowing his blindness normality. On August 29, 1998, in Reston, Virginia, he succumbed to a lengthy illness. Johnnetta B. Cole, a next generation anthropologist whose life is documented in this volume, remarks in an obituary that "he embarked on a remarkable journey that would lead him to corridors of anthropology and render him a gatekeeper of black core culture, and innovator of native anthropology" ("John Langston Gwaltney," 614).

This chapter is an overview of Gwaltney's life and his work as a scholar, teacher, writer, ritual wood carver, and native anthropologist. I also explore the complex factors that enabled this anthropologist to transcend his visual impairment to participate in fieldwork under the guidance of famed anthropologist Margaret Mead. Finally, I consider his development of a "core black" ethnography of African Americans' social exclusion and his analysis of African American lives as "drylongso" (a black English term meaning "ordinary" or "not unusual") as well as his participation in African American museology.

Gwaltney's Personal Life

Gwaltney became known to me through his artistic and intellectual contribution to urban ethnography, the humanities, and native anthropology. He was a prolific writer and a sagacious observer of black people and everyday life. Gwaltney's publications and biographies about him, as well as obituaries and census records provide insight into his personal life. He was most interested in studying African American culture. For most of his active academic career he maintained that a "core black culture" exists in the United States, that it is centered around large family groups and church affiliations, and that its main features are communal responsibility, tolerance, conviviality, awareness of repression, and a rich language. Gwaltney cultivated his anthropological skills by seeking to understand and give voice to his natal community. In "Choosing Anthropology as a Career" he reminds readers that "black American culture, the one I was born into, has a rich mythic past and a lively proverbial oral tradition. Many things from that heritage made me think about my past and other people's pasts. My elders taught me slave counting games and clapping figures and spoke to me of the time when the animals could talk and of the holy men and women who conducted the secret slave church" (69).

Gwaltney's parents were Stanley and Mabel (Harper) Gwaltney. Stanley Gwaltney spent most of his life traveling the world by sea, at times as a member of the US Navy. He also worked as a merchant seaman as a means of providing for himself and his family. A census search reveals that he registered to fight in World War I for the US Navy in 1918.[1] At that time, he was twenty-two years old and single, living with his parents, Gus and Ida Gwaltney. A second registration found through census data search shows him married and the father of five children.[2] His registration card from 1942 for World War II provided a physical description of this seafaring man. He was 5'4" and weighed 175 pounds; his hair was black, his complexion was dark, and he had a scar on his nose. He was born on December 27, 1896, in Orange, New Jersey. He would be the first to introduce his son to the wonders of the world: "My father was a sailor full of vivid talk about Nagasaki, Marseilles, and Veracruz." Stanley Gwaltney's travels inspired in his son a curiosity of geography and a desire to learn about the lives of the people who were living in the places his father had described so vividly as he was growing up. According to an Ancestry.com search, his father died on February 24, 1964, and is buried in the Beverly National Cemetery, in Beverly, New Jersey. John would begin his first independent field research in Mexico the following year at the age of thirty-seven under the guidance of one of the most well-known anthropologists of that time, Margaret Mead.

Mabel Harper was born in Virginia. She married Stanley Gwaltney and they had five children: Lucy, Laurel, Hattie, John, and Robert. While her husband provided for the family as a sailor, she was a homemaker. She was tenacious when it came to John's well-being. John once said of his mother in this regard that she "enlisted the aid of medical doctors, chiropractors, faith healers and root doctors in vain attempts to restore my sight" ("Choosing Anthropology as a Career," 69). Once she resigned herself to the fact that there was no cure, she was the first to become proactive in securing the best quality of life she could for him despite his visual impairment. She made sure that her son had every opportunity to achieve success in whatever endeavor he decided to undertake. Even in his early childhood his mother experimented with potential occupations for the visually impaired. Her first attempts were the arts, where there were many role models from singers to musicians to artists (sculptors). She would cut pieces of cardboard into the shapes of letters, numbers, and animals so that he could "see" them with his hands. She encouraged him to play the piano, because she thought that music might be a good career for a blind black person. She enlisted the help of her uncle Julius, a famous wood carver from Virginia, when she saw what John was skilled with a piece of wood and a file. John recalled how one time he was outlining previously cut shapes with a pin, thereby creating a Braille image on the reverse side of the paper. He says, "I inundated my mother with a flood of these copies until she finally gave me a piece of wood and a file and said, "now let's see what you can do" ("Afro-American Ritual Carving," 70). She made another attempt to tap into potential outlets for his abilities when he was nine years old, arranging for him to attend a summer camp despite his concerns of the dangers he might face. He enjoyed the experience and attended the camp every year until he was sixteen years old (Hillstrom and Hillstrom, "John Langston Gwaltney," 85). Mabel Gwaltney mounted an effort to get John in the programs that would give him the best education. In this excerpt from his 1976 article "A Native Replies," John recounts the lengths to which his mother was willing to go to get the help her son might need.

> I was certainly born a native of the natives as a kindly fortune saw fit to deposit me in a great, extended Black American family. Like most people I suppose, I felt that I had been fortunately situated by the great god chance. The only disadvantages I was sensible of as a child were those that were the necessary consequence of blindness. It was to minimize this disability that my mother, who held the portfolios for defense and foreign relations in our family, initiated a lengthy exchange with the demon officialdom. Eventually these negotiations reached White House level as our "first lady" Eleanor Roosevelt was believed to be a member of a pitifully small company for whom a Caucasoid status had not proven to be an insurmountable moral impediment. All this summitry culminated in the decision to dispatch me to what were then known as sight-saving classes. Because such classes were conducted in schools located beyond the boundaries of my Casbah, my formal education involved an inordinate amount of dealing with foreigners. (8)

John Gwaltney's paternal grandparents were Gustave "Gus" Gwaltney and Ida George Gwaltney; they were both Virginia natives who married on April 15, 1886. At the time of the 1900 census the Gwaltney family was living in Virginia and they had four children; Velma, twelve years old; Elnora, seven; Clarence, five; and Stanley, three.[3] They migrated to New Jersey, where they raised their children and became essential figures in the lives of their grandchildren. When John reflects in his article "The Native Replies" about the ways of coming to understand being a native in a native vs. settler dichotomy he draws his example from his grandfather Gus's philosophies. "More than a shadow of this schism" between native and settler

> had been cast upon my preschool consciousness by the most reverend of those Black elders, my paternal grandfather, who was a sagacious, self-taught classicist and Hausa scholar whose equanimity, integrity, and encyclopedic knowledge made him the leader of a large kindred. He, like most Black elders I knew, held privately but tenaciously to the view that White people were genetically incapable of the broad process of civilization. He did not question the Caucasoid capacity as a perfectly adequate tribe of smiths and tinkers, but he did entertain formidable reservations about the ability of White men to use the strange and awesome fruit of their forges with anything like wisdom and deliberation. The evidence of individuals and groups that seemed to Caucasoid pretensions to more than purely mechanical sufficiency was attributed to the antiquity and pervasiveness of the practice of "passing" or charged to that reprehensible mania for co-option that had moved Europeans to "whiten up" the Lower Nile Valley and every other square centimeter of the historically better neighborhood. (8, 10)

Just as John Gwaltney's father planted the seed for travel and the wonders of the world in his heart and mind, it can be said that his interests in anthropology, and specifically understanding the anthropology of his people—black people/native people, in relationship to white people/settlers—was fostered by the seeds planted by his paternal grandfather.

Raising children in a sighted household is an all-out effort if we want them to be healthy and productive members of society. It is equally the case in families with children who have disabilities. The Gwaltneys wholly embraced the "it takes a village to raise a child" concept. In the acknowledgments for his books, Gwaltney shows his appreciation for two of his siblings in particular, his oldest sister, Lucy, and his younger brother, Robert, and thereby lets his readers know how much his family means to him. He dedicated his book *Drylongso* (1980) to Lucy, who was seven years older than him and who, as the oldest child in the Gwaltney household, appears to have taken on a lot of the responsibility

104 · DEBORAH JOHNSON-SIMON

for helping her mother with her younger brother. He says that from his earliest days, she was a constant source of inspiration and an exemplar of the core black way. He goes on to say that

> there is no one to whom I am so deeply indebted for the profound satisfactions which proceed from the exercise of the mind and the imagination. She bore us both on wings of print to Troy and Thebes and Xanadu. Her command of the art of puppetry lent substance to many of the shadowy characters which have their being in the realms of books and art. She showed me what a campfire was by kindling one in a great iron pot in the center of our living room. She showed me how to make everything from exquisite cheese biscuits to perfume of dubious quality. But the success of those experiments has much less to do with their immediate product than with the habit of inquiry which she strove so patiently and graciously to inculcate in me. Lucy was a prime mover in my introduction to almost everything that is excellent in life and creditable in character. (x)

Robert is John's only brother, and they were two years apart in age. But it appears that this gap was not as big a gulf as it sometimes is, as they seem to have been more like buddies or twins. Robert (Bob) was John's sidekick, although he allowed John to have the limelight. In the acknowledgments in *Drylongso*, Gwaltney remarks that his brother's "disinclination to be interviewed was more than compensated for by his never-failing material assistance in transportation, sustenance and lodging" (x). The biography on Gwaltney in James Kessler, J. S. Kidd, Renee A. Kidd, and Katherine A. Morin's *Distinguished African American Scientists of the 20th Century* reveals more about the relationship between the two brothers, especially when it comes to a family support system: "In his last year of high school John bought an old second-hand car and that purchase allowed him more freedom than he had ever had before. His brother or his friends drove John and his mother to the countryside where they had many happy outings" (132).

In the preface and acknowledgments for his first book, *The Thrice Shy* (1970), Gwaltney mentions that for invaluable assistance in the acquisition and expedition of field equipment he was greatly indebted to his brother, Robert Gwaltney. He also notes that he is "deeply appreciative of the diverse vital contributions of readers, researchers, and braillists," among whom he lists his big sister (vii).

In 1956 in the Bronx, New York, Gwaltney married Judith Lucille Jacobson. They raised two children, Karen and Peter. They lived near Syracuse, New York (Hillstrom and Hillstrom, "John Langston Gwaltney," 92). Judith was absolutely devoted to her husband. They embarked on their marriage in the same year that John began his field-work in Mexico, which was followed by a year of analyzing the data collection and writing the dissertation and then another year of turning that dissertation into his first book. Judith's devotion and his appreciation and love for her is evident in the preface and acknowledgments in *The Thrice Shy*, where he applauds her: "Training in the vital field skill of riding and the burden of library research are only two of the indispensable contribution of my wife, Judith, to this project" (vii). In the acknowledgments to *Drylongso*, he likewise notes that "most special thanks are due and lovingly tendered to my wife, Judy. Her proficiency in editing, her skill and patience in typing and her lively, diligent mind were all absolutely indispensable in the translation of these data into book form. It is no exaggeration or perfunctory domestic duty but a statement of plain fact to say that without her assistance it would not have seen the light of print" (x). Judith would again play an essential role in bringing *The Dissenters* to fruition: "It would be impossible to overestimate the contributions of my wife, Judy, to the forging of this project and volume. In addition to all the typing she also did much of the drudgery of tape transcription. A sagacious and probing interviewer with a genius for rapport, her editing and research skills are manifest throughout the entire work. For her general discernment, intrepidity, and aplomb in a very serendipitous field of endeavor, I am profoundly grateful" (xii).

Education

Mabel Gwaltney mounted an effort to get John in the program that would give him the best education her visually impaired son could receive. So she wrote a letter to First Lady Eleanor Roosevelt about John and the hopes she had for him. In response, Mrs. Roosevelt helped place John in a special public school program for blind children. In grade school his favorite subject was geography, in part because of the stories of his father's travels but also because of the CBS national radio program *American School of the Air* and one of the show's special guests, anthropologist Margaret Mead, who talked about various societies she had researched and observed.

During John's senior year in high school, his mother became ill with diabetes, a chronic disease that can lead to cardiovascular problems and death. Despite her illness, however, she still insisted that John go on to college. He decided to attend Upsala College in East Orange, so that he could be close to home. Sadly, his mother died shortly before

106 · DEBORAH JOHNSON-SIMON

he graduated from Upsala in 1952 with a bachelor's degree in history and sociology.[4]

After graduating from college, Gwaltney received a scholarship to continue his education at the New School for Social Research in New York City. One of his primary areas of study was the effects of European colonialism in Africa. Gwaltney earned his master's degree in political science and sociology from the New School in 1957. Shortly after graduating, Gwaltney accepted a teaching job at the Henry George School of Social Sciences in New York City. The job enabled Gwaltney to develop his teaching skills as well as earn money to continue his education. In 1959, he began taking courses toward a doctoral degree at Columbia University. One of his professors there was Margaret Mead, the anthropologist who had sparked his interest in studying other cultures twenty years earlier. Gwaltney had always wanted to conduct research as a field anthropologist, which would involve living among the people he was studying for a period of time. Dr. Mead was very encouraging and helped him to plan a research project that took him to San Pedro Yolox, Mexico.

Upon returning to the United States in 1966, Gwaltney wrote a dissertation outlining all that he learned about life in San Pedro Yolox. One thing he discovered was that the Chinantec people treated the blind with profound respect and believed that they were protected from harm by supernatural forces. In fact, each blind person was assigned a child as a helper and guide, and the children viewed this sort of assignment as an honor.

In 1967, Gwaltney completed his dissertation and earned his PhD from Columbia. The faculty of the school was so impressed with his research project that they presented him with the Ansley Dissertation Award, the highest award for a doctoral candidate at Columbia. Out of several hundred people who received doctoral degrees that year, only thirteen people were even recommended for the award. His doctoral defense was praised by his mentor and advisor, Margaret Mead, as "one of the most brilliant PhD oral examinations in my long experience." (Freedman, "On the Occasion of John Gwaltney's Retirement from University of Syracuse," 62).

Career

John Gwaltney launched into a stellar career as a scientist, a native anthropologist, and an educator. In 1967, he took a job as an assistant professor at the State University of New York College at Cortland, and he became an associate professor of anthropology in 1969. He remained at SUNY Cortland until 1971, when he moved to Maxwell Graduate School of Citizenship and Public Affairs at Syracuse University, where he would remain until his retirement in 1989. He was introduced to the folks at the University of Syracuse through a letter of recommendation from his mentor, Margaret Mead, who wrote, "He is a most remarkable man. Blinded at two months, he manages his life and work with extraordinary skill and bravery, including the most onerous fieldwork alone in a Mexican village" (Freedman, "On the Occasion of John Gwaltney's Retirement from University of Syracuse," 62).

Even with this demanding career, John found the time to serve as a consultant to projects of national science organizations. The Smithsonian Institution and the New York Council for the Humanities list him as a board member, and he was an active consultant to the New York State Creative Artist Public Service.

Fieldwork

Gwaltney used his first independent field experience for his doctoral dissertation, and he later recounted these experiences in *The Thrice Shy*. Gwaltney helps us understand his field experience via his reflections on that experience in this excerpt from his *Dialogue* article:

> My doctoral dissertation was based on a year's field work in a very remote Indian village in the Mexican Sierra Madre Occidental. I knew that this type of terrain would present certain problems in mobility. I knew much travel would be by muleback so I acquired some acquaintance with the horse before I left. I knew there would be much walking over very rough ground so I had some extra long, extra strong solid steel canes made and I relied heavily upon guides. The use of guides in the field work context is often a necessity for any stranger, sighted or not, so this did not represent any great divergence from common practice.
>
> Field work is often narrowly interpreted as meaning some protracted stay in a rain forest, arid desert, or frozen tundra environment, but in a larger sense, the field is wherever you do your research. An increasing amount of anthropological research is being conducted in modern industrialized cities. I have conducted field research in such commonplace setting as classrooms, bars, street corners, and hospital rooms, as well as rain forests. ("Choosing Anthropology as a Career," 69)

Gwaltney also conducted fieldwork among urban African Americans at the Ethiopian Hebrew Congregation and Commandment Keepers in Harlem, among the Shinnecock and Poospatuck Indians of Long Island, and among the Maroons of St. Elizabeth Parish, Jamaica ("John Langston Gwaltney").

Memberships

I first gained knowledge of John Langston Gwaltney when his name appeared in the 1983 *Blacks in Museums* directory published by the Smithsonian Institution and the African American Museums Association (AAMA). This was the first directory of museum professionals who were African Americans. The directory included a listing of anthropologists, a category that is rarely associated with African Americans engaged in museum work. Six black anthropologists were listed: Joan B. Waite, Theresa Ann Singleton, Melvin D. Williams, Laura Henley (now Laura Henley Dean), Reginald Jackson, and John Gwaltney. Thus I began my research of that museum association. I was encouraged by Elgin Klugh and Angela Howell (both of whom are contributors to this volume) to participate with them on an Association for Black Anthropologists (ABA) panel during the American Anthropological Association meeting in 2011 to share the connections between black anthropologists, HBCUs, and black museology. After our session, Ira Harrison shared his new list of African American anthropologists with the panel participants. He let us know there would be an opportunity to sign up to be a contributor to an upcoming publication on the second generation of black anthropologists in the United States. Once I saw John Gwaltney's name on the list, I knew that I wanted to research his life and work and more importantly how he came to be associated with AAMA and the other anthropologists listed in that directory.[5] Gwaltney's appearance in the first directory of blacks in museums under the anthropologist category solidified his status as not only a native anthropologist, a title to which he readily lays claim, but also as a black museum anthropologist.

In addition to being a member of the ABA and the AAMA, Gwaltney was associated with the following organizations: the American Anthropological Association (fellow), American Ethnological Society, American Association for the Advancement of Science (member of Committee on Opportunities in Science), National Science Foundation, the Latin American Anthropology Group, and the Society for Applied Anthropology. When it came to memberships, Gwaltney believed in not just joining up but joining in. He was never just a name on a roster that would look impressive on the resume. He was a regular contributor to the ABA's newsletters. In an early ABA publication, "Notes from the ABA," John shared with readers the fruits of his research and his thoughts on the evolving area of native anthropology. In his connection with the AAMA, he participated in its first national workshop in Atlanta, Georgia, April 22–24, 1982, hosted by the Atlanta University Center Coordinated Arts Program.[6]

Mentors

Gwaltney explains that "I owe much of the persistence curiosities of my life to the radio of my youth": "It was, for example, on the excellent series, the CBS *School of the Air of the Americas* that I first heard Dr. Margaret Mead, who directed my first piece of foreign field work a generation later" ("Choosing Anthropology as a Career," 69–70). In her acclaimed book *Margaret Mead: A Life* (1984), Jane Howard expounds on the extent of Mead's mentorship abilities. She states that Mead's work in cultural anthropology called the world's attention to her profession. She recruited hundreds of students to anthropology, moving far beyond Columbia University, where she taught, and the American Museum of Natural History, where she was a curator. Howard remarks that Mead's "generosity was staggering. She didn't just write letters of recommendation and maneuver for grants and fellowships; she gave of her time and her attention and made connections no one else would have imagined" (13).

John Gwaltney took the time during the summer of 1976 to write about his experiences and his other mentors. He tells us that "the opinions and judgment of intelligent, civil teachers at every level were very important in forming my choice of a career. Elder John Robinson, who taught me most of what I know about the old-time religion of my slave ancestors, and professors like Robert Rockwood, Fredric Barth and Gilbert Highet did much to establish in me some notion of the splendid country of the mind where no one has any greater need of 'travel techniques' than any other" ("Choosing Anthropology as a Career," 70).

Gwaltney's Influence on African American Anthropology

Gwaltney left us in his physical presence in 1998, but his legacy continues to affect the field through his views on anthropology and African Americans, native anthropology, and core black ethnography. A search for anthropology syllabi will still yield Gwaltney's books and papers as required texts. His influence on anthropology is still far reaching. In "Gwaltney's Influence on African American Anthropology," Cheryl Rodriquez expresses eloquently how many of us who are introducing young minds to the rewards of understanding African American anthropology can look to the work of Gwaltney. Rodriquez sees *Drylongso* as the quintessential reference, arguing that it "reflects unyielding and diverse black views on many of life's key issues" (71). "Gwaltney's data," she notes, "recorded during 'folk seminars' held in churches as well as taverns, was critical in illuminating and supporting

110 · DEBORAH JOHNSON-SIMON

the existence and legitimacy of 'Core Black Culture'" (71). With "his field methodology—the collecting of 'good and profound dialogue,'" he "sought to reveal the integrity of core black culture and to dismiss historical images of black people as marginal or exotic beings." She concludes that his "respect for his informants, his sense of connectedness to his field community, his belief in the theory-building and analytical capacities of black people, all compose a model for native anthropology that I have attempted to utilize in my teaching" (71). Rodriguez reminds us that one of the rare treasures of being trained to do anthropology is to be able to use that training as a native in your native communities. She points out that this was a quality of Gwaltney's work that will forever be recognized for its splendor.

Gwaltney and Native Anthropology

Gwaltney delivered the rallying call for the embrace of native anthropology to the members of the ABA in Washington, DC, on December 5, 1980, during the awards ceremony at the AAA annual meeting. In this remarkable presentation, he defines this discipline and explains how it became an important practice for his work and why it must be embraced by black anthropologists: "I believe that native anthropology, which is one voice, is a very important voice which has got to be heard more and which will be heard more if you as Black anthropologists turn your attentions to your natal communities and do what the soji did" ("Some Thoughts on Native Anthropology," 67). No doubt sensing the questioning looks on the faces of his audience and knowing that in years to come, when his commentary on his thoughts on native anthropology would be read, this statement would need clarification, he adds that

> I did not know the word "soji" until Ruth Shays, another octogenarian, told me that it was the word for an unbaptised person in the old-time religion. Such unbaptised persons learned the core Black way by listening to their elders. And the other thing that those people had to pledge to do was to follow the truth wherever it leads you. That's what native anthropology has to do. And that's a sort of simple statement of a very difficult mission, because if you follow the truth wherever it leads you, you will have difficulty in this world with publishers, with universities, and occasionally with your own constituents. But, one of the most important things about this research was that almost all the sober people who contributed the data said that if all we could do is sit here and tell more lies, then we might as well forget it. The truth is good enough, whatever it is. (67)

Gwaltney was convinced, and wanted to convince his colleagues, that the truth would come from the mouths of black people who became comfortable sharing their experiences with other natives who would not be willing to manufacture more of the same lies. Gwaltney wanted to encourage fellow black anthropologists to become like the soji. His energy was renewed by this practice. He found it sobering not to put his words in their mouths. He found it liberating to be able to go back into those communities where he conducted his fieldwork and share their published words along with the astounding reviews that his scholarship was receiving. I believe that Gwaltney wanted succeeding generations of black anthropologists and natives to be pillars, as in the prayer of the Baptist deacons of old: "Lawd, prop us up on all leaning sides." Black anthropologists embracing native anthropology would be the "bridge over troubled waters." John had a love for the truth of his people and saw that truth in the practice of native anthropology.

African American Ritual Carving

My account of John L. Gwaltney and his work would be remiss if I did not mention his love of ritual carvings. I believe that this extraordinary talent is one of the things that drew him to museums and galleries and that resulted in his being included in the *Blacks in Museums* directory in 1983. The arts have been a tremendous vehicle for expression and truth in native communities. Gwaltney found refuge in the arts and derived energy from them for his work. In one of his articles he shared his introduction into this world: "My Great Uncle Julius was a famous carver from Virginia who made the first dala I ever touched. Friends, relatives and neighbors taught me the art and its accompanying ideology. It is a largely undocumented and clandestine art with no uniformity of orthnography or formal codification" ("Afro-American Ritual Carving").

Native anthropology and being like the soji was for Gwaltney the essence of a core black theology. The methodology he used with his ritual carving and the arts became one with his administration of anthropology. His carvings provided him with another opportunity to be a part of his native community, to hear what they had to say, and then to express it through the medium of wood carvings. The ritual or sacred carving tradition of old-time religion is the translation into wood sculpture of the basic philosophy, conventions, and reasoning of that core Black theology. Sculpture, in very general terms, expresses elements of old-time religion in the form of sacred motifs called parables. Although old-time religion was necessarily decentralized, the symbols

112 · DEBORAH JOHNSON-SIMON

of authority were remembered from West Africa and elaborated on in the New World. Yams, gourds, and mythic creatures were combined according to the codes devised in the many slave neighborhoods ("Afro-American Ritual Carving").

Gwaltney's Influence and Museum Anthropology

Gwaltney could not have predicted that his love of native anthropology would land him in the midst of museum professionals. Nevertheless, when his mother gave him a piece of wood and said, "Let's see what you do with this," or when his elders led him through old-time religion, they may have encouraged him on a path that would end there.

So much of Gwaltney's life and work as an anthropologist and as a ritual carver centered on what he called the "will of black people to preserve and celebrate our rich and worthy way of being human." I believe that it is within this spirit that he was invited to present at the first workshop for the AAMA and now is not only among the ranks of the next generation of African American anthropologists but among the pioneers of African American museums.

John Langston Gwaltney, you have left an indelible footprint on the paths that you have graciously traveled. You have also carved your way into the arts and humanities with your African American museum anthropology and core black ethnography.

Notes

1. 1930 census, East Orange, Essex, New Jersey, roll T626-1330, page 6B, enumeration district 0388.

2. 1940 census, East Orange, Essex, New Jersey, roll T627-2332, page 11B, enumeration district 7–134.

3. 1900 census, Orange Ward 4, Essex, New Jersey, roll 968, page 11A, enumeration district 0165.

4. Upsala suffered from lack of funding and declining enrollment over the course of the second half of the twentieth century and closed in 1995.

5. A group of colleagues and I searched the Smithsonian archives for the original applications filled out by the directory participants. After going through six large boxes, we were thrilled to discover a copy of the directory in the pristine form in which it was presented to the grant administrators. Sadly, we were not able to recover the original applications. We did, however, find the solicitation documents for participants that verified the national search for Black museum professionals. A copy of the directory, which had been owned by James E. Lewis, the director of the art gallery and museum at Morgan State University and never used by him, was gifted to the Center for the Study of African and African Diaspora Museums and Communities. In our preliminary search

among the members of this still thriving network, we have unfortunately been unsuccessful in recovering other copies of it.

6. Gwaltney is mentioned in a 1982 *Columbus Times* article titled "Ms. Shabazz is Chosen to Attend Workshop" in connection with the AAMA conference.

Bibliography

Cole, Johnnetta B. "John Langston Gwaltney (1928–1998)." *American Anthropologist* 101.3 (1999): 614–16.

Freedman, Michael. "On the Occasion of John Gwaltney's Retirement from University of Syracuse." *Transforming Anthropology* 7.2 (1998): 62–64.

Gwaltney, John L. "Afro-American Ritual Carving." *Transforming Anthropology* 7.2 (1998): 70.

———. "Choosing Anthropology as a Career." *Dialogue* (Summer 1976): 68–70.

———. *The Dissenters: Voices from Contemporary America.* New York. Random House, 1986.

———. *Drylongso: A Self Portrait of Black America.* New York. Random House, 1980.

———. "A Native Replies." *Natural History*, December 1976, 8–14.

———. "On Going Home Again—Some Reflections of a Native Anthropologist." *Phylon* 30 (1976): 236–42.

———. "Some Reflections of a Blind Anthropologist." *Dialogue* (Winter 1975): 81–83.

———. "Some Thoughts on Native Anthropology." *Transforming Anthropology* 7.2 (1998): 67–69.

———. *The Thrice Shy: Cultural Accommodation to Blindness and Other Disasters in a Mexican Community.* New York. Columbia University Press, 1970.

Harrison, Ira E., and Faye V. Harrison, eds. *African-American Pioneers in Anthropology.* Urbana: University of Illinois Press, 1999.

Hillstrom, Kevin, and Laurie Hillstrom. "John Langston Gwaltney, 1928–1998." In *Biography Today: Scientists and Inventors Series Profiles of People of Interest to Young Readers,* ed. Laurie L. Harris and Cherie D. Abbey, 84–93. Detroit, MI: Omnigraphics, 1999.

Howard, Jane. *Margaret Mead: A Life.* New York. Simon and Schuster, 1984.

"John Langston Gwaltney." *Contemporary Authors Online.* Detroit, MI: Gale, 2001.

Kessler, James H., and J. S. Kidd, Renee A. Kidd, and Katherine A. Morin. *Distinguished African American Scientists of the 20th Century.* Phoenix, AZ: Oryx Press, 1996.

Rodriguez, Cheryl R. "Gwaltney's Influence on African American Anthropology." *Transforming Anthropology* 7. 2 (1998): 71–72.

9

Ira E. Harrison

Activist, Scholar, and Visionary Pioneer

ALISHA R. WINN

This chapter explores the professional journey of scholar, activist, and pioneer Ira E. Harrison and documents the many intricate components shaping his life's work. Harrison was cofounder of the Association of Black Anthropologists (ABA) and the organization's first archivist. His educational path, activism in the 1960s, ethnographic research in the black Church, and commitment to preserve and recognize the contributions of African American anthropologists epitomize a revolutionary pioneer in anthropology.

Ira E. Harrison
Courtesy of Ira E. Harrison

"Without history you are just a mystery," a line from a poem by Harrison, captures what drove black people to fight for civil rights for all and to seek to preserve, recognize, and disseminate the contributions of black scholars and black people. Harrison's life is one of activism and scholarship. I first met Harrison at the Southwest Regional Library in Atlanta, Georgia, after his poetry session with other poets and poetry lovers. A true artist and archivist, he shared some of his poetry with me and showed me images and documents related to the ABA.

I first came to know of Harrison through a former classmate; he suggested I ought to meet Harrison, since I had recently signed on as archivist of the ABA. At the time, my former classmate was conducting interviews with Harrison to record his life history. I never imagined that a few years later, at the annual meeting of the American Anthropological Association (AAA) in November 2011, I would be among the first anthropologists to sign on as one of the contributors to this volume. The members of my panel, entitled "Anthropology and Historically Black Colleges and Universities," had an informal conversation about the need for a book that would cover the second generation of pioneers. Harrison had attended our panel. After our panel, among many other topics, he and my colleagues talked in detail about the challenges facing anthropologists and the importance of anthropology at historically black colleges and universities (HBCUs). As a result of this meeting, the ball for the second volume of the African American pioneers in anthropology got rolling.

Harrison was born in Coatesville, Pennsylvania, on June 1, 1933, the only child to Isaiah Michael "Ike" Harrison and Sarah Louisa Richardson. After his mother passed when he was nine, his aunt Mary raised him until he was eleven. He then moved to Syracuse, New York, to live with his father and stepmother, Janie Ruth Godwin Harrison, and spent his junior and high school years in New York, attending Syracuse Central High School. His parents, both social workers in Syracuse communities, molded his mind in the direction of solving social problems and engaging in activism. His parents encouraged him to make a contribution and a difference. His father had been a great athlete in high school in New Orleans and at Lincoln University in Pennsylvania. In Syracuse, he was a key figure in the community who urged children to focus on their studies in his capacity as an administrator and coach of the Dunbar Community Center. His stepmother received her degrees at Syracuse University and was awarded a women's achievement award in 1969.

Growing up in Syracuse, Harrison "always wanted to know more," a desire he sees as being "part of an exploratory frame of mind." He notes that he was "always looking for something, . . . always searching" and wanting to find answers to problems, and that set him on his journey to become a pioneer for activism and applied anthropology.

Education

Isaiah Harrison sent his son to Morehouse College in Atlanta, Georgia, in 1951, wanting to ensure a good foundation for his future (Spadey, "Ira E. Harrison Reveals the Lives and Works of Pioneers in Anthropology"). Atlanta was a city full of rich history and African American culture and thus was the perfect place for molding a future academician and activist. Morehouse's president at the time, Benjamin Mays, shaped his academic life, raised his consciousness, and encouraged his activism. According to Harrison, Mays said, "Young man, you are here to get your act together, go forth, and make your contribution to society." This was the "Morehouse spirit." At Morehouse, Harrison served as president of the Academic Sociology Honor Society. Majoring in sociology, with minors in psychology, English, and the humanities, he became interested in anthropology at this time, taking his first class at Atlanta University. He earned his bachelor of arts in 1955 and then served in the US Army as a medical aidman in Colorado and Germany from 1956 to 1957. He returned to Atlanta University and earned a master of arts in sociology and anthropology. His interests in travel and research resulted in summer sessions in the late 1950s and mid-1960s at Atlanta University, Syracuse University, and the University of Puerto Rico.

Harrison took a job teaching history and geography at Boggs Academy in Keysville, Georgia, which allowed him to experience working in the rural South (he had already worked in the urban South). In the summer of 1960, after a year of teaching, Harrison moved back to Syracuse and entered the PhD program at Syracuse University. He remained busy taking summer sessions, and by fall he was working as a course coordinator and instructor, teaching introductory courses in sociology at Syracuse University.

In 1962, Harrison experienced "culture shock" at his first AAA conference in Chicago because he saw only three persons that looked like him. One looked surprised, and they were all speechless seeing each other. (Later he learned that the one who looked surprised was William Alfred Shack. The other two were Diane Lewis and Delmos Jones). This meeting was a pivotal point in Harrison's career. The lack of representation of black scholars in the field of anthropology initially made him question his decision to enter the discipline but ultimately motivated Harrison to work toward ensuring the visibility of his fellow colleagues.

Activism in the 1960s

The 1960s was marked by unrest and a demand for equality and civil rights; it was an era of social change and protest. The first protest Harrison participated in was the March on Washington on August 28, 1963, after he had returned from a summer session at the University of Puerto Rico. When there was a call for individuals to attend the March on Washington, thirty-year-old Harrison did not hesitate to respond. "I had to be there," as he recalls. "It was in the spirit of the '60s." He and his wife drove from Syracuse to the Raleigh-Durham area of North Carolina to meet Asa T. Spaulding Jr., a friend of Harrison's from Morehouse, to ride the bus together to DC.[1] It was very hot, he recalls, but just before King delivered his speech, there was a breeze that came through the area. The march was a family affair, for his parents and grandparents attended as well. To Harrison's surprise and interest, he saw Puerto Ricans at the march. Staying in DC for that day, Harrison and his wife got back on the bus and then drove back to Syracuse.

Syracuse in the early 1960s faced new challenges. The city was changing, promoting urban renewal, and tearing down old housing residences. Although the number of places to live was decreasing, the population was increasing. PhD graduate student Harrison believed it was an unhealthy situation and argued that housing units should not be torn down until residents could find reasonable housing. However, contractors of the city said no, and residents had to move their belongings out on schedule. He and others who disagreed with this protested. Harrison, students, along with George Wiley, a chemistry professor at the university, were water hosed and beaten. Harrison's father had to get him out of jail. The people in jail shouted, "What are you doing in here? You shouldn't be here." According to Harrison, the jailers knew what was going on. His right arm was twisted, and his father sent a family friend who was a doctor to examine him. The doctor in turn sent him to the hospital. The arrest of the son of the director of the Dunbar Community Center made the local newspaper.

Research on Churches

By the mid-1960s Harrison had entered the PhD program in social science in the areas of anthropology, sociology, and metropolitan area studies at Syracuse University's Maxwell School of Citizenship and Public Affairs. This new interdisciplinary program was ahead of its time, as well as evolving. Harrison always wanted to attend Syracuse; his mother graduated twice with honors from Syracuse University.

Harrison, who at one time thought he would go into the ministry, examined black churches and storefront churches for his dissertation, "A Comparative Case Study of Church Desegregation in a Midwest Metropolitan Area." During this time, Harrison also undertook research for his first publication examining the black church, "The Storefront

118 · ALISHA R. WINN

as a Revitalization Movement." Harrison argues that "case studies on storefront churches and former storefront churches are needed. They may provide us with the answers to such questions as why some storefront churches always remain storefronts, why other storefronts pass out of existence, and why still others become organized churches" (163).

From 1961 to 1964, Harrison also worked under S. M. Miller at Syracuse University's Youth Development Center, in the fifteenth ward, the same area where his father served as an administrator, researching on junior and senior high school dropouts. From 1964 to 1968, he served as associate director of research and planning for the Ohio Council of Churches and the Southwest Ohio Regional Church Planning Board. This position resulted in a series of essays on the inner city of Canton, Ohio, church desegregation in metropolitan areas, and church and community linkages. He also developed a church planning group in northeast Ohio. This group consisted of communities from Dayton to Youngstown, Ohio. He commuted from Dayton to Youngstown to conduct the studies. In 1966, in Lordstown, Ohio, and Jefferson Township, he conducted two phases of a church planning and strategy study, as well as the Bath-Beavercreek survey examining church locations in two Green County townships.

Medical and Applied Anthropology in Public Health

By 1967, Harrison had earned his PhD. In 1968, he moved to Harrisburg, Pennsylvania, to take up a position as a behavioral scientist with the commonwealth's health department in medical and applied anthropology in public health. Harrison asserts that he had not planned to be an applied anthropologist but rather evolved into one. Coming out of the 1960s, he remembered an adage he had heard to the effect that "we can march to freedom but we can't stumble and stagger to freedom." Harrison realized that in order to fight for rights, individuals had to be in good health. His 1969 *Observations in a Black Neighborhood Clinic: A Progress Report* helped pave the way for the US Office of Economic Opportunity to fund neighborhood health centers. The report highlighted the importance of not dismissing patient perceptions in clinics. Harrison continued to serve on several boards and committees and to consult in the public health field.

In May 1971, Harrison earned a second master's degree in public health from the School of Hygiene and Public Health at Johns Hopkins University; in his research for this degree, he focused on how communities can impact policy. In 1978, he published "The Agricultural Migratory Farm Labor System as an Adaptive Mechanism for Afro-Americans," in which he describes African American pickers as contemporary products of the slave plantation system, examining migratory farm workers' attitudes toward health in the Harrisburg, Pennsylvania, area. In "Traditional Medicine in Africa," Harrison and coauthor Collins O. Airhihenbuwa identify a culturally appropriate health education model for involving traditional healers in Africa in the planning, implementation, and evaluation of health policy. Throughout his work, Harrison is careful to take indigenous knowledge regarding health and health education and cultural beliefs into account.

Harrison also worked with Airhihenbuwa and Leonard Jack on "Ethnicity and the Health Belief System*s*," which examines health beliefs related to common origins, customs, and styles of living within a given ethnic group. The goal of the research was to increase understanding of cultural aspects of health and illness to assist with developing more effective and culturally appropriate health education programs for various ethnic groups that have unique cultural beliefs. He also coedited a two-volume bibliography on the implications of traditional medicine in contemporary medicine with Sheila Cominsky (1976–84).

Harrison left the Pennsylvania Department of Health for Meharry Medical College in Nashville in 1972. During the 1970s, he traveled to many countries, including Nigeria. While in Lagos, Harrison served as consultant for African chief Opral Mason Benson. Harrison's consulting work extended beyond academia and health education, as he also served as a judge for the Miss Lagos State Beauty Contest and the Miss Black Universe Pageant in Columbia, South Carolina.

The Search for Anthropology in Black Institutions

The year 1984 was a critical one in Harrison's career as an African American anthropologist. He conducted research at the Hampton Institute in Hampton, Virginia, as part of the NEH Summer Institute, that surveyed African American participants about when they first became familiar with anthropology and anthropologists. He wanted to understand why anthropology was not an established discipline in predominantly black colleges. His study explores the origin of anthropology as a discipline at Hampton, a historically black university. Pioneer St. Clair Drake and even Margaret Mead had spent a brief period there. Harrison also sent out a survey to HBCU institutions to try to find out how many HBCUs had anthropologists on staff.

Association of Black Anthropologists

Harrison was one of the founding members of the ABA in 1970, representing the southern region, along with Vera Green (eastern), Sheila Walker (western), and Glenn Jordan (midwestern) ("The Association of Black Anthropologists," 19). According to Harrison, the four founding members represented and articulated a "consistent commitment to the original purpose of the Black Anthropology Caucus," which itself had emerged out of the Minority Caucus in 1968 ("The Association of Black Anthropologists," 19).[2] By 1975, the organization had become the ABA. The ABA's purpose was to encourage the anthropology of black people and support blacks involved in anthropological study internationally. The ABA sought to identify black people in the discipline of anthropology to foster communication between them on issues pertaining to their professional interests ("The Association of Black Anthropologists," 19). Harrison's life and career paralleled the ABA's purpose and function. At the time Harrison was associate professor in the department of anthropology at the University of Tennessee, Knoxville. Harrison served as the southern regional representative of the ABA from 1975 to 1984 and as ABA president from 1985 to 1987.

ABA Installation in AAA

As president of the ABA, Harrison was not satisfied with the ABA remaining in one place, and he wanted the ABA to be a part of the AAA. This was a controversial issue. During the ABA meeting in Washington, DC, on December 7, 1985, a number of members voiced concerns that the ABA risked losing its identity if it became a part of the AAA, while others embraced a dual identity for the association.[3] By vote, the ABA decided to merge with the AAA in February 1986, and on December 14, 1986, at the AAA meeting in Philadelphia, it became part of the AAA. In the status report on the ABA, Harrison discussed the merger. He stressed that in order to be visible, vital, and virtuous in anthropology in the 1980s, individuals and groups had to organize and affiliate. He assured ABA members that affiliation did not mean amalgamation, and that forming linkages would not denigrate ethnic identity or African ancestry. The AAA would handle the ABA newsletter, *Notes from the ABA*, ABA elections, and the billing and collection of dues. The ABA would, however, publish another separate newsletter and occasional papers series.

November 19, 1987, the twelfth anniversary of the ABA, offered an opportunity for everyone to get together and learn about each other's research and interests. It was at this particular meeting that the idea for the book that became *African-American Pioneers in Anthropology* was first discussed. Harrison believed, as he documents in "The Association of Black Anthropologists," that the history and contributions of African American anthropologists had been neglected. Four years later, Harrison organized and chaired an invited session at the AAA annual meeting titled "Black Anthropologists and the African-American Experience."

As a historian and preserver of history, Harrison wanted to locate and identify past and present African American anthropologists. As the ABA's first archivist, Harrison sought to ensure that the accomplishments and works of ABA members as well as ABA events and meetings were recorded and preserved. The Moorland-Spingarn Research Center provided a place to house both Harrison's papers and the works and papers of other ABA members. At the AAA meeting, in 1993, Harrison gave a speech about the installation of the Archives of the Association of Black Anthropologists at the Moorland-Spingarn Research Center.

Activist and Practitioner Intertwined:
Social Consciousness and Activism

Harrison's work reflects what Uzoechi Nwagbara identifies as "intellectual activism." This form of political activism seeks to encourage the masses to pursue justice in society via ideo-political engagement and education. In the February 1988 issue of *Anthropology News*, Harrison challenged fellow anthropologists to become more politically active, noting "we have come a long way" but "we have a long way to go" (6). He asked why so many academic associations like the American Sociological Association, the American Historical Association, and the American Political Association had had African American presidents (E. Franklin Frazier, John Hope Franklin, and Ralph Bunche, respectively) but the AAA had not.

Vindication

Harrison's work is part of what he and Faye Harrison identify as the tradition of vindication emerging "in reaction to racist assertions that Africans are degraded savages, that Africans and African Americans have no culture that blacks are inherently inferior, and that miscegenation is degenerative to whites and white culture" (introduction, 12). Vindicationist scholars study racist ideas and behavior. They correct distorted interpretations of the African American past or they develop counterideologies for coping with the present. They may decide to take direct action, often giving up an otherwise comfortable existence in the interest of tackling racist beliefs and behaviors head-on (Baber, "St. Clair Drake," 193).

Harrison's research on the University of Tennessee–Knoxville's black faculty exemplifies the vindicationist approach (Baber, "St. Clair Drake," 193). Harrison and his colleague Earl Riggins in religious studies compiled a list of African American achievements (*Black Shadows in Big Orange Country*) documenting the intellectual interests and output of black academicians during the 1979–80 academic year. They had their colleagues, representing all departments, complete a form outlining their education, publications, achievements, and so forth.

In 1997, during his tenure at the University of Tennessee, Harrison wrote an article for the university's newspaper *Context* titled "Silver Anniversary History of the UTK Black Faculty and Staff Association," marking the twenty-fifth anniversary of the organization's existence. In an attempt to provide background on the perspective of black faculty and staff at a white southern university, Harrison looked at the leadership structure of the organization and its objectives over its history. In 1998, the association, of which Harrison was a member, submitted a position paper to address the University of Tennessee's failure to recruit, retain, and promote African American faculty and staff in general and in positions of authority. The association also addressed the problem of positions not held by African Americans. They demanded that the university acknowledge their concerns and make the changes the association was requesting.

Harrison conceived and conducted his research as a form of activism. In *African American Pioneers,* he and coeditor Faye Harrison identify racism as a "central problem in the contemporary world," stressing "race's intersection with class on both national and international levels" (introduction, 13). The volume documents the "life stories, career paths, and intellectual agendas from the black experience in American anthropology" (introduction, 2), highlighting African American anthropologists such as Caroline Bond, Katherine Dunham, Zora Neale Hurston, and William D. Willis. Like Harrison, many of the pioneers were activists, advocates, and public servants.

Ellen Irene Diggs's intention, as described by A. Lynn Bolles, to dispel the myth that Africans in the Americas had no histories except what Europeans or European-Americans had constructed for them ("Ellen Irene Diggs," 159) is similar to Harrison's intention to dispel myths about black anthropologists. Although Harrison did not seem to follow a particular anthropologist's work, his early anthropological work was part of a time that was dominated by a Margret Mead type of framework. As the coeditor of the *African American Pioneers*, Harrison had an opportunity to write chapters on Louis Eugene King and Hubert Ross. In fact, Harrison's motivation for writing about King and recognizing the African American pioneers in anthropology came unexpectedly. During his time as a behavioral scientist in 1969 with the Pennsylvania Department of Public Health, he met King, who would be the first African American to graduate from Columbia University with a PhD. He later found out that King was an anthropologist. As Harrison states in his article on King, he mentioned to a friend at the time that he "doubted that were ten African Americans with Ph.D.'s in anthropology at the time," but the friend "insisted that King was an anthropologist with a Ph.D. from Columbia University. . . . [W]hen I heard the story, I was shocked and angry, wondering how many other blacks who studied anthropology had been forgotten" ("Louis Eugene King," 70).

Harrison promised King and his family that he would tell his story and try to situate him properly in the history of anthropology. Harrison knew and met many of the pioneers. In addition to King, Harrison also wrote about the life and work of Hubert B. Ross. He had met W. Montague Cobb, St. Clair Drake, and Ellen Irene Diggs. Harrison was familiar with another unofficial pioneer, Manet Helen Fowler. She was the first African American woman to earn a PhD in the United States and to establish a professional practice as consultant in policy analysis. From 1966 to1971, Fowler worked at Syracuse University in the Family Service Center in the School of Social Work.

Legacy and Achievement

Harrison's work in medical and applied anthropology through public health and in the black church and his editing of *African American Pioneers* demonstrate intellectual activism at its finest. His legacy is centered on advocacy, which follows "naturally from the practice of anthropology" and is "an integral part of the process of representing other people's views" (Fuller, Layton, Parish, and Rowlands, *Advocacy in Anthropology*, 40). It is an "active, politically-committed, morally engaged anthropology" (Scheper-Hughes, "The Primacy of the Ethical," 419). He has received numerous awards for his anthropological contributions and his service in the community. He is the recipient of the Distinguished Fellow Award for his fifty-year membership in the AAA, and in 2010, he was awarded the Legacy Scholar Award by the ABA at the AAA annual conference. Harrison's achievement resonates not only in the academic world but in the artistic world of oratory. He is the

124 · ALISHA R. WINN

second African American president of the thirty-seven-year-old Georgia
Poetry Society. He has published eight books and still shares his love of
poetry in the community.

Notes

1. Asa Spaulding Jr. is the son of the former president of the North Carolina
Mutual Life Insurance Company.

2. The Caucus of Black Anthropologists was formed during an experimental
session on the Black curriculum in anthropological studies at the AAA meeting
Seattle, Washington, in 1968. The session, whose panel was chaired by Council
Taylor and included Delmos Jones, Diane Lewis, Johnnetta Cole, and Oliver
Osborne, agreed that a caucus was needed to discuss the issues and problems
concerning the lack of minorities and their contributions in anthropology and
the social sciences (Jones, "Association of Black Anthropologists"; Harrison,
"The Association of Black Anthropologists," 17). As Harrison asserts in his
article on the history of the ABA, the caucus was committed to providing a
structure for social scientists from the Black world and to participate in and
to coordinate as much information and as many resources as possible about
anthropology's relevance for Black people.

3. See *Notes from the ABA* 12. 4 (1986): 9.

Bibliography

Airhihenbuwa, Collins O., and Ira E. Harrison. "Traditional Medicine in Africa: Past, Present, Future." In *Health and Health Care in Developing Societies*,
ed. Peter Conrad and Eugene B. Gallagher, 122–34. Philadelphia: Temple
University Press, 1993.

Baber, Willie. "St. Clair Drake: Scholar and Activist." In *African-American Pioneers in Anthropology*, ed. Ira E. Harrison and Faye V. Harrison, 191–212.
Urbana: University of Illinois Press, 1999.

Bolles, A. Lynn. "Ellen Irene Diggs: Coming of Age in Atlanta, Havana, and
Baltimore." In *African-American Pioneers in Anthropology*, ed. Ira E. Harrison
and Faye V. Harrison, 154–67. Urbana: University of Illinois Press, 1999.

Fuller, Chris, Robert Layton, Jane Parish, and Michael Rowlands. *Advocacy in
Anthropology: The Seventh Annual GDAT Debate*. Ed. Peter Wade. Manchester,
UK: Department of Social Anthropology, 1996.

Harrison, Faye, and Ira E., Harrison. Introduction to *African-American Pioneers
in Anthropology*, ed. Ira E. Harrison and Faye V. Harrison, 1–28. Urbana:
University of Illinois Press, 1999.

Harrison, Ira E. "The Agricultural Migratory Farm Labor System as an Adaptive Mechanism for Afro-Americans." *Tennessee Anthropologist* 3.2 (1978):
168–86.

———. "The Association of Black Anthropologists: A Brief History." *Anthropology Today* 3.1 (1987): 17–21.

9. IRA E. HARRISON · 125

———. *Church Desegregation in a Metropolitan Area: A Study in Church and Community Linkages*. Dayton, OH: Ohio Council of Churches, 1967.

———. "A Comparative Case Study of Church Desegregation in a Midwest Metropolitan Area." PhD diss., Syracuse University, 1967.

———. *Impressions*. Dayton, OH: Ohio Church Planning, 1965.

———. "Louis Eugene King, the Anthropologist Who Never Was." In *African-American Pioneers in Anthropology*, ed. Ira E. Harrison and Faye V. Harrison, 70–84. Urbana: University of Illinois Press, 1999.

———. "The Search for Anthropology at Hampton Institute." Paper presented at the 1984 National Endowment for the Humanities Summer Seminar for College Teachers, "History in Higher Education, 1865–84." Hampton Institute, Hampton, VA, July 3, 1984.

———. "Silver Anniversary History of the UTK Black Faculty and Staff Association." *Context* 15.4 (1997): 7.

———. "Status of ABA as Reported at the 86th Annual Meeting." *Anthropology Newsletter* 29.2 (1988): 6.

———. "The Storefront Church as a Revitalization Movement." *Review of Religious Research* 7.3 (1966): 160–63.

———. *The Youngstown Church Survey: Church Locations and Socio-Economic Trends*. Dayton, OH: Ohio Church Planning, 1965.

Harrison, Ira E., and Sheila Cominsky. *Traditional Medicine: Implications for Ethnomedicine, Ethnopharmacology, Maternal and Child Health, Mental Health, and Public Health—An Annotated Bibliography of Africa, Latin America and the Caribbean*. 2 vols. New York: Garland, 1976–84.

Jack, Leonard, Jr., Ira E. Harrison, and Collins O. Airhihenbuwa. "Ethnicity and the Health Belief Systems." In *The Multicultural Challenge in Health Education*, ed. Ana Conseulo Matiella, 51–72. Santa Cruz, CA: ETR Associates, 1994.

Jones, Rhett S. "Association of Black Anthropologists." In *Organizing Black America: An Encyclopedia of African American Associations*, ed. Nina Mjagkij, 63–64. New York: Routledge, 2001.

Nwagbara, Uzoechi. "Political Power and Intellectual Activism in Tanure Ojaide's *The Activist*." *Nebula* 5.4 (2008): 225–53.

Scheper-Hughes, Nancy. "The Primacy of the Ethical: Propositions for a Militant Anthropology." *Current Anthropology* 36.3 (1995): 409–40.

Spadey, James. "Ira E. Harrison Reveals the Lives and Works of Pioneers in Anthropology." *New Observer*, February 17, 1999.

10

Audrey Smedley

A Pioneers' Pioneer Anthropologist

JANIS FAYE HUTCHINSON

Throughout the world people are hopeful that the twenty-first century will bring positive changes to their lives. In the United States, the reelection of the first African American president, Barack Hussein Obama, gave hope that this nation could be a land where everyone matters and where equality is the norm. Despite these dreams of a better world, the 2012 election revealed that racism, sometimes overt and at other times cloaked in politically correct language, persists. While some may assume that Obama's presidency reflected the advent of a postracial world, attitudes and behaviors in the nation indicated the opposite. As suggested by the Trayvon Martin shooting, other racially motivated crimes, and, as attested by a 2012 AP poll, racial attitudes toward blacks did not improve during the first four years of Obama's presidency, and in fact racial prejudice increased slightly.[1]

It is in this climate that black organizations, black publication venues, and discussions of the first black "this and that" in various disciplines become salient. Organizations such as the Association of Black Anthropologists and Association of Latina and Latino Anthropologists present a view that is marginalized or a voice that even when spoken is not heard. They also provide an opportunity for people of color to collectively share experiences and perspectives that can affect their disciplines as well as feed and validate their work. That is why this volume is important. *People of color are less likely to be cited, and their work is more likely to be co-opted by the dominant group, renamed, and published without the original author being cited.* For all of these reasons, volumes like this are a treasure. One jewel within the discipline is a scholar whose work has had an impact not only on anthropology but on many other disciplines as well: Audrey Smedley.

Audrey Smedley
Courtesy of Audrey Smedley

The Birth of an Antiracist Anthropologist

Smedley is definitely a pioneer in anthropology and in the social sciences. Her classic book *Race in North America: Origin and Evolution of a Worldview* provides a historical and sociocultural context with which to understand the history and legacy of the race concept. Born in Detroit, Michigan, in 1930, she attributes her focus on the idea of race to her father, Ulysses Smedley: "My father made me conscious of racism." He did not have a high school diploma, but he was a skilled welder and toolmaker. She notes that "he knew that he needed a skill, one that white bosses desired, so he went to night school and took courses in welding and tool making. . . . He had skills that most people didn't have. When he died, we found that he had fifty-six certificates for welding."[2]

One of the things he talked about was training young white immigrant men who could barely speak English in welding and other factory jobs. As a black man he could not be a boss or foreman because they wouldn't put him in a senior position over white men. He found himself training these immigrants who were subsequently promoted over him. They became his bosses. Although there were few blacks with any kind of training, these bosses still wanted to keep him oppressed, used the "N" word, and treated him like an unskilled worker, but he always made more money than the skilled white men, and with his skills he always had a job.

Smedley understood what was happening to her father and other black men who managed to get the "good jobs" in the factories. She also remembers her dad coming home and "pacing the floor" out of frustration because he was treated so unfairly. In the 1930s and 1940s such treatment was a daily occurrence, part of the norm of American culture.

Smedley thus became committed to fighting racism at an early age. In high school she wrote essays in different courses about discrimination, which her teachers did not like. She went to predominantly white schools during her elementary and middle school years, but by the time she got to Northwestern High School it was in transition and about 30 percent black because the neighborhoods had changed. The teachers, however, were still all white.

> We all knew that certain teachers were very racist. I remember one teacher keeping me after her class and making me miss another class because I dared to talk back to her. She had argued that she didn't want black salesgirls in the high status downtown stores helping her try on her girdles and other things. I came back with, well you hire them in your home to wash your underwear! She didn't like that at all so she kept me back a whole hour; but she had to give me an A because I was always doing A-level work. We all hated her and understood where she came from.[3]

Racism was as pervasive within the school system as it was in society in general. In her senior year of high school she was awarded a Student Aid Foundation scholarship based on her grade point average, which had helped her get into the University of Michigan. At eight o'clock in the morning the day after the award had been announced, the principal of her high school confronted her at the top of the steps ("he *never* got there at 8 o'clock in the morning") and told her he tried to stop the organization from giving her the award. She said she cried but didn't let him see the tears. She merely replied, "You'll have to do better next time," and turned her back and walked off. "I saw the racism," she recalls. "Colored students were told to take classes like sewing and cooking instead of calculus and algebra. . . . I resented having to learn how to sew and cook, although my mother said those were good skills to have."[4]

While Smedley had racist experiences, she also was sometimes chosen to give talks about race and racism off campus by a social science teacher "who was my friend." Another friend was the woman who taught Latin, a white woman from Alabama. "She knew how we were treated. She stood up for us. That was my initiation into the world of racism. At that time I knew I would be fighting racism for the rest of my life."[5]

This dedication continued at the University of Michigan, where she entered a prelaw program. As in the rest of the country, segregation was the rule of the day at the University of Michigan in the 1950s. There were about two hundred black students out of a total population of approximately twenty-five thousand ("Travels and Adventures in an Uncharitable Field," xvii). Smedley was the only black girl in her dorm, so she had white friends, "mostly Jewish kids from New York who befriended me." During the 1950s, the university began allowing blacks to live in the dorms in segregated rooms. At first she roomed with another black girl who was a senior, but after her roommate graduated there was concern about where she would live since there were no other black girls in the dorm. Eventually, a white student agreed to room with her, and in her third year she moved to another dorm where there were more black students.

In her second year Smedley ran for student legislature and won. "The dean remarked that I was the best adjusted Negro girl in the university. She meant I got along with people." Smedley was surprised to win but was not surprised by the political complexities that went with being a member of the legislature. That year she was also elected to Wyvern, the sophomore women's honor society. She was more engaged in campus life than ever, which put her in more direct contact with racial prejudice and discrimination. In the legislature, for example, during a discussion about integrating certain groups, a representative from a famous fraternity vigorously stated, "We don't have any Negroes in our fraternity! We don't want any Negroes in our fraternity!"[6]

In her third year a friend told her about a French language and literature course that was cheap and was taught in Paris. "I was tired of racism, and so I talked it over with my parents; I worked every summer, saved all my money and sailed to Europe."[7] When she got to Paris she realized it was a different world. There was no segregation and none of the mean looks of contempt that she often experienced in the States ("Travels and Adventures in an Uncharitable Field," xviii). Smedley thrived in Paris because it was before the proliferation of American tourists in Europe, so it was less contaminated by racial bias. "I didn't experience racism anywhere in Europe like in the United States, although it was clear I was different. When we traveled around in Spain kids often followed me and called me Gypsy, but the kids were always friendly and smiling. You know the Gypsies were originally from India. Many have brown skin." She also remembers meeting "Africans in Paris, people whom I had never met before. They were friendly, but I realized they were culturally different from Americans. I met blacks from Haiti who were different from ones in Africa and America. Meeting culturally different peoples was one of the major things that made me think about anthropology."[8]

African students had a strong sense of themselves and were assertive. The only visible hostility was between some Frenchmen and some North Africans, particularly Algerians, which was political in nature. (Algerians

130 · JANIS FAYE HUTCHINSON

and other North Africans were rebelling against the French colonialists.) She met many Africans from sub-Saharan Africa who appeared to suffer little from racism, although she learned about colonialism and was aware of the feelings of inferiority engendered by the colonial experience. This sense of cultural variation stayed with her and was enhanced as she met people in Paris from all over the world.

Smedley, along with a couple of other girls, began traveling around. "We were hitchhiking. I hitchhiked all over Europe to Spain and the tip of Spain. We sailed to Morocco, and that was interesting, living in cheap hotels and experiencing the cultures of African Islamic people. We got lost in the Medina, major part of the indigenous city. This was a different world all together."[9]

Through her experiences in Paris and other parts of Europe she learned a fundamental anthropological truth: physical appearance does not provide evidence of ethnic or racial identity. Blacks in France were French in culture just as blacks in America manifest that culture. When she met blacks who were born and raised in Russia, it further confirmed her sense of the distinction between physical characteristics and cultural behavior.

One example stayed with her. In the American library in Paris, she met a young man whom she thought was African American. He told her that his name was "Jimmy" and that he was a student from Chicago. As he started showing her around Paris, she soon realized that there was something unusual about him. His English was clearly American, but she discovered that he spoke several other languages, apparently fluently. On one occasion he took her to a storefront market on the Right Bank where there were a dozen or so men in Arab garb and several women. They looked at her with suspicion, but a strange thing changed the mood. Jimmy had been carrying a large book for her, *An American Dilemma*, by Gunnar Myrdal, which she was researching to give a talk. "He suddenly took the book from under his arm, placed it on the table, opened it and started translating from it."[10] All of the people in the room were interested; they started nodding, talking, and looking at her. Now they were smiling and greeting her, welcoming her.

After this incident, Jimmy admitted that he had never been to the United States, but learned his American English from watching American movies! Like the people in that room, he was from North Africa. She remarks that as a Moroccan, Jimmy "was classified as an Arab and thus 'white' in the American scheme of racial ideology," but "in Chicago, he most certainly would have been seen as 'black'" ("Travels and Adventures in an Uncharitable Field," xix). She realized that when we expect individuals to behave in a certain way because of perceptions

Back at the University

In her fourth year, Smedley returned to the University of Michigan, where she finished her degree. She could have continued on to law school and graduated in two years, but her experiences in Europe had convinced her she wanted to do something else. She liked traveling and seeing the world, so in her senior year she decided to go into anthropology at the graduate level. Smedley entered the master's in anthropology program at the University of Michigan, where her mentors were Elman Service, Marshall Sahlins, and Leslie White. They promoted a neo-evolutionist view of society that posited that the process of evolution explained cultural variation. She read White's *Theory of Culture Change* (1949) and Julian Steward's *The Science of Culture* (1955) to gain an understanding of the ecological perspective that emphasized the connections between culture and the social and natural environment.

Many evolutionists came to regard cultural change over time as an index of progress. According to Smedley, progress was construed in terms of the "historical trajectory of Europe" ("Travels and Adventures in an Uncharitable Field," xx). She realized later as she worked on *Race in North America* that the development of the social sciences corresponded with the rise of a racial ideology that made all achievements a function of racial identity.[11]

The person who influenced her most was Leslie White. He "was very fair and a very good person. He was a southerner who, like a lot of southern whites, had a lot more experience dealing with blacks" than northern whites. Leslie White was convinced that culture was learned and that Blacks were not naturally lazy or stupid. Evolutionists like Elman Service, Leslie White, and Marshall Sahlins influenced her views on the human condition by focusing on culture as learned and as something that should be studied separately from biology.[12]

In her second year of graduate school, White asked Smedley to be a teaching fellow:

> All of the teaching fellows had their master's and I was in my second year of graduate work, didn't have a master's but he thought I could do the job. I appreciated the fact he didn't ignore me. He invited people to his house for barbecue and steak and I was included. He made anthropology seem very important and very real. The fact that he believed strongly that race, biology, and culture were separate things impacted what I would do later. He was an early proponent of separating biology from culture.

> He was a seminal figure in anthropology and everyone knew his school would not use race as an explanation for people's behavior.

While White was supportive and could protect her, she knew that blacks were treated differently in the States, so she "just dealt with what came."[13]

Friends and professors at the University of Michigan (David Aberle) and Manchester (Kathleen Gough) encouraged her to go to the University of Manchester for her doctorate. At Manchester, she moved from a neo-evolutionary perspective to British functionalism, which was good for her because to understand cultural change over time one needs to understand the functions of social systems. The group of social anthropologists she joined "were drawn to the recognition of social *processes* and their transformations over time" rather than to "static structural-functionalist analyses" (xxiii). She was interested in social relations and the production of strategic resources needed for survival.

Social anthropology flourished at Manchester from the 1950s through the 1970s. With Max Gluckman at the helm, the reputation of the department was at its height. Gluckman was her mentor at Manchester, and "he read everything I sent him and liked my work." The next stage in her career was, of course, fieldwork. Smedley wanted to leave the United States and the racism and felt the best thing to do was to get funding to go to Africa. She got a Ford Foundation fellowship that awarded her enough money for two years of fieldwork. Some of her professors tried to discourage her from going because they thought she would not function well in an environment with no toilets or electric lights. To them she did not seem "like a rough-it type girl."[14] But she went to Nigeria by herself and decided to do her fieldwork in an area in the north where Europeans were involved in tin mining.

Fieldwork

"Before leaving for Nigeria I read a lot about the Nigerians and tin mines. It was a pristine situation on the Jos plateau, a small-scale society where people lived in mud brick houses. The indigenous people had been mining for tin for ages and smelting iron. When the British learned about this early in the twentieth century, they quickly established control over the region and by the First World War were producing tin for the war effort."[15] Europeans still dominated the industry at the time of Smedley's stay. In 1960, Nigeria became an independent nation.

Smedley sailed from Liverpool to West Africa on the Elder Dempster Line. She experienced racism from the British people who ran the ship and especially passengers from the States. On the ship she met American missionaries who argued—and really believed—that Africans mated with apes. She was shocked by their lack of education and, of course, "they looked down on me. When you meet people like that you may argue some until you realize how stupid they are and then you don't."[16] She also met college students on the ship who were returning to West Africa who contradicted everything the missionaries believed.

Her fieldwork took place between 1959 and 1961, the last years of colonial rule in Nigeria and the beginning years of independence. She planned to study the history and culture of the Birom of Northern Nigeria; her goal was to assess how the culture was changing as a result of tin mining. She took a cultural ecological approach in this project. "I followed them around and talked to them about things. The thing that impressed me the most was how independent and strong and self-confident the women were. My perception of the women was so different from what other people had written about them. They gave me a Birom name, Katchallom, which means 'bush cow' but refers to a strong survivor."[17]

She had planned to study tin mining but ended up turning most of her attention to social life: "I lived in a compound with eight buildings. What they did was move a family out of one, and I rented one room. I saw everything going on at the compound. The houses opened out the back, and I would ask questions about everything, and mostly children would help me. I discovered that they knew everything that was going on."[18] With the emergence of feminist consciousness in the 1960s, there were numerous publications by women scholars that corrected the interpretations of older ethnographies. A certain theoretical perspective held that women around the world were subordinate in all societies, which prevented them from fully participating in political, social, and religious institutions and processes, and many writers set about describing and explaining women's global oppression. Feminist researchers were interested in inequality in women's access to and use of power and control of strategic resources. "Scholars focused on analyzing the sexual division of labor, the cultural construction of gender and its relationship to kinship patterns, and how inequality is manifest in practice and in symbolic form" (*Women Creating Patrilyny*, 2).

Evolutionary theories about the origin of the family postulated an early stage of promiscuity followed by matriliny. Subsequently, matriliny was replaced by patriliny because of the importance of property rights, the need to protect these rights, and the need to provide for the orderly transmission of these rights through the generations. It was considered a superior form of social organization and therefore became common in human societies. In Africa, patriliny was and still is the main organizing principle (3).

In the States, feminists in the 1970s saw matriliny as providing greater freedom and higher status for women because it allowed them to have more control over resources and their children. While men did hold positions of power in matrilineal societies, feminists who embraced matriliny believed that women experienced less oppression in such societies. There are numerous biases in this construction, and the assumption that women everywhere prefer matriliny has been proven false (3).

With this challenge to the assumption that women prefer matriliny illustrated in her field notes, Smedley came back to Detroit and began to write her dissertation. Soon she was approached by Wayne State University to teach introductory courses and eventually the history of anthropology and the history of theory. Since she also taught courses on African ethnography, she became involved in Afro-American studies. While reading her notes she realized African women were very much their own persons. They are "independent, assertive, and self-assured" (3). Smedley began to argue that freedom for women must be viewed in the context of freedom, or lack of it, for men in their societies. Economic and political options for men and women are limited by Western domination, colonialism, dictatorships, and the global market, among other things. In her dissertation, "Kinship and Social Organization among the Birom of Northern Nigeria," she questions the idea that men have more rights, powers, and resources than women in such societies. In *Women Creating Patrilyny* she contends that scholars

> in the West were using concepts and imposing categories of reality on Third World women derived from the experiences of Western societies. . . . [T]he gauges by which we have measured women's status (such as property ownership, control over the means of production, access to public office, and the exercise of public forms of power) clearly reflect Western cultural values and emphases on visible power and control. (4)

While Smedley does not argue that there is no male dominance in patrilineal societies, she suggests that it assumes different forms in different societies. Birom women appear to conform to traditional portrayals of women in a patriarchal society, barred from power and resources, but they did not display attributes associated with people in subordinate positions except in specific circumstances. Patriliny in Birom society turned out to be "radically different" from what she thought it was: "My interpretation of gender roles in this patrilineal society was an important part of my dissertation."[19]

On one occasion, Smedley was asked to give a paper on the women of Africa, "but the white anthropologists in particular didn't accept it or assumed that I didn't observe what I claimed or that I was so incompetent I didn't realize that women were being oppressed." On the other hand, Paul Bohannon read the manuscript and called it "superb." Max Gluckman said it was first class and asked Manchester University Press to publish it, but in the 1970s it was difficult to get published, and despite his recommendation, the press did not end up publishing it.[20]

By this time Smedley was a single mother with two children and was teaching at Oakland University. Looking to improve her situation, she applied for and received a Radcliffe Institute fellowship for women who needed a place and time to publish their work. While in Cambridge, she worked on a revised manuscript based on her fieldwork among the Birom that focused on the social construction of gender roles ("Travels and Adventures in an Uncharitable Field," xxvii).

This became *Women Creating Patrilyny: Gender and Environment in West Africa*. Smedley realized that the problems women faced stemmed not from conflict with men but from their efforts to function in societies dominated by exploitative policies of overseas companies, world markets, food shortages (i.e., overproduction of cash crops), "development programs, unstable currencies, intractable diseases, lack of clean water, lack of schools, inadequate health care," and many other problems that they confront on a daily basis" (8). The relationships among men, Smedley discovered, were more rigidly structured than those of women. In addition, women were involved in political and economic decisions and in maintaining patriliny. Smedley saw the pattern of the Birom among African American women in the States. For example, in the early twentieth century, many in Detroit were migrants and were independent women from the South. "Black women always had to work and weren't totally dependent on their husbands."[21]

Smedley sent her manuscript to several publishers, but they would not publish it because it not only went against the prevailing feminist ideology regarding the universal oppression of women but also suggested that women may have invented some aspects of patrilineal ideology. A heretical perspective like hers was not going to sell ("Travels and Adventures in an Uncharitable Field," xxvii). She published a couple of papers on Birom women ("Women of Udu" [1974], "The Implications of Birom Cicisbeism" [1980]), but the larger manuscript was placed on the shelf. After the publication of *Race in North America*, she returned to her study of the Birom people, and the book was finally published in 2003. This decision was motivated by new publications by African and African American anthropologists about the use of Western feminist theory to explain African societies, including Ifi Amadiume's *Male Daughters, Female Husbands*, Gwendolyn Mikell's *African Feminism*, Leith Mullings's *On Our Own Terms*, and Christine Oppong's *Female and Male*

136 · JANIS FAYE HUTCHINSON

in West Africa. These scholars were at last reporting results similar to her findings among the Birom. Her work has also stimulated interests in questions such as whether women introduced aspects of patriliny to further their own particular interests. Since its publication, I have not found any reviews of the book.

Race in North America

When she was in Cambridge, Smedley met black faculty at Harvard who encouraged her to write a book on race. After leaving Cambridge and taking a position at the State University of New York at Binghamton, she got another Ford Foundation grant to work on the history of race. By 1978 she had amassed a fair amount of material and introduced a new course on the origin and evolution of the idea of race. Since there was no textbook for her course, by the mid-1980s she decided to write one. This became her classic textbook, *Race in North America: Origin and Evolution of a Worldview*, which has seen five editions to date and in which she examines the power of a racial way of viewing the world and how this came about.

In *Race in North America* she not only describes the racial worldview but provides a sociohistorical context that was not apparent in previous historical works. In particular, she shows how race was popularized as a part of folk culture and then given authority as a scientific concept through white power and privilege. Under this folk classification people were ranked based on the social, economic, and political experiences of expansionist, conquering, and dominating nations that pursued power and wealth. The primary purpose of race, Smedley maintains, is to rank individuals and populations and allocate resources. In the edition she co-wrote with Brian Smedley, she traces the origin of the race concept in North America in large part to the English. Smedley argues that their knowledge system is marked by "extreme obsession with property, particularly as a measure of human worth and a symbol of personal identity" (304). The race concept is maintained in US society because it continues to identify who has access to wealth, power, and privilege and who does not. The book is a cultural and historical account of the evolution of the race concept in North America and its legacy today.

While it has stood the test of time, when it was first published, it received mixed reviews. Some reviewers suggested in their assessment of the first edition in 1993 that the social construction of race was already an established idea, and some others seemed to resist race as a worldview concept. Other scholars such as Ashley Montagu (1942) had put forth the idea that race is not a biological concept, that it is a cultural invention and social construction with an eco-adaptive relationship to phenotype. Smedley, of course, was aware of this; what she does instead in the book is attempt to uncover the historical events and attitudes that led to the creation of race ideology. The importance of her book, as noted by Smedley, is that she stresses the significance of the origin of race and its evolution as a social concept. In particular it is a comprehensive examination of the sociohistorical contexts within which populations are racially classified.

She also wrote the book because in anthropology, little attention was given to race during or after the civil rights movement: "I became aware that anthropologists were really no different from individuals in other fields who would rather not deal with the phenomenon of race" ("Travels and Adventures in an Uncharitable Field," xxviii). By the 1970s and 1980s, whites were tired of black activism and the realities of racism in America. Whites "are not even aware that they view the world through a racialized lens and consider that their beliefs about human variation are normal and shared with all others" (xxxviii). The next year, 1994, *Race in North America* was awarded the Gustavus Myers Center Outstanding Book Award for the Study of Human Rights in North America.

With the publication of this book she began to get letters and emails from scholars in a variety of fields such as history, sociology, and psychology. Encyclopedia Britannica asked her to write major articles on race ("Race"), and other encyclopedias wanted articles on slavery or race. She began publishing a number of journal articles (e.g., "Race and the Construction of Human Identity") and book chapters (e.g., "Science and the Cultural Construction of the Idea of Race") as well as giving talks at meetings. The book surprised some people and angered others, especially those who firmly believed in the inferiority of blacks.

The second edition in 1999 got more attention, and scholars other than anthropologists accepted her arguments. It was during this period that the American Anthropological Association (AAA) returned to the issue of race, and she was asked to prepare the official 1998 statement on race for it. In 2006 the AAA developed a major project on race titled "Understanding Race and Human Variability: A Public Education Program" that consisted of a traveling museum exhibit, website, and printed publications. Smedley was a consultant on that project, and the museum exhibit continues to traverse the United States. She was also a contributor to a widely discussed video that is often used in the classroom: *Race: The Power of an Illusion*, aired on public television. Larry Adelman, the head of California Newsreel, the company that produced this film, told her years earlier that it was reading the first edition of her book that inspired him to make this film.

In 2007, the third edition of *Race in North America* was published, and it became the top selling anthropology textbook for Perseus Books.

138 · JANIS FAYE HUTCHINSON

This was very reaffirming for Smedley because throughout her career many white colleagues had assumed she was their intellectual inferior. Unfortunately, she knows that this experience is not unique to her; nearly all black American scholars she knows have had similar experiences of being presumed to be inferior. As she has analyzed, a belief in black inferiority is central to racial ideology in the United States and other places, and it is a major barrier to reducing racism.

A fourth edition of the book was published in 2012 with her son Brian as coauthor. The 2012 edition includes a chapter on health in which she and her son, Brian, focus on the extent and causes of racial health disparities in the United States. Here, as in previous chapters, structural racism is viewed as the primary determiner of health inequities. The fact that this book is a comprehensive discussion of race and racism, has gone through so many editions, and is widely read attests to Smedley's impact on anthropology and the social sciences. The fifth edition, coauthored with Vilna Bashi Treitler, was published in 2016.

Thoughts on Anthropology

Decades before the publication of the race textbook, Smedley terminated her membership in the AAA (although she is a member now). She did this because she felt that the organization was moving toward "esoteric, irrelevant, and uninteresting" topics and approaches to social reality. The postmodernists, at least some, seemed to be ego driven and focused on American individualism rather than productive attempts to understand the human condition ("Travels and Adventures in an Uncharitable Field," xxix). Another sticking point for her is that not all anthropologists accept the distinction between biology and culture: "Anthropologists still don't agree on race."[22]

What she realized is that the level of racism found in society as a whole is present in the anthropology community too. "As a matter of fact," she notes, "they may be more racist. Too many white anthropologists are uncomfortable with black people and cannot seem to think of them outside of racial terms just like the larger society. Race is a thing that's always present." Considering how the AAA is structured, it's not possible for power to be distributed: "The president of the association does not have the power to make changes, and opposition to change comes out of racialized mindsets." Just as the racial reality of many Republicans in Congress "appears to be that a black man should not be president, similar attitudes occur in anthropology." Other than the race exhibit the AAA put together, there is little evidence that anthropology is concerned with racism as an area of research or as an issue to be dealt with. "We used to be a liberal social science, and that has changed. By

10. AUDREY SMEDLEY · 139

'liberal' I mean aimed at doing good for people and for humanity. I'm not sure what good anthropology does. There is no impact of anthropological thinking on public policy."[23] Smedley hoped anthropology would reflect a nonracial philosophy and that courses would include such tenets, but she has not stopped alerting people to inequalities and the history and legacy of race. She continues this work in communities in the Washington, DC, area.

Notes

Audrey Smedley is currently a professor emeritus at Virginia Commonwealth University in anthropology and African American studies. She has two sons: Brian, who is vice president and director of the Health Policy Institute of the Joint Center for Political and Economic Studies in Washington, DC, and David, who is a professor of sculpture and head of the sculpture program at Howard University. She also has two grandchildren.

1. See Euroweb, "AP Poll: Negative Racial Attitudes Harbored Against Blacks," October 28, 2012, archive.curweb.com/2012/10/new-ap-poll-negative -racial-attitudes-harbored-against-blacks/#.
2. Audrey Smedley, phone interview with Janis Faye Hutchison, 2012.
3. Audrey Smedley, phone interview with Janis Faye Hutchison, 2012.
4. Audrey Smedley, phone interview with Janis Faye Hutchison, 2012.
5. Audrey Smedley, phone interview with Janis Faye Hutchison, 2012.
6. Audrey Smedley, phone interview with Janis Faye Hutchison, 2012.
7. Audrey Smedley, phone interview with Janis Faye Hutchison, 2012.
8. Audrey Smedley, phone interview with Janis Faye Hutchison, 2012.
9. Audrey Smedley, phone interview with Janis Faye Hutchison, 2012.
10. Audrey Smedley, phone interview with Janis Faye Hutchison, 2012.
11. Audrey Smedley, phone interview with Janis Faye Hutchison, 2012.
12. Audrey Smedley, phone interview with Janis Faye Hutchison, 2012.
13. Audrey Smedley, phone interview with Janis Faye Hutchison, 2012.
14. Audrey Smedley, phone interview with Janis Faye Hutchison, 2012.
15. Audrey Smedley, phone interview with Janis Faye Hutchison, 2012.
16. Audrey Smedley, phone interview with Janis Faye Hutchison, 2012.
17. Audrey Smedley, phone interview with Janis Faye Hutchison, 2012.
18. Audrey Smedley, phone interview with Janis Faye Hutchison, 2012.
19. Audrey Smedley, phone interview with Janis Faye Hutchison, 2012.
20. Audrey Smedley, phone interview with Janis Faye Hutchison, 2012.
21. Audrey Smedley, phone interview with Janis Faye Hutchison, 2012.
22. Audrey Smedley, phone interview with Janis Faye Hutchison, 2012.
23. Audrey Smedley, phone interview with Janis Faye Hutchison, 2012.

Bibliography

Amadiume, Ifi. *Male Daughters, Female Husbands: Gender and Sex in an African Society*. London: Zed Books, 1987.

140 · JANIS FAYE HUTCHINSON

Harrison, Ira E., and Faye Harrison, eds. *African-American Pioneers in Anthropology*. Urbana: University of Illinois Press, 1999.

Mikell, Gwendolyn. *African Feminism: the Politics of Survival in Sub-Saharan Africa*. Philadelphia: University of Pennsylvania Press, 1997.

Montagu, Ashley. *Man's Most Dangerous Myth: The Fallacy of Race*. New York: Columbia University Press, 1942.

Mullings, Leith. *On Our Own Terms: Race, Class, and Gender in the Lives of African American Women*. New York: Routledge, 1997.

Oppong, Christine. *Female and Male in West Africa*. New York: Allen Unwin, 1983.

Smedley, Audrey. "The Implications of Birom Cicisbeism." In "Women with Many Husbands: Polyandrous Alliance and Marital Flexibility in Africa and Asia," special issue, *Journal of Comparative Family Studies* 11.3 (1980): 345–57.

———. "Kinship and Social Organization among the Birom of Northern Nigeria." PhD diss., University of Manchester, 1967.

———. "Race." In *Encyclopedia Britannica's Guide to Black History*. Chicago: Encyclopedia Britannica, 2007.

———. *Race in North America: Origin and Evolution of a Worldview*. 1st ed. Boulder, CO: Westview, 1993.

———. *Race in North America: Origin and Evolution of a Worldview*. 2nd ed. Boulder, CO: Westview, 1999.

———. *Race in North America: Origin and Evolution of a Worldview*. 3rd ed. Boulder, CO: Westview, 2007.

———. "Race and the Construction of Human Identity." *American Anthropologist* 100.3 (1998): 690–702.

———. "Science and the Cultural Construction of the Idea of Race." In *Many Americas: Critical Perspectives on Race, Racism, and Ethnicity*, ed. Gregory R. Campbell, 41–61. Dubuque, IA: Kendall/Hunt, 1998.

———. *Slavery*. Southfield, MI: Black History Project, 1969.

———. "Travels and Adventures in an Uncharitable Field." *Annual Review of Anthropology* 30 (2001): xvii–xxxii.

———. *Women Creating Patrilyny: Gender and Environment in West Africa*. New York: Altamira Press, 2003.

———. "Women of Udu: Survival in a Harsh Land." In *Many Sisters: Women in Cross-Cultural Perspective*, ed. Carolyn J. Matthiasson, 205–28. Glencoe, IL: Free Press, 1974.

Smedley, Audrey, and Brian Smedley. *Race in North America: Origin and Evolution of a Worldview*. 4th ed. Boulder, CO: Westview, 2012.

Smedley, Audrey, and Vilna Bashi Treitler. *Race in North America: Origin and Evolution of a Worldview*. 5th ed. Boulder, CO: Westview, 2016.

Steward, Julian. *Theory of Culture Change: The Methodology of Multilinear Evolution*. Urbana: University of Illinois Press, 1955.

White, Leslie. *The Science of Culture: A Study of Man and Civilization*. New York: Farrar, Straus Giroux, 1969.

11

George Clement Bond

Anthropologist, Africanist, Educator, and Visionary

RACHEL WATKINS

> Africa is not an historical continent; it shows neither change
> nor development. Whatever may have happened there belongs
> to the world of Asia and Europe.
>
> G. F. W. Hegel, 1834

> Perhaps, in the future, there will be some African history to
> teach. But at present there is none, or very little: there is
> only the history of the Europeans in Africa. The rest is largely
> darkness. . . . And darkness is not a subject for history.
>
> Hugh Trevor Roper, 1963

George Clement Bond's study of social and political change among the Yombe of Northern Zambia during emerging independence challenged dominant paradigms that situated Africa as a static continent made up of "people without history." His work offered important critiques of dominant approaches to research on Africa that reified the continent as the place where the "savage in modernity" could be found. In addition to seeking to write Africa and Africans into modern history, Bond aimed to represent the voices of Africans as participants in and producers of their own history before, during, and after colonialism.[1] Bond also produced scholarship demonstrating how his theorization of social and political organization and arguments against dominant social and historical framings of Africa applied to discussions outside of African studies and anthropology. This includes his critical examinations of how social scientists construct the past, in which he explores the relationships between knowledge production and distributions of power and the study of race in the United States.

George Clement Bond
Courtesy of Teachers College, Columbia University. Samantho Isom.

This chapter offers a thematic examination of Bond's work that underscores early innovations, later developments, and connections between his scholarship and that of the previous generation of black anthropologists. The discussion highlights three aspects of Bond's research agenda evident throughout his career: his reimagining of Africa and Africans within modernity, his challenging of dominant methodological and analytical approaches to social and political organization, and his application of his work to discussions and debates outside of African studies and anthropology.

Bond's work demonstrates that African American vindicationist intellectual projects involve more than countering narratives that cast Africans and their descendants in a negative light. Rather, Bond asserts that approaches to the study of Africa that counter its positioning as peripheral to the modern world are a critical part of refining method and theory in the social sciences.[2]

Intellectual and Biographical History

Bond was born into a family of esteemed educators and activists, and information about his family and history is readily available on line. The Columbia Teacher's College added to numerous existing entries when it created a tribute page chronicling his esteemed career as a scholar and activist shortly after his death in 2014 (Levine, "George Bond, TC Education Anthropologist, Dies at 77").[3] Bond spent periods of his childhood in Haiti, Liberia, and Afghanistan as well as the American South as a result of his father's various posts. J. Max Bond Sr. was a notable educator with a doctorate in sociology from the University of Southern California.[4] He retired in 1966 from the United States Agency for International Development (USAID), where he oversaw educational programs during tours of duty in Afghanistan, Tunisia, Sierra Leone, and Malawi (Pace, "J. Max Bond Sr., 89, an American Who Headed Liberian University").

Bond's mother, the former Ruth Clement, was also an educator and civic leader born into a prominent black family.[5] Ruth received bachelor's and master's degrees in English literature from Northwestern University. She is also known for her work on a quilting project with the wives of men building dams for the Tennessee Valley Authority. During this time, she designed what is thought to be the first "black power quilt."[6]

Also of note is Bond's paternal grandfather, James Bond. Bond worked at North Carolina's Livingstone College with James Aggrey, Ghanaian educator and founder of Achimota School in Ghana, in the early 1920s. It was during this time that Aggrey visited Livingstone's sister school in Zambia, Livingstonia, and delivered his acclaimed "Africa for the Africans" speech. George heard about this speech and its significance from his grandfather as a child (Peel "George Clement Bond," 183). Many years later, Bond encountered elders in Zambia who were students at Livingstonia when James Aggrey came to the school.[7]

In 1959 Bond graduated from Boston University with a degree in sociology. He then pursued doctoral studies in anthropology at the London School of Economics. Under the supervision of Lucy Mair and mentors Raymond Firth and E. E. Evans-Pritchard, he began dissertation research on the Yombe of Northern Zambia. In keeping with the work of these scholars, he also drew on structural functionalists such as Emile Durkheim, Max Weber, Alfred Radcliffe-Brown, and Bronislaw Malinowski (Levine, "George Bond, TC Education Anthropologist, Dies at 77"). Bond's dissertation, based on fieldwork conducted between 1963 and 1965, was published as a monograph titled *The Politics of Change in a Zambian Community* in 1976.

Bond made his first trip to Zambia in 1962 and lived for extended periods of time in Uyombe over a span of forty years. The data he collected was expansive in scope and covers a range of subjects, including inequality, social organization, migration, education, and local constructions of history and religion. Data Bond collected include records of the British colonial administration and interviews with male and female Yombe elders.

Bond notes in his monograph that he was drawn to the study of Zambia because it had been neglected in anthropological studies of Central Africa (1976, x). More broadly, he was interested in contributing to studies of nations emerging from colonial rule and in exploring the attendant changes in political and social organization. His study of the continuities and changes during this transitional period focused on local-level politics. His focus on the relationship between continuity and change, which he also describes as the study of "social forces and the persistence of social principles" (2), played a key role in his identification of the limitations of dominant analytical approaches at the time of his study. Specifically, Bond noticed that structural functional analyses did not have the ability to capture the complexities of social and political change he observed among the Yombe. This discovery led Bond to consider that the tools developed to understand social organization during colonialism might lend to analyses that oversimplify postcolonial African situations. Bond believed that innovative approaches to understanding postcolonial social and political organization in Africa could serve as a model for refining method and theory in the social sciences more broadly.[8]

In 1968, Bond joined the Department of Anthropology at Columbia University as an assistant professor and moved to the Teachers College in 1974. In 2001 he was appointed William F. Russell Professor of Anthropology and Education and held that title until his death.

A Profile of the Yombe

The Yombe of Northern Zambia and are more closely tied to fellow Tumbuka speakers in northern Malawi than to groups in Southern Zambia. The social and political organization of the Yombe is evident in the social spheres Bond selected as the focus of his study of changes associated with newly independent nations and how the Yombe fit into modern history. The first sphere of interaction was Muyombe, the capital of Uyombe chiefdom and lesser villages, because policies coming from central, province, and district governments were funneled through Muyombe before being presented to the lesser villages. Therefore, the relationship between Muyombe and lesser villages was a contentious one that saw them battling over resource allocation. The relationships between the six branches of the Wowo clan that comprised the traditional elite was another sphere of social and political activity that Bond examined. At the time of research, two branches were in competition: that of the chief and that of the deputy chief, appointed by the district commissioner. Each represented different interests. A third sphere was the relationship between the Wowo clan, the native administration, and the local constituency that made up a subregional branch of the United

National Independence Party (UNIP). The latter group represented a "party based elite" that competed with the royal clan and native administration for control of the chiefdom. A fourth sphere considers the relationship between people with different levels of education. Most political leaders during field research were from the more educated group, which cooperated with imposing policies established by the government, province, and district on the chiefdom. However, lesser-educated members were beginning to regain control, as independence facilitated the movement of more educated members away from the chiefdom for civil service political party work.

These spheres of interaction, as well as the interaction between them, reflect the complexity that Bond observed and that he makes visible in his analyses. Making this complexity visible was central to his project of situating the Yombe as agents in the present and participants in and producers of their own history.

Analytical Frameworks and Publications

Bond elaborates on these spheres in essays that preceded and followed the publication of his dissertation. Research and writing on the Yombe after his dissertation considers subsequent periods of social and political transition in Northern Zambia in the context of class, religion, and gender, specifically examining the effects of transitions related to agriculture, education, privatization, climactic changes, and health crises. Moving beyond structural functionalism, Bond draws on the work of Gramsci to analyze the coexistence of dominant and countering ideologies in various social spheres. In addition to looking at ideologies within local spheres of interaction, Bond considers how dominant ideologies regarding Africa are naturalized and coexist with organic and nonorganic counterideologies.[9] Foucault's work informs Bond's ongoing discussion of the relationship between knowledge and power.

However, while Bond's analyses benefited from Gramscian and Foucauldian perspectives, the complexities of African social and political organization also required going beyond the parameters of their arguments (Sanjek, "The Bond Legacy," 267).[10] For instance, Bond draws on Foucault's categorization of subjugated knowledge in a number of publications, but at the same time, he considers his approach to uncovering that knowledge to depart from the archaeological or genealogical. The ethnographic study of social interaction reveals the immediate processes involved in the construction of dominant and subjugated positionalities.[11] Similarly, Bond notes the limitations of Gramsci's intellectual scheme in light of the fact that Bond and the Yombe elders shared knowledge of Aggrey's speech. Colonial administrators assumed that Bond would not be accepted by the Yombe owing to the hegemonic notions of tribal differences that informed their social organization. However, shared knowledge of the speech connected him to the elders "in a fundamental way, one so very different from the fragmented constructs of central African 'tribes' set out by colonial administrators. . . . We were a part of a broad social and intellectual field whose contacts communicated through the images and rhetoric of African nationalism" ("Historical Fragments and Social Constructions in Northern Zambia," 88).

The nationalism reflected in Aggrey's rhetoric was one of many elements of the highly charged and complex political struggle among the Yombe in the early 1960s. Members of the royal clan, commoners, and elites in the emerging anticolonial political party and other allegiances between people of various status created spheres of potential influence and power outside of established social hierarchy. Thus, Bond notes that "the distinction that Gramsci might have made between traditional and organic intellectuals proved inappropriate during this period of Zambian history" (88). Bond's discussion of his connection with the elders through James Aggrey also highlights another one of his intellectual priorities: understanding African social organization and constructs of history outside of precolonial, colonial, and postcolonial temporal frames. In other words, Bond's approach to the study of the Yombe (and Africa more broadly) includes perspectives from a number of disciplines that were represented among the conversations he facilitated in various published forms.

Vindicationist and broader elements of his work are captured in his introduction to *The Social Construction of the Past: Representation as Power*, which he coedited with Angela Gilliam (1994). In the introduction, he and Gilliam argue that social constructions of the past contain multiple social paradigms and principles that not only lend to domination and collusion but also resistance (1). It is important to note that while most of Bond's work focuses on some aspect of social and political organization, he also holds that the same history and dynamics are revealed in the study of African languages. One of his many edited volume projects focuses on the intersection of African languages and education, another recurring theme in his work.[12]

Bond views the identification of relationships between the production of knowledge and distributions of power as part of the larger project of decolonizing anthropology, which aims to expose the partisan renderings of history that undermine the agency of subjugated people as creators of their own histories as well as the complexities of social life obscured in dominant historical renderings.[13] One example is the framing of histories outside of traditional periodizing and the decentering of colonial narratives.[14] Related to these strategies is the destabilizing of dichotomies that position Africa as just having emerged from "traditionalism."[15] The "rhetoric of Africa's marginality" conceals how deeply it is implicated in the development of the modern world.[16] Bond's work explores how neoliberal projects that underwrite structural adjustment impact individual states within Africa as well as the continent as a whole. In an article titled "Globalization, Neoliberalism, and Historical Conditionalities," Bond notes that Africa inherited states that were constructed by colonial powers and that had little capacity for autonomy and so became "dependent associates" in the global economy, subordinate to the policies of international agencies that provide financial aid (330). At the same time, he recognizes how those policies impact a number of world regions: "States in Africa are operating within the confines of a global capitalism that is weakening national state structures everywhere" (Bond and Gibson, introduction, 10). Bond's critique of the separation of traditional and Western knowledge is a key maneuver for opening up space for Africans to be situated as participants in and producers of their own histories. Bond's scholarship can thus be seen as part of a critique of anthropology, rooted in his commitment to identify with and address the paucity of theories that locate Africa as a complex participant in global history:

> Anthropologists are in the unique position of advancing themselves and their discipline through the fabrication of the subjects they study. The bind is that anthropologists usually develop paradigms to explain or interpret that which they themselves have created. The crisis lies in the limitations of the anthropological paradigm to explain historical and ethnographic constructions and look at the appropriateness of our data to contemporary theory and political issues . . . , the focus being on texts and textual analysis and not on actual physical circumstances and consequences of subjugation." (Bond and Gilliam, introduction, 13–14)

Bond associates the postmodern turn with the obscuring of connections between representation and relations of domination and with the ignoring of scholarship within and outside of the discipline that renders those relationships visible (Mullings, "Ethnicity and Representation, 25").

Myth

Bond published two papers about the Yombe before publishing the monograph based on his dissertation. "Kinship and Conflict in a Yombe Village: A Genealogical Dispute" (1972) centers on two lesser villages within the chiefdom in conflict over land use. The paper details the components of mythical charters of Yombe descent groups, explaining that the genealogical component that deals with generations descending from the founders is subject to multiple interpretations and configurations (278). Bond's ethnographic data demonstrate how each village attempts to situate its ancestors so as to justify rights to land and other aspects of power. This introduction to the use of myth among the Yombe demonstrates how the narrative history of the clan has been manipulated by various actors according to individual and descent group interests. More importantly, this illustration belies functionalist assumptions that myth exclusively serves as a form of social cohesion and control. Bond argues that myth should be seen as a form of flexible social tradition that can be shaped to suit different interests ("Kinship and Conflict in a Yombe Village," 286).

Bond published "New Coalitions and Traditional Chieftainship in Northern Zambia: The Politics of Local Government in Uyombe" in 1975. This paper addresses the third sphere of interaction noted in *The Politics of Change in a Zambian Community*: relations between more and less educated people before and after independence. In keeping with his recognition of the complexity of these interactions and connections between spheres, Bond uses the changing role and power of the chiefdom as a frame for his examination.

During colonial rule, Yombe children acquired skills from mission schooling that encouraged them to migrate to cities to seek work and that led them to be counted among the urban African elite of the towns (352). Some were unable to find employment or remain employed, and because they still had ties with the chiefdom, they returned to Uyombe and assumed positions of leadership. Their return shifted interactions between commoners and the chief, as members of the educated elite became the majority of his advisers. This in turn freed the chief from traditional forms of political reciprocity with commoners, which impacted their willingness to provide labor (353). Nonetheless, the imposition of the native administration secured the chief's position. The discontent of the commoners in turn gave rise to the acceptance of UNIP, which created a sphere of influence for commoners and elites not counted among the chief's advisers.

The power of the chief was minimized during the rise of UNIP. However, the opportunities that came with independence led to more educated members of UNIP leaving Uyombe for jobs elsewhere. This helped to restore the power of the chief and less educated, more conservative members of the chief's clique. Bond concludes that independence paradoxically allowed for the power of the chiefdom to be restored, along with promoting the less progressive interests of members without social mobility (360). The multiple dynamics between colonial and postcolonial structural constraints and assertions of agency underscored the value of analyses that did not assume societies to be closed or fixed systems.

Bond elaborates on his discussion of myth in "Historical Fragments and Social Constructions in Northern Zambia: A Personal Journey"

11. GEORGE CLEMENT BOND · 149

(2000). The paper demonstrates how the construction of local history is a crucial element in processes of domination, subjugation, resistance, and collaboration between rulers and the ruled (76). Bond draws on ethnographic data to illustrate how various hegemonic elements, such as lineage, are used to legitimate authority and how the Yombe employ these elements to assert agency in the making of their own local histories. Returning to the issue of manipulating genealogical aspects of the charter myth to access power, this paper deals more directly with the role of myth in determining the eligibility of clan branches for chiefdom. Bond provides rich ethnographic data on narrative forms that include, exclude, add, or omit various historical actors. In keeping with his interest in documenting local and extralocal interactions, he details the role of colonial authority in settling genealogical disputes and shaping clan history, drawing on district commissioners' reports. Bond's discussion illustrates the control that colonial authorities had over the dispute resolution process and authority of the chiefdom. At the same time, Bond shows that their involvement was a component of the organic legitimization of chiefly authority (85). This is significant because of the strain colonial authorities placed on rule by attempting to collapse groups into homogenous tribes and citizens who recognized and affirmed colonial rule (81). This informed the production of carefully crafted historical texts—to be used as a vehicle for British recognition of chiefly authority on the part of the British and local subjects.

Bond uses a 1913 dispute to foreground contemporary disputes over genealogical aspects of the mythical charter. The district commissioner thought Uyombe was not an autonomous chiefdom but rather a satellite of the non-Tumbuka speakers in close proximity. The Uyombe subsequently sought to prove their autonomy through the auspices of a member of the mission-educated elite. This individual structured his own narrative that synthesized mission accounts and Yombe poetic historical narrative and that referenced Livingstonia as a source of authority (85). Although the narrative privileged the position of the educated elite, the narrative also wrote colonial influence on the establishment of the chiefdom and its boundaries out of the history, attributing them to military activities of the Wowo clan instead. The narrative thus posed a threat to secular authority, which in part set the tone for the emergence of self-identified prophets who were also mission-school educated. However, unlike the majority of mission-schooled elite, these individuals operated without adherence to traditional secular and religious authority. Bond details a specific case in *African Christianity: Patterns of Religious Continuity*, coedited with Walton R. Johnson and Sheila S. Walker (1979).[17]

The story continues in 1981 with the chief of the Wowo clan asking Bond to write the history based on a section from his book. The result was the removal of all but two branches from the possibility of rule. The status of some branches declined as a result of the lack of mission school education. Bond saw this as an example of the way agency is obscured in traditional historical treatments of Africa; such treatments ignore how "the classes of intellectual and political leaders known as elites create themselves by taking control of their own historical narratives," the acknowledgment of which is "essential for a colonized people to assume its own identity and assert itself against its master" (quoted in Levine, "Bond, George Bond," 12).

The final history rendered in the paper links the founder of the clan to major historic places, fusing Yombe and African history in a way that produces what Bond refers to as a "pan-Africanist overlay to local history" ("Historical Fragments and Social Constructions in Northern Zambia," 90). This term could also be used to characterize Bond's connection to the Yombe elders through their common knowledge of James Aggrey and the speech he delivered at Livingstonia in 1924.

Education, Religion, and Gender

In "Education and Social Stratification in Northern Zambia: The Case of the Uyombe" (1982), Bond discusses education in the context of change that does not situate the West as a "prime mover" of social organization and change within Africa. Destabilizing the notion of education as a Western construct, Bond presents an anthropological understanding of it as a social force of continuity, intimately related to the social institutions and production mode of the society (251). He juxtaposes that conception with the socially intrusive Western style of formal education that the Uyombe received in the form of mission schooling. In previous papers, Bond focuses on the social and political effects of mission education. In this paper, he provides a political and economic analysis tying mission schooling to wage earning—a particular type of production that imposes a system of social status based on educational achievement instead of domestic productive modes. Prior to mission schooling, social status was determined by productive and political arrangements (253).

Bond's research illustrates that Western education had more of an impact on social organization than commercial agriculture did. Bond collected statistical data indicating the level of importance Uyombe attached to Western-style education over time. During Bond's first phase of research in 1964, the majority of the sixty-three heads of household he interviewed were educated for an average of 4.2 years (259). By 1971, there was an increase in average years of education of roughly 1.5 years. By 1981, 69 percent of male heads of household had seven years of formal education. Bond analyzes this change as signaling the end of small-scale economies and the imposition of a uniform national state system in which a citizen's assuming a position within the social structure requires that he or she be educated (267). As noted in "Historical Fragments," the lack of mission-school education is directly correlated with the decline in the status of some clan branches.

Bond's writings on Yombe religion equally demonstrate the need for macro- and microlevel analyses of social interactions and processes that challenge dominant paradigms of Africa constructed within Western frameworks. "Ancestors and Protestants: Religious Coexistence in a Social Field of a Zambian Community" (1987) is one such example. Again, Bond's rich ethnographic data and historical grounding of social organization demonstrates that the coexistence of domestic and commercial economic spheres is related to the coexistence of Christianity and indigenous ancestor cults. For instance, the Yombe take the money they are paid for labor and ritually imbibe it with the spirit of the ancestors. In doing so, they construct local meanings of capitalism and assign new meaning within both spheres of production.[18] Bond also identifies the decision-making processes and choices that maintain Christianity and ancestor cults as distinct religious forms (57). One of two primary examples in the paper focuses on a Christian woman who lost her husband and was thus posed to lose her rights as a wife as well as those for her children because she no longer had ritualized ties to her husband's relatives (presumably a brother). To secure her position on both fronts, she strategically participates in ancestral rights that allow her eldest son to be recognized as her late husband (66–67). This example also illustrates how Bond's ethnographic data belie assumptions about the hegemony of Christianity over indigenous, parochial religions.[19]

Bond addresses the issue of gender and religion more directly in "Ideology, Dominance, and Inequality: Gender and Control in Muyombe" (2002). After outlining the fundamental role that Yombe ancestor cults play in social stratification, he goes on to illustrate how they impact distributions of power along lines of gender. Religion provides the basis for understanding Yombe individuals as organic and spiritual beings. Male dominance is mediated through the differential value and power assigned to male- and female-associated substances and essences.[20] Bond argues that this in turn supports the maintenance of the agnatic kinship structure and daily gendered interactions. Keeping himself attuned to social complexity, Bond looks at interactions in which women are operating outside of a traditional gendered context and shows how they are tied to the cross-cutting fields of capitalist and domestic activities, meanings, and valuations (231). He also takes care not to overstate the role of the economic transitions in gender dynamics. This is because women influence decision making in traditional rituals of negotiation

152 · RACHEL WATKINS

and dispute settlement even though they are forbidden from being a part of the council that handles these matters.[21] He also notes the organic changes in women's status that accompany getting older and entering menopause.[22] After locating the Yombe's foray into capitalist production within their colonial history, he details changes in interactions between men and women that coincided with the increase in subsidized hybrid maize agriculture from 1972 until the late 1990s. He goes on to illustrate the relationship between an uptick in legal actions and the increase in female-household-led hybrid maize farms. By the mid-1990s, hybrid maize farming declined due to the central government's privatization policies, which disproportionately affected the women who owned hybrid maize farms. He asserts in the conclusion of the paper that climate changes associated with El Niño and the growing HIV/AIDS crisis in the early and mid-1990s likely impacted gendered social interactions and stratification. Social changes associated with environmental and health changes are more specifically addressed in papers discussed in the following section.

"Religion, Ideology and Property in Northern Zambia" (1987) illustrates how property ownership across space, time, and life cycles is mediated through religious ritual and ancestor worship. The essay opens with Bond describing a discussion he had with Yombe elders in which they compared Western society and kinship with their own. Rejecting its validity for their own society, the conversation reflected a sort of disruption of the Western gaze on Africa that is one of the key themes of Bond's work. Bond argues that the elders' view of the West served to obscure growing inequalities in part resulting from Western influence. Nonetheless, the discussion fundamentally demonstrated what Bond calls an astute understanding of the inherent ideological forms of Western society. This is an important example of how Bond imparts the agency of Zambians in modernity and as participants and producers of their own history.

Edited Volumes

In addition to publishing his own scholarship, Bond brought African studies scholars from various disciplines together in the form of edited volumes to interrogate existing dominant and counternarrative knowledge around Africa. The contributions to these volumes include research conducted in Africa as well as work by African intellectuals who studied in the United States. Another component of Bond's project involves considering how belief systems and practices ideologically relegated to Africa (such as witchcraft) operate similarly outside of the continent.[23] Bond also contributed to volumes edited by colleagues within and outside of African studies and anthropology that demonstrated the wider applicability of his work.[24]

Contested Terrains and Constructed Categories: Contemporary Africa in Focus (2002), which Bond edited with Nigel Gibson, focuses on how dominant ideologies regarding Africa become organic and thus mapped in society and on the human body (introduction, 11). The contributions to this volume created intellectual space for contesting and interrogating dominant paradigms regarding Africa. Bond's chapter in the volume, "The Moving Frontier of AIDS in Uganda: Contexts, Texts and Concepts," coauthored with Joan Vincent, addresses the problem of treating Africa as a totality. Bond and Vincent illustrate how disregarding the regional differences in Uganda undermined treatment and prevention efforts in the North in the 1980s. Drawing on the spheres of interaction Bond documented in Zambia, Bond and Vincent provide historical context that enables us to see why data collected from the South was used to represent the entirety of the country. The overattention to the South went hand in hand with the political and economic power concentrated there, which fostered a sense of hegemony in which capitalism was privileged and the North was rendered peripheral. The North was also embroiled in warfare and civil strife that impeded research. To point out the unintended complicity of research in obscuring conditions in which AIDS was regionally embedded, Bond and Vincent analyze two neglected research texts: the Social and Institutional Profile (SIP) of Uganda and the report on AIDS-related mortality and orphans. Their analysis of these texts indicates that the most vulnerable, women and children, were not front and center in them. Decentralization campaigns in the 1990s helped to address the underrepresentation of the North and Northeast in research efforts.

Bond coauthored another paper with Vincent titled "Community-Based Organization in Uganda: A Youth Initiative" for *AIDS in Africa and the Caribbean,* which Bond coedited with John Kreniske, Ida Susser, and Joan Vincent (1997), that focuses on an HIV/AIDS prevention initiative created by university-based youth in 1988.[25] This study reveals another aspect of the disproportionate attention given to specific groups in addressing the AIDS crisis. Although the Ministry of Health stated that it aimed to reach the masses, most of its materials and initiatives were directed toward the young, educated Ugandan middle and upper classes (110). As with "The Moving Frontier of AIDS in Uganda," they situate this misguided attention in the historical context of colonialism, noting that the Ministry of Health complex has been the primary site of medical and public health research since the colonial period (102). Bond and Vincent chronicle the development of the student organization within and outside of the context of colonialism. They discuss how the medico-moral values of the organization were rooted in its understanding of Westernized "enlightenment," which it believed called for the adoption of English and shunning of "traditional" social and sexual mores.[26] Volunteers within the organization focused on sharing that knowledge with the uneducated people in their rural places of nativity, although Bond and Vincent point out how the emphasis on this Western idea of enlightenment came into conflict with rural values. Interrogating the perceived traditional-Western dichotomy used to situate Africa outside of modernity, Bond and Vincent point to the Catholic Church's condemnation of condom use as an example of how modern power contributed to sexual practices often defined as "traditional." Bond and Vincent also situate the organization as one that shows adolescents to be self-conscious agents in AIDS intervention. The students founded the organization in part to contribute to developing a "Ugandan solution" to the AIDS crisis in response to their sense that Ugandans were overrelying on international efforts. As in "The Moving Frontier of AIDS," here Bond and Vincent are modeling social science research that considers the social and historical context of AIDS with an eye toward developing more effective interventions and situating people with AIDS in a social and medical framework. The focus on college students who represent the privileged educated class is yet another dimension of Bond's ongoing study of the role of Western education in creating elites and its impact on social organization and distributions of power within societies.

Where *Contested Terrains* looks at various dominant constructions used to frame Africa, *Witchcraft Dialogues: Anthropological and Philosophical Exchanges* (2001) focuses on dominant interpretations of witchcraft that represent it as signifying an intrinsic difference between indigenous/traditional and Western knowledge and that use it as a vehicle for locating Africa outside of the realm of modernity. Constructing a counternarrative to this interpretation, Bond and his coeditor, Diane Ciekawy, redefine witchcraft as a system of belief that assists with understanding the relationships between individuals and their communities (introduction, 6). As such, it has a role in subverting and reinforcing social order. This includes creating space for individual action when collective interests are privileged. For instance, Bond and Ciekawy also turn a gaze on the West and show how racial formations are constructed and operate in a similar fashion to witchcraft (Fields, "Witchcraft and Racecraft," 285).

Bond's chapter in the book, "Ancestors and Witches: Explanations and the Ideology of Individual Power in Northern Zambia," presents another dimension of the coexistence of Christianity and indigenous religious forms discussed in "Ancestors and Protestants," "Historical Fragments" and "The Prophecy that Failed," documenting how witchcraft was syncretized with Christian religion in Zambia and became part of a larger explanatory framework for circumstances and events, including witches, ancestors, God, Jesus, and the Holy Spirit. Bond's ethnographic evidence reveals dynamics between syncretism and political shifts that affected the degree to which witchcraft was acknowledged by governing bodies. For instance, colonizers declared that witchcraft was not real and dismissed it, and local chiefs eventually prohibited witch finding. However, Bond also notes later circumstances that facilitated the secret involvement of local officials in witchcraft-related venerations. Bond highlights two case studies to show how witchcraft emerges in accounts of disasters (such as the AIDS epidemic) as a part of the modern explanatory social and political fabric. Rather than supplanting indigenous beliefs, Christianity merely added to the scope of spheres of influence.

Broader Applications and Connections to Early Pioneers

Bond's belief in the ability of African studies to refine social science methods and theory led him to apply his research insights to anthropological concerns outside of African studies. This research falls into three main areas. First, his study of social inequality and the emergence of elites in Africa extends to research on African American elites. A published interview with first-generation pioneer St. Clair Drake is one such example ("A Social Portrait of John Gibbs St. Clair Drake," 1988). The presence and scholarship of anthropologists such as Drake informs Bond's interest in the role of organizations like the Rosenwald Phelps-Stokes Funds in providing education to blacks in the early twentieth century (Levine, "Bond, George Bond"). A number of first-generation pioneers received funds from these organizations to complete their education, including Allison Davis and Bond's grandfather (Baber, "St. Clair Drake," 204). Second, Bond's interrogation of the social construction of Africa and African history has been complemented by publications bringing scholars from different fields within and outside of anthropology together to explore social constructions of the past more broadly.[27] Third, a heavily cited literature review article on achievement and education levels in the US (in which he cites the work of his uncle) is related to his research on the role of education in the emergence of elites in Africa. Scholars have followed suit, using Bond's work to address broader questions and issues in the sciences and social sciences.[28]

In addition, George Bond's career can be connected to the earlier generation of pioneering black anthropologists in many ways. To start, there is a long history of African Americans receiving anthropological training at Columbia University. This includes well and lesser-known scholars in the field, ranging from Zora Neale Hurston to Louis King and William Willis.[29] Most notably, Elliott Skinner (1924–2007), the first African

156 · RACHEL WATKINS

American trained in anthropology to study in Africa, received his doctorate from Columbia and subsequently was offered a post there and became the first black tenured professor at an Ivy League institution (Mwaria, "The Continuing Dialogue," 283). Bond's connection to Skinner extends to their shared interest in the political organization in African states on the verge of independence. Bond's arguments regarding the limitations of a functionalist approach to studying complex social processes and cultural change in Zambia echo those Skinner expressed some five years before Bond began his research as he studied political change in the former Upper Volta (Skinner, *The Mossi of the Upper Volta*, 376).

There are also noteworthy connections between Bond's work and the pioneering work of Ellen Irene Diggs and Hubert Ross. Both Diggs and Ross contributed to the development of alternative approaches to African studies in an American context. Diggs's research on transplanted Africans in South America sheds light on their agency in a way that is similar to Bond's approach to situating Africans as participants in and producers of their own history. A. Lynne Bolles notes that Diggs changed the focus of scholarship on slavery to the perspective of the enslaved, giving visibility to their lives as bullfighters, teachers, actors, and freedmen ("Ellen Irene Diggs," 162). Going against the prevailing study of African continuities in the Americas, Ross examines South American dietary influences on West and Central Africa during the sixteenth century (Ross, "The Diffusion of the Manioc Plant from South America to Africa").

There are also apparent connections between the work of earlier anthropologists and Bond's broader interests in education and the role of education in producing elites.[30] Dallas Browne's chapter on the work of Allison Davis in *African-American Pioneers in Anthropology* highlights the particular aspects of research on class and caste in the United States.

Finally, there are the literal familial connections between members of Bond's relatives and the earlier pioneers: his uncle Horace Mann Bond was president of Lincoln University while Lawrence Foster and Hubert Ross taught there (Moses "Laurence Foster," 97).

Conclusion

Bond's work is a part of the ongoing project of decolonizing anthropology, a project that addresses inequalities in the larger society and within the discipline both intellectually and politically). While recognition of this movement has gained traction over the years, its role in maintaining the integrity of anthropology as a discipline, which includes retaining and increasing the presence of minorities in the discipline, has yet to be fully appreciated. Colleague Mamadou Diouf notes that in the 1960s and '70s, in particular, George, particularly as an African American, was a key actor in an international conversation that sought to frame a de-colonized social sciences. He was asking, what does it mean to be an anthropologist, when anthropology is so linked to the colonial project, when it, itself, has been a colonizing intervention? Others among his cohort had begun calling themselves "sociologists," to distance themselves from these associations, but George chose to work from within the discipline and reframe it. (Levine, "Bond, George Bond," 14)

In one such example of working to change the discipline from within, Bond mobilized with colleagues to offer a necessary and public critique of the American Anthropological Association conference structure as it relates to the participation of minority colleagues. A session titled "Race, Cultural Pluralism, and the Anthropological Promise" was scheduled for the 1995 annual meeting. The session was slated to be a presidential session to illustrate the commitment of the association to the contribution of native anthropologists and those concerned with and a part of the subaltern class.[31] A scheduling conflict left a senior minority anthropologist in the position of having to shuffle between sessions—a conflict for which the association was initially unapologetic. On a matter of principle, the session participants followed the lead of the senior anthropologist and withdrew altogether. Bond and his colleagues publicly announced the cancellations of the session in *Anthropology News*. Toward the end of the statement they ask, "How do we address the structural parameters and institutional ethic, that at one level, through our individual voices, becomes a sincere concern for the plight of the canon and its practitioners, yet paradoxically continues to shun and reproduce action that peripheralizes and supports the status quo?" (Alvarez et al., "Cancellation of the Anthropological Promise," 2). Bond's research and writing as an anthropologist helped to change the study of Africa within the discipline. His efforts to apply his work more broadly and to engage in political action with colleagues contribute to an important legacy that helps to bring much needed change to the study of anthropology.

Notes

Thanks to Faye V. Harrison, Ira Harrison, and Deborah Johnson-Simon for inviting me to contribute to this important volume. Thanks to Nikhat Ghouse for early guidance and Kamela Heyward-Rotimi for guidance and feedback throughout the development of this essay.

1. See Bond, "New Coalitions and Traditional Chieftainship in Northern Zambia," Bond, "Ideology, Dominance, and Inequality," Bond, "Globalization, Neoliberalism, and Historical Conditionalities," and Levine, "Bond, George Bond."

158 · RACHEL WATKINS

2. Bond's vindicationist approach also goes beyond merely reclaiming or salvaging in the form of critically situating Africans as agents. For instance, he does not romanticize the role that preindependence leaders played in postcolonial political and social change. In "Globalization, Neoliberalism, and Historical Conditionalities," he discusses the failure of African leaders to meet stated goals and fulfill promises to engage in development and provide public services (331).

3. There are abundant digital and print media sources with information about Bond and his relatives. Numerous accounts of Bond's life and career published after his death in 2014 can be found online.

4. J. Max Bond was director of an interracial commission in Kentucky from 1928 to 1931, a personnel and training official of the Tennessee Valley Authority from 1934 to 1938, dean at Dillard University in New Orleans from 1938 to 1940, and an administrator at Tuskegee Institute in Alabama from 1940 to 1944 (Pace, "J. Max Bond Sr."). From 1944 to 1947 he represented the Inter-American Educational Foundation in Haiti and also directed a commission working with the Haitian school system to improve its instruction in health and other fields. From there he became director of the School of Education at Atlanta University for three years, after which he moved to Liberia to assume the post of president of the University of Liberia, which position he held from 1950 to 1954 (Pace, "J. Max Bond Sr.").

5. See Fox, "Ruth Clement Bond, 101, Quilter and Civic Leader, Is Dead," and Levine, "Bond, George Bond." Ruth Clement's father, George, was a bishop of the African Methodist Episcopal Zion Church. Her mother, Emma Williams Clement, was, in 1946, the first black woman to be named American Mother of the Year (Fox, "Ruth Clement Bond"). George's paternal grandfather, James Bond, was a minister who served at Congregational churches across the South, often associated with historically black colleges. Bond's paternal grandfather and grandmother were graduates of Oberlin College and encouraged their children in academic achievement (see the finding aid for the J. Max and Ruth Clement Bond Papers at Columbia University Library, http://findingaids.cul.columbia .edu/ead/nnc-rb/ldpd_7031632/summary#history). Bond's uncle, Horace Mann Bond (father of civil rights figure and former Georgia state legislator Julian Bond) graduated from Lincoln University in 1923 and received his doctorate from the University of Chicago in 1936. He was appointed the first president of Fort Valley State University in Georgia in 1939 after guiding its transition from a two-year normal and industrial school to a four-year college. In 1945, he became president of Lincoln University, his alma mater. Horace Bond is also known for his research and writing that critiques racial claims about the intelligence of blacks (see the finding aid for the Horace Mann Bond papers, University of Massachusetts, Amherst Library, https://asteria.fivecolleges.edu/ findaids/umass/mums411_bioghist.html).

6. Among Bond's quilt designs for this project was that of a black fist, seeming to rise straight from the earth. The fist clutches a jagged red lightning bolt, symbolizing the Tennessee Valley Authority's promise of rural electrification. The women referred to it as the "black power" quilt, and it is regarded as the first of its kind (Fox, "Ruth Clement Bond, 101, Quilter and Civic Leader, Is

Dead"; Levine, "Bond, George Bond"; Levine, "George Bond, TC Education Anthropologist, Dies at 77").

7. See Bond, "Globalization, Neoliberalism, and Historical Conditionalities," and Peel, "George Clement Bond." Livingstonia was established by the Free Church of Scotland missionaries in Zambia and was the sister school to Livingstone College in North Carolina. James Aggrey delivered the speech on Africa for the Africans there in 1924.

8. See Bond, "Ideology, Dominance, and Inequality."

9. See Gramsci, *Selections from the Prison Notebooks*, Comaroff and Comaroff, *Of Revelation and Revolution*, Bond and Gilliam, eds., *The Social Construction of the Past*, Bond, "Historical Fragments and Social Constructions in Northern Zambia," and Bond, "Ideology, Dominance, and Inequality."

10. Bond also provided thoughtful critiques of Durkheim, Marx and other "fathers" of the social sciences (Sanjek, "The Bond Legacy," 266).

11. See Bond and Gilliam, eds., *The Social Construction of the Past*, and Bond "Ideology, Dominance, and Inequality."

12. See Kleifgen and Bond, eds., *Languages of Africa and the Diaspora*.

13. See Faye Harrison, ed., *Decolonizing Anthropology*, Angela Gilliam, "Militarism and Accumulation as Cargo Cult," Stuart Hall, "Marxism and Culture," and Gayatri Spivak, "Can the Subaltern Speak?"

14. See Bond, "Ideology, Dominance, and Inequality," and Bond, "Globalization, Neoliberalism, and Historical Conditionalities."

15. See Bond and Gilliam, eds., *The Social Construction of the Past*, and Spiegel, "Struggling with Tradition in South Africa."

16. See Bond and Gibson, introduction, 7, Bond "Historical Fragments and Social Constructions in Northern Zambia," Bond, "Ancestors and Witches," and Bond, "Ideology, Dominance, and Inequality."

17. In "The Prophecy that Failed" (1979), Bond details the rise of a particularly divisive prophetic movement led by Leshina Mulenga. As Bond points out in "Ancestors and Protestants," prophetic movements constitute a threat to colonial, chiefly, and traditional, religious authority. The Lumpa church was different from those of most Zambian prophetic movements in that many of the prophetic movements Bond references were founded by mission educated elites, but Mulenga had little education. Although the church did originate in part in opposition to colonial rule, it ended up in a violent conflict with the anticolonial UNIP. This conflict led to a particularly aggressive suppression of the church and subsequent reintegration of the members back into the chiefdom. Bond makes a point of noting that the Lumpa church was made up of individuals associated with a minimally influential clan branch. The Lumpa church, like the churches described in "Historical Fragments" and "Ancestors and Protestants," reflected the way the political and the religious coexisted in African religious movements.

18. See Bond, "Ancestors and Protestants," and Bond, "Ideology, Dominance, and Inequality."

19. See Bond, "New Coalitions and Traditional Chieftainship in Northern Zambia," Bond, "Religious Coexistence in Northern Zambia," Herskovits, *Cultural Anthropology*, and Turner, *The Drums of Affliction*.

160 · RACHEL WATKINS

20. Only men, for example, are imbued with spirit and able to become ancestors. Narratives reflect this. People Bond interviewed would share narratives in which sperm was described as imbued with spirit and the egg as lacking spirit and as less powerful. Another representative narrative states that men's sperm is more powerful than women's blood.

21. Women, for example, make the ritual beer, and by manipulating the level of fermentation, they are able to influence decisions and have an effect on the outcome of disputes.

22. Bond suggested that older and menopausal women were regarded as being like men and so treated similarly.

23. See Fields, "Witchcraft and Racecraft: Invisible Ontology and Sensible Manifestations."

24. See Markovitz, ed., *Studies in Power and Class in Africa*, and Nugent, ed., *Locating Capitalism in Time and Space*.

25. The organization is called the Makerere University Students AIDS Control Association.

26. Such as sexual norms around premarital sexual liaisons, sanctioned polygamy and anticipated extra-marital relations (Bond and Vincent, "Community-Based Organization in Uganda," 105).

27. See Bond and Gilliam, eds., *The Social Construction of the Past*.

28. See Johnson, "George C. Bond on Inequality," Newkirk, "Tuskegee's Talented Tenth: Reconciling a Legacy," and Young, "Ghanaian Woman and Dutch Wax Prints." Johnson draws on Bond's writings on inequality, particularly social constructions of the past and organic ideologies, to analyze the discussion and debate following what he calls a "race crisis" that occurred at Rutgers University in 1995. The crisis was the result of the university president at the time, Lawrence Francis, stating that African Americans received lower scores on the SAT because of a "genetic hereditary background." The local meanings of capitalism that Bond identifies among the Yombe (such as imbibing money with the spirits) serve as a guide for Young's study of how Ghanaian women culturally define Dutch imported textiles. Bond's interests in drawing connections between Africa and the United States, especially as it relates to the emergence of elites through the medium of education, serves as a model for Newkirk's study of the transfer of the Hampton-Tuskegee model from the US South to British colonial Ghana during the early years of the twentieth century.

29. See Mikell, "Feminism and Black Culture in the Ethnography of Zora Neale Hurston," I. Harrison, "Louis Eugene King," and Sanday, "Skeletons in the Anthropological Closet."

30. See Carpenter, "Arthur Huff Fauset, Campaigner for Social Justice," and Browne, "Across Class and Culture."

31. See Alvarez, Bond, Chavez, Gregory, Harrison, Johnson, Rodriguez, Rosaldo, Sanjek, Zavalla, "Cancellation of the Anthropological Promise."

Bibliography

Alvarez, Robert R., George C. Bond, Leo Chavez, Steven Gregory, Faye V. Harrison, Walton R. Johnson, Sylvia Rodriguez, Renato Rosaldo, Roger Sanjek, and Patricia Zavella. "Cancellation of the Anthropological Promise." *Anthropology News* 36.8 (1995): 2, 6.

Baber, Willie. "St. Clair Drake: Scholar and Activist." In *African-American Pioneers in Anthropology*, ed. Ira E. Harrison and Faye V. Harrison, 191–212. Urbana: University of Illinois Press, 1999.

Bolles, A. Lynne. "Ellen Irene Diggs: Coming of Age in Atlanta, Havana, and Baltimore." In *African-American Pioneers in Anthropology*, ed. Ira E. Harrison and Faye V. Harrison, 54–67. Urbana: University of Illinois Press, 1999.

Bond, George C. "Ancestors and Protestants: Religious Coexistence in the Social Field of a Zambian Community." *American Ethnologist* 14.1 (1987): 55–72.

———. "Ancestors and Witches: Explanations and Ideology of Individual Power in Northern Zambia." In *Witchcraft Dialogues: Anthropological and Philosophical Exchanges*, ed. George C. Bond and Diane Ciekawy, 131–57. Athens: Ohio University Press, 2001.

———. "Education and Social Stratification in Northern Zambia: The Case of the Uyombe." *Anthropology and Education Quarterly* 13.3 (1982): 251–67.

———. "Globalization, Neoliberalism, and Historical Conditionalities." *Journal of African American History* 88.4 (2003): 330–38.

———. "Historical Fragments and Social Constructions in Northern Zambia: A Personal Journey." *Journal of African Cultural Studies* 13.1 (2000): 76–93.

———. "Ideology, Dominance, and Inequality: Gender and Control in Muyombe." In *Locating Capitalism in Time and Space: Global Restructurings, Politics, and Identity*, ed. David Nugent, 229–46. Stanford, CA: Stanford University Press, 2002.

———. "Kinship and Conflict in a Yombe Village: A Genealogical Dispute." *Africa* 42.4 (1972): 275–88.

———. "Labour Migration and Rural Activism: The Yombe Case." *African Urban Notes*, ser. B, 1 (1974–75): 21–35.

———. "New Coalitions and Traditional Chieftainship in Northern Zambia: The Politics of Local Government in Uyombe." *Africa* 45.4 (1975): 348–62.

———. *The Politics of Change in a Zambian Community*. Chicago: University of Chicago University Press, 1976.

———. "A Prophecy That Failed: The Lumpa Church of Uyombe, Zambia. In *African Christianity: Patterns of Religious Continuity in Africa*, ed. George C. Bond, Walton R. Johnson, and Sheila S. Walker, 137–60. New York: Academic Press, 1979.

———. "Religion, Ideology, and Property in Northern Zambia." In *Studies in Power and Class in Africa*, ed. Irving L. Markovitz, 170–88. New York: Oxford University Press, 1987.

———. "Religious Coexistence in Northern Zambia: Intellectualism and Materialism in Yombe Belief." *Annals of the New York Academy of Sciences* 318 (1978): 23–36.

———. "Social Economic Status and Educational Achievement: A Review Article." *Anthropology and Education Quarterly* 12.4 (1981): 227–57.

———. "A Social Portrait of John Gibbs St. Clair Drake: An American Anthropologist." *American Ethnologist* 15.4 (1988): 762–81.

162 · RACHEL WATKINS

Bond, George C., and Diane Ciekawy. Introduction to *Witchcraft Dialogues: Anthropological and Philosophical Exchanges*, ed. George C. Bond and Diane Ciekawy, 1–38. Athens: Ohio University Press, 2001.

Bond, George C., and Nigel C. Gibson. Introduction to *Contested Terrains and Constructed Categories: Contemporary Africa in Focus*, ed. George C. Bond and Nigel C. Gibson, 1–34. Boulder, CO: Westview, 2002.

———, eds. *Contested Terrains and Constructed Categories: Contemporary Africa in Focus*. Boulder, CO: Westview, 2002.

———, eds. *Witchcraft Dialogues: Anthropological and Philosophical Exchanges*. Athens: Ohio University Press, 2001.

Bond, George C., and Angela Gilliam. Introduction to *The Social Construction of the Past*, ed. George C. Bond and Angela Gilliam, 1–24. London: Routledge, 1994.

———, eds. *The Social Construction of the Past*. London: Routledge, 1994.

Bond, George C., and Joan Vincent. "The Moving Frontier of AIDS in Uganda: Contexts, Texts, and Concepts." In *Contested Terrains and Constructed Categories: Contemporary Africa in Focus*, ed. George C. Bond and Nigel C. Gibson, 345–63. Boulder, CO: Westview, 2002.

Bond, George C., John Kreniske, Ida Susser, and Joan Vincent, eds. *AIDS in Africa and the Caribbean*. Boulder, CO: Westview, 1997.

Bond, George C., Walton R. Johnson, and Sheila S. Walker, eds. *African Christianity: Patterns of Religious Continuity in Africa*. New York: Academic Press, 1979.

Boone, Catherine. "Poststructuralism as a Historical Condition." *American Anthropologist* 105.2 (2003): 359–63.

Browne, Dallas L. "Across Class and Culture: Allison Davis and His Works." In *African-American Pioneers in Anthropology*, ed. Ira E. Harrison and Faye V. Harrison, 168–90. Urbana: University of Illinois Press, 1999.

Carpenter, Carole H. "Arthur Huff Fauset, Campaigner for Social Justice: A Symphony of Diversity." *African-American Pioneers in Anthropology*, ed. Ira E. Harrison and Faye V. Harrison, 213–42. Urbana: University of Illinois Press, 1999.

Comaroff, John L., and Jean Comaroff. *Of Revelation and Revolution*. Chicago: University of Chicago University Press, 1991.

Fields, Karen E. "Witchcraft and Racecraft: Invisible Ontology and Sensible Manifestations." In *Witchcraft Dialogues: Anthropological and Philosophical Exchanges*, ed. George C. Bond and Diane Ciewaky, 283–315. Athens: Ohio University Press, 2001.

Fox, Margalit. "Ruth Clement Bond, 101, Quilter and Civic Leader, Is Dead." *New York Times*, November 13, 2005. www.nytimes.com/2005/11/13/obituaries/ruth-clement-bond-101-quilter-and-civic-leader-is-dead.html?_r=0.

Gilliam, Angela. "Militarism and Accumulation as Cargo Cult." In *Decolonizing Anthropology: Moving Further toward an Anthropology for Liberation*, 2nd ed., ed. Faye V. Harrison, 170–91. Arlington, VA: American Anthropological Association, 1997.

Gramsci, Antonio. *Selections from the Prison Notebooks*. New York: International Publishers, 1971.

Hall, Stuart. "Marxism and Culture." *Radical History Review* 18 (1978): 5–14.

Harrison, Faye V., ed. *Decolonizing Anthropology: Moving Forward toward an Anthropology for Liberation*. Washington, DC: American Anthropological Association, 1997.

Harrison, Ira E. "Hubert B. Ross: The Anthropologist Who Was." In *African-American Pioneers in Anthropology*, ed. Ira E. Harrison and Faye V. Harrison, 265–73. Urbana: University of Illinois Press, 1999.

———. "Louis Eugene King: The Anthropologist Who Never Was." In *African-American Pioneers in Anthropology*, ed. Ira E. Harrison and Faye V. Harrison, 70–84. Urbana: University of Illinois Press, 1999.

Herskovits, Melville J. *Cultural Anthropology*. New York: Knopf, 1995.

Jacobs, Sylvia M. "James Emman Kwegyir Aggrey: An African Intellectual in the United States." *Journal of Negro History* 81.1 (1996): 47–61.

"J. Max Bond Sr.: Founding President of University of Liberia." *Los Angeles Times*, December 20, 1991. http://articles.latimes.com/1991-12-20/news/mn-363_1_j-max-bond-sr.

Johnson, Walter R. "George C. Bond on Inequality." *Journal of Asian and African Studies* 51.3 (2016): 217–82.

King, Kenneth. "James E. K. Aggrey: Collaborator, Nationalist, Pan-African." *Canadian Journal of African Studies* 3.3 (1969): 511–30.

Kleifgen, Jo Anne, and George C. Bond, eds. *Languages of Africa and the Diaspora: Educating for Language Awareness*. Bristol, UK: Multilingual Matters, 2009.

Levine, Joe. "Bond, George Bond." *TC Today* 33.2 (2009): 13–17.

———. "George Bond, TC Education Anthropologist, Dies at 77." Teachers College Newsroom, May 7, 2014. www.tc.columbia.edu/articles/2014/may/george-bond-tc-education-anthropologist-dies-at-77.

Markovitz, Irving L., ed. *Studies in Power and Class in Africa*. Oxford: Oxford University Press, 1987.

Mikell, Gwendolyn. "Feminism and Black Culture in the Ethnography of Zora Neale Hurston." *African-American Pioneers in Anthropology*, ed. Ira E. Harrison and Faye V. Harrison, 51–69. Urbana: University of Illinois Press, 1999.

Moses, Yolanda. "Laurence Foster: Anthropologist, Scholar, Social Advocate." In *African-American Pioneers in Anthropology*, ed. Ira E. Harrison and Faye V. Harrison, 85–100. Urbana: University of Illinois Press, 1999.

Mullings, Leith. "Ethnicity and Representation." In *Social Constructions of the Past: Representation as Power*, ed. George C. Bond and Angela Gilliam, 25–28. London: Routledge, 1994.

Mwaria, Cheryl. "The Continuing Dialogue: The Life and Work of Elliot Skinner as an Exemplar of the African American/African Dialectic." In *African-American Pioneers in Anthropology*, ed. Ira E. Harrison and Faye V. Harrison, 274–92. Urbana: University of Illinois Press, 1999.

Newkirk, Pamela. "Tuskegee's Talented Tenth: Reconciling a Legacy." *Journal of Asian and African Studies* 51.3 (2016): 328–45.

Nugent, David, ed. *Locating Capitalism in Time and Space: Global Restructurings, Politics, and Identity*. Stanford, CA: Stanford University Press, 2002.

Pace, Eric. "J. Max Bond Sr., 89, an American Who Headed Liberian University." *New York Times*, December 18, 1991. www.nytimes.com/1991/12/18/nyregion/j-max-bond-sr-89-an-american-who-headed-liberian-university.html.

Peel, J. Y. D. "George Clement Bond, 1936–2014." *Africa: The Journal of the International African Institute* 85.1 (2015): 183–84.

Ross, Hubert Barnes. "The Diffusion of the Manioc Plant from South America to Africa: An Essay in Ethnobotanical Culture History." PhD diss., Columbia University, 1954.

Sanday, Peggy Reeves. "Skeletons in the Anthropological Closet: The Life and Work of Willliam S. Willis Jr." In *African-American Pioneers in Anthropology*, ed. Ira E. Harrison and Faye V. Harrison, 243–64. Urbana: University of Illinois Press, 1999.

Sanjek, Roger. "The Bond Legacy." *Journal of Asian and African Studies* 51.3 (2016): 265–70.

Skinner, Elliott P. *The Mossi of the Upper Volta: The Political Development of a Sudanese People*. Stanford, CA: Stanford University Press, 1964.

Spiegel, A. 1994. "Struggling with Tradition in South Africa: The Multivocality of Images of the Past." In *Social Constructions of the Past: Representation as Power*, ed. George C. Bond and Angela Gilliam, 185–202. London: Routledge, 1994.

Spivak, Gayatri Chakravorty. "Can the Subaltern Speak?" In *Marxism and the Interpretation of Culture*, ed. Cary Nelson and Lawrence Grossberg, 271–313. Urbana: University of Illinois Press, 1988.

Turner, Victor. *The Drums of Affliction*. Oxford: Oxford University Press, 1968.

Weber, Max. *Economy and Society*. Berkeley: University of California Press, 1978.

Young, Paulette. "Ghanaian Woman and Dutch Wax Prints: The Counter-appropriation of the Foreign and the Local Creating a New Visual Voice of Creative Expression." *Journal of Asian and African Studies* 51.3 (2016): 305–27.

12

Oliver Osborne

African American Nurse-Anthropologist Pioneer

BERTIN M. LOUIS JR.

Oliver Osborne was born in 1931 in Brooklyn, New York, where he grew up with his parents and three siblings: two brothers, including his twin brother, and one sister. He grew up in south Brooklyn near downtown, bordering the Fort Greene area.[1] His family migrated to the United States from Barbados in the 1920s and was one of the first generation of Barbadians in the United States. The Osborne family settled in the New York and Philadelphia metropolitan areas. Women in the Osborne family migrated to the United States first due to their ability to gain employment as housekeepers and in factories and stores. This migration intersected with the migration of African Americans from the South to the industrial North. Men in his family migrated to these areas soon after and then moved into independent business practices such as driving cabs in the 1930s. Oliver's father and his father's twin brother opened up a trucking company and would transport items to New York's garment district, where Osborne recalls that his father's white clients would address them as "sir."

The Osborne family lived in a row house that they owned in a racially mixed neighborhood. In his interview Osborne fondly recalled walking to school with his siblings, participating in a segregated Boy Scouts troop, playing stickball in the streets of Brooklyn, and performing in the all-city high school chorus. The schools he attended in his youth were predominantly white schools. Osborne and his brothers attended Boys High School (currently Boys and Girls High School), located in the Bedford-Stuyvesant area of Brooklyn; they were some of the first black students the school admitted. Some of the notable alumni from this school include the author Isaac Asimov and Shirley Chisholm, who

Oliver Osborne
Courtesy of Oliver Osborne

in 1968 became the first black woman elected to Congress and who in 1972 became the first woman to run for president of the United States.[2] Osborne remembers different forms of institutional racism structuring the organizations and schools he attended. For instance, the racial stratification within his high school was reflected in how faculty and administrators favored white students over black students. Institutional racism was also reflected in the fact that the white YMCA was a nice building, as he recalls it, whereas the black YMCA was small and underfunded.

Over the course of his life Osborne worked different jobs—sometimes working two or three jobs while attending school. He was a Western Union messenger, worked in factories, did metal stamping, was a commercial clam fisherman and a construction worker, and also painted. Growing up, Osborne was considered the scholar in his family, and his family's Barbadian middle-class culture was such that he was expected to become a lawyer, a minister, or a doctor. Medicine and the ministry did not interest him because of how those professions, in his opinion, "captured" their practitioners (meaning that people spent too much time working those types of jobs), so he studied to become a lawyer at Brooklyn College while he continued working other jobs.

The Psychiatric Nurse

While attending law school in 1949, Osborne also worked as a messenger in an emergency room in a hospital in Brooklyn. One night he saw a man getting out of an ambulance. This person was wearing a white uniform, and Osborne asked him what his job was and learned that the man was a nurse. Osborne had never heard of a male nurse before. The man told him that nursing was a great profession. Since he was dissatisfied with law school, Osborne took the male nurse's advice and started along a path of becoming a nurse. He began his nursing career at Central Islip State Hospital on Long Island, New York, working as a staff nurse. He also went back to school and earned his RN and a bachelor's degree in nursing, specializing in psychiatric and mental health nursing. When he wanted to pursue his master's degree in nursing in 1958, a nursing supervisor informed him that the profession was not for him," which made him determined to earn the degree. Osborne ended up winning a competitive New York Regents scholarship for advanced nursing.

After completing his master's degree in psychiatric and mental health nursing from New York University, Osborne accepted an assistant professorship at Michigan State University. In this job, he worked at integrating behavioral concepts into the nursing curriculum. He craved greater intellectual discipline and also required a doctorate to have the type of university faculty career he wanted. So within a year of arriving at Michigan State, Osborne had entered the Department of Sociology and Anthropology ("The Way of One Nurse-Anthropologist," 829). After forays into social psychology and sociology, he settled on anthropology, which was an ancillary component of the sociology-heavy joint department. When the joint department split, he decided to go with the newly formed Anthropology Department. In his words, "In anthropology, I found a discipline that captured my imagination. It is an extraordinarily broad field of study and I found its methodologies, particularly its commitment to field studies, peculiarly compatible [with nursing]" (829).

Osborne developed interests in the burgeoning anthropological subdiscipline of medical anthropology and conducted his dissertation research in Nigeria, where he investigated traditional African health care systems and their relationship to Western biomedical systems. Osborne studied in the Nigerian village of Ibara Orile and focused on how Yoruba villages served as therapeutic communities for the mentally ill. His research interests brought him back to Nigeria several times, and during one of these visits his Yoruba research consultants made him Chief Adila of Ibara, associating his visits with preserving peace during times of violent unrest.[3]

Osborne produced an article from his fieldwork in Nigeria titled "The Yoruba Village as a Therapeutic Community" that discusses village psychiatric treatment programs among the Egba-Egbado Yoruba peoples and how this approach contrasts with those in Western societies. He describes the social structure of Egba-Egbado Yoruba villages

168 · BERTIN M. LOUIS JR.

by noting gender relations, village political structures, power relations, and patterns of interpersonal relations and exploring how those relate to a collective response to the treatment of the mentally ill by traditional healers (190–92). Osborne's approach is anthropological in that it focuses on the need to understand, analyze, and appreciate village social and cultural systems and how they relate to the development of community psychiatric programs. Among one of his conclusions is that studying Yoruba villages reveals specific processes related to community health programs, processes that should stimulate the development of dynamic therapeutic programs ("Cross-Cultural Social Science Research and Questions of Scientific Medical Imperialism," 199). His work in Nigeria also implies that cross-cultural studies can improve Western health delivery systems. Osborne would tout the importance of delivering community-based health services in his later US-based work.

Nurse-Anthropologist

In 1969, after Osborne had completed his dissertation and had spent nearly two years serving as a faculty member in the School of Nursing at Wayne State University, the dean of the University of Washington School of Nursing invited him to become the chair of their psychiatric–mental health nursing program. In Washington, Osborne worked on integrating a small program focused on psychiatric–mental health nursing into a department focused on psychosocial nursing. In an interview, Osborne explains the impetus for integrating psychiatric and mental health nursing into psychosocial nursing:

> At that time and even today most departments and schools of nursing had departments or programs in psychiatric and mental health nursing. Previously, in the 1950s and '60s it was psychiatric nursing because most of us were in state hospitals or in psychiatric units in general units. These hospitals were very, very big. . . . [T]he state hospital I was in had something like nine thousand patients. . . . Up north, or north of central Manhattan [New York], there were several other state hospitals with thousands of patients, and the nurses in there were prepared in these state hospitals, and they were known as psychiatric nurses. . . .
>
> When I came to the University of Washington, there was a program in psychiatric and mental health nursing, and I wanted, as I said, to introduce social and cultural concepts in there. . . , [and] so I and the faculty sat down and agreed to go in the direction of psychosocial [nursing] in order to directly set our interest in the continuum from the biological to the cultural-psychosocial/psychological and social or sociology were in the middle. So we ranged from interests in biology, psychiatry, sociology and cultural interests.[4]

The pressures of creating a doctorally prepared research faculty, competing for and managing National Institute of Mental Health training and research grants, publishing and presenting at conferences, and raising five children prevented Osborne from continuing his overseas research and anthropological teaching. Nevertheless, he dedicated himself to building the University of Washington's psychiatric–mental health nursing program up into a department. One way he did this was by hiring nurses with social science backgrounds and developing a doctoral program, which became, in his opinion, the top doctoral nursing program in psychosocial nursing.

The majority of his publications are in nursing journals like the *Archives of Psychiatric Nursing*, *Communicating Nursing Research*, the *Journal of Psychosocial Nursing and Mental Health Services*, *Nursing Research*, and the *Western Journal of Nursing Research*. A lot of his research was generated through fieldwork at state psychiatric hospitals ("The Way of One Nurse-Anthropologist," 832). I have identified four themes in his research: the political and economic aspects of health care delivery, the contributions of alternative health care systems, the needs of the oppressed, and the systemic changes needed in the way care was delivered to mental health patients. The first two themes are reflected in his work in Nigeria. The last two themes are central to his work in the United States. In "Forced Relocation of Hospitalized Psychiatric Patients," for example, Osborne and his coauthors argue for the development of humane transfer procedures for mentally ill patients when forced relocation from one hospital to another was necessary and to also keep patients in their home community as much as possible (227).

A common thread in Osborne's work is that psychosocial nursing practice should be informed by careful analysis of the cultural and how such an analysis would benefit the oppressed. In some psychiatric cases, undertaking this kind of analysis would translate to advocating for change in mental health systems and to making an overall commitment to social change in Osborne's care-oriented profession of nursing. By and large, Osborne's application of anthropological method and theory to psychosocial nursing reflects an applied and critical anthropological engagement with the nursing profession. His work also resonates with a humanistic approach to anthropology.

Program and Institution Builder

While directing the University of Washington's psychosocial nursing program, Osborne focused on changing the nature of the role of the psychosocial nurse through the systems-oriented community mental health graduate program, a program he supported by securing grants.

Osborne used another grant he secured to deliver services to the marginalized and oppressed through public sector nursing in the state hospitals. Osborne was also a member of a faculty group that designed and implemented the PhD nursing science program.[5]

During the early 1980s, the Reagan years, funding for education, nursing, and social sciences dried up across the United States, and Washington State experienced a financial crisis. Departments across the University of Washington were asked to make budgetary sacrifices, and the Department of Psychosocial Nursing was on the cutting block. Even as Oliver worked within the school to save the department, he knew that the department's practicing graduates were its best hope for keeping it alive. He asked faculty members Marilyn Whitley and Linn Larson to identify and work with community-oriented graduates who were willing to actively lobby to preserve the department. The joint efforts of the faculty and these community activists helped to save the department. These community activists formed the Northwest Association of Clinical Specialists in Psychosocial Nursing, which is now the Association of Advanced Practice Psychiatric Nurses (AAPPN). It was founded in 1982, with Osborne and Marilyn Whitley serving as cofounders. According to its website, the AAPPN is the only organization committed to advanced practice psychiatric nursing in the state of Washington. The organization provides a forum in which advanced psychiatric nurses can "exchange ideas, identify issues pertaining to advanced practice, and foster networking and professional visibility." The AAPPN also "advocates for patients' rights and access to care," an important aspect of Osborne's work as a nurse-anthropologist.[6] Oliver's vision for the organization was that it would belong to the community of advanced practice psychosocial nurses as an entity distinct from the university. He also believed that as such, this organization could support the Department of Psychosocial Nursing and that his psychosocial nursing department could support the organization.

Osborne would also establish a public sector nursing project. Founded in 1979, the project encouraged career development of hospital staff by teaching them how to give workshops, which they then offered at area hospitals. The program also offered graduate-level courses to interested nurses and provided support for research projects at each hospital. The research projects investigated factors that affected outcomes for individuals with schizophrenia as they transitioned from the hospital setting to the community. The public sector project also resulted in research and consultation programs within prisons and the greater community.

In collaboration with David Allen, Osborne developed and, for a number of years, taught the graduate multidisciplinary course People of Color, Psychosocial Nursing, and the Culture of Oppression. In his final professional years, Oliver returned to teaching Africa-related courses in the University of Washington's Department of Anthropology and completed an article on African health care systems for Microsoft's Encarta encyclopedia. Osborne retired in 2001. He currently runs a bed and breakfast in the Capitol Hill area of Washington State with his wife and splits his time between the United States and a home in Altea, Spain, where he spends several months of the year.

Pioneer African American Nurse-Anthropologist

Osborne is a pioneer in many senses of the term. He is a pioneer because he is a black man who blazed a trail for African Americans and other people of color in the white woman–dominated profession of nursing.[7] Whether it was using participant observation as a method to understand the meanings of being a nurse working in a state hospital or advocating for the use of other qualitative methods in nursing settings, Osborne was also a pioneer in using cultural anthropological methods in the nursing profession.[8] He was one of the first nurses to articulate a holistic view of nursing as well as touting the utility of anthropological studies for nurses. He is also recognized as being part of the first generation of nurse-anthropologists in the United States (De Chesnay, "Overview of Ethnography," 17).

Osborne is also a pioneer because of the role he played in the formation and maintenance of important programs and institutions that have informed the direction of the nursing profession. By creating one of the first psychosocial nursing programs in the country and graduating nurse practitioners in psychosocial nursing, Osborne helped to swing the focus of mental health away from the study of individual mental health care and toward an understanding of the larger context in which mental illnesses occur. Focusing on the minutiae of the lives of patients and nurses can illuminate aspects of the care of mentally ill patients. This contribution is particularly anthropological because cultural anthropologists focus on studying the day-to-day aspects of a culture. Osborne brought this attention to detail to nursing in Washington State.

His life's work offers a number of lessons for younger generations of black anthropologists. An immediate takeaway from Osborne's story is the way he used cultural anthropological methods to solve real-world problems in the field of nursing. A subtext of his work with marginalized and oppressed peoples, like the mentally ill and homeless populations, demonstrates the importance of having an ethic of care in one's work.

Another important lesson that newer generations of black anthropologists can draw from Osborne's life is the importance of having more than one job and multiple streams of income so that one does not have to rely solely on a salary derived from academic employment. In his life, Osborne had a series of jobs (worked two or three jobs at a time at certain points), even while he was director of the University of Washington's psychosocial nursing program, so that he always had the options and the security that money provides. This is a very important lesson for current and future generations of anthropologists when we consider the difficulties many of us encounter in trying to land a tenure-track academic appointment and the uncertainty and anxiety that comes with that reality.

Here is the advice that he leaves black anthropologists:

> The tradition of the African American anthropologist has been to study small groups and societies within those societies. I . . . say to African Americans: . . . [they] must . . . be internationalists. If they are studying Haiti, they must realize [that] it's irrelevant [to study only Haiti] unless they understand, study, and communicate that society in terms of international community and international processes. In terms of everything, the acquisition of health, the acquisition of food, the acquisition of education and the type of education they are getting right down to the smallest village. . . . Take a look at all the immigration that's going on—the migration of people across the world. This is a fantastic time! Any anthropologist [only studying] one little village is missing the point all together. . . .
>
> If you are focused on the locals, don't forget the universal because the universal is always local.[9]

Notes

I am grateful to Oliver Osborne for his help and to Whitney Wright and Hannah Zechman for their comments, research, and interview transcription services, which assisted in the completion of this manuscript.

1. Osborne mentioned in his interview that he lived by where the new sports arena is. He was referring to Barclays Center, an entertainment and sports arena where the Brooklyn Nets of the National Basketball Association and the New York Islanders of the National Hockey League currently play.

2. See http://boysandgirlshigh.org/about-our-school/testimonials.

3. The Ibara people have three traditional chieftaincy societies: merchant, warrior, and Ogboni (the Holders of the Earth). Osborne was invited to become a member of the Ogboni. During that time, despite violent unrest in other Nigerian communities, Ibara Orile remained peaceful.

4. Oliver H. Osborne, phone interview with Bertin M. Louis Jr., September 2, 2015.

12. OLIVER OSBORNE · 173

5. www.zoominfo.com/p/Oliver-Osborne/1526026128.

6. www.aappn.org/pages/about.html.

7. According to the Bureau of Labor Statistics, in 2003, women comprised 92.1 percent of RNs, 81.9 percent of RNs were white, 9.9 percent were black, 7.0 percent were Asian, and 3.9 percent were Hispanic (www.dol.gov/wb/fact sheets/Qf-nursing.htm).

8. See Thomas, Beaven, Blacksmith, Ekland, Hein, Osborne, and Reno "Meanings of State Hospital Nursing," and Bush, Ullom, and Osborne, "The Meaning of Mental Health."

9. Oliver H. Osborne, phone interview with Bertin M. Louis Jr., September 2, 2015.

Bibliography

Bush, Mary, Jean Ullom, and Oliver H. Osborne. "The Meaning of Mental Health: A Report of Two Ethnoscientific Studies." *Nursing Research* 24.2 (1975): 130–38.

De Chesnay, Mary. "Overview of Ethnography." In *Nursing Research Using Ethnography: Qualitative Designs and Methods in Nursing*, ed. Mary De Chesnay, 1–14. New York: Springer, 2015.

Osborne, Oliver H. "Cross-Cultural Social Science Research and Questions of Scientific Medical Imperialism." *Bioethics Quarterly* 2.3 (1980): 159–63.

———. "The Egbado of Egbaland." *African Urban Notes* 3.4 (1968): 5–6.

———. "The Way of One Nurse-Anthropologist." *Western Journal of Nursing Research* 23.8 (2001): 828–35.

———. "The Yoruba Village as a Therapeutic Community." *Journal of Health and Social Behavior* 10.3 (1969): 187–200.

Osborne, Oliver H., Ruth Jalane Hagerott, Illa Hilliard, and Mary Durand Thomas. "The Rise of Public Sector Psychosocial Nursing." *Archives of Psychiatric Nursing* 7.3 (1993): 133–38.

Osborne, Oliver H., Helen Murphy, Suzanne Sexton Leichman, Myra Griffin, Ruth Jalane Hagerott, Ethel Stitt Ekland, and Mary Duran Thomas. "Forced Relocation of Hospitalized Psychiatric Patients." *Archives of Psychiatric Nursing* 4.4 (1990): 221–27.

Thomas, Mary, Jane Beaven, JoAnn Blacksmith, Ethel Ekland, Jan Hein, Oliver H. Osborne and Jackie Reno. "Meanings of State Hospital Nursing," pt. 1, "Facing Challenges." *Archives of Psychiatric Nursing* 13.1 (1999): 48–54.

Thomas, Mary, Ruth Jalane Hagerott, Illa A. Hilliard, Jo Kelly, Suzanne Leichman, Oliver H. Osborne, and Jeff Thurston. "Meanings of State Hospital Nursing," pt. 2, "Coping and Making Meaning." *Archives of Psychiatric Nursing* 13.1 (1999): 55–60.

13

Anselme Remy and the Anthropology of Liberation

ANGELA MCMILLAN HOWELL

Long before concepts such as native anthropology or activist anthropology became rooted in the anthropological canon, Haitian anthropologist Anselme Remy's life and work reflected these complex intersectionalities.[1] Initially attracted to the academic life because of its potential to spur social movement, Remy left Haiti in 1962, after having finished his bachelor's degree at Université d'etat d'Haiti and having become publically critical of François "Papa Doc" Duvalier. He fled to Puerto Rico and the United States, embracing life as an anthropologist and a diasporan intellectual. However, his identities as a Haitian and an activist have continued to drive his scholarship and his decision to pursue an anthropology of liberation (Gordon, "Anthropology and Liberation," 155–57).

Anselme Remy has taught and researched all over the United States and the world. He has been on the front lines of social activism and politics in the Caribbean, the United States, and Haiti, at times paying a high price for his commitment to social justice and his grounded representations of peoples of African descent. Through his several published scholarly works he has offered insightful ethnographic portrayals of Haiti (Remy and Houtart, *Les référents culturels à Port au Prince*; Remy and Houtart, *Haïti et la mondialisation de la culture*), the Dominican Republic ("The Limitations of the Segmented Model in Explaining Race Relations in the Caribbean"), Grenada, Barbados ("Men's Clique in a Barbados Community"), and Martinique ("The Unholy Trinity"); theoretical contributions to sociopolitical development and social change ("The Duvalier Phenomenon," "The Unholy Trinity," Remy and Houtart, *Haïti et la mondialisation de la culture*); and critiques of those whose agendas

Anselme Remy
Courtesy of Deborah Johnson-Simon

were thinly veiled behind weak scholarship (review of *Haiti: The Politics of Squalor*, by Robert I. Rotberg; review of *Lecture en anthropologie haïtienne*, by Gerson Alexis; and review of *Les marrons de la liberté*, by Jean Fouchard). Anselme Remy also helped to cofound the Association of Black Anthropologists (ABA) during an era when the collective organization of people of color within the discipline was impugned by some.[2] This chapter examines a scholar whose choices reflect boldness and fierce individuality yet a true love of collaboration and community at the same time. The lack of citation of Remy's work, despite the proliferation of work on Haiti in recent years, should inspire continued reflection on the problematic stratification of scholars and scholarship within the political economy of the discipline of anthropology.[3]

Roots of a Native Anthropologist

Anselme Remy's activism and scholarship are rooted in a love for his home: Haiti. He was born in Port-au-Prince, Haiti on May 13, 1934.

Remy's parents separated when he was a young teenager, and thereafter he was raised by his mother. In recounting the story of his childhood, Remy speaks with reverence and abiding respect for his mother, who chose to leave his father after a period of abuse.[4] He says that despite having to raise five children and a younger brother, his mother "never came crawling back to his father." Remy's analysis of his early childhood experiences is complex. His mother, who was from a family that was involved in politics, was a seamstress, while his father was self-employed as a mechanic. Though his mother chose to leave his father, he still sees his father as having texture, as being worthy and complex. His father grew up on a plantation in Cuba and moved back to Haiti in 1928, around the end of the first US occupation of Haiti. Describing his family as lower middle class, Remy links his family struggles to intrafamily class dynamics and larger issues of colorism, class, and the social upheaval that took place in Haiti in 1946 when, after massive student protests, a three-man military junta deposed the mulatto president, Élie Lescot, and took control of the government.

The changing social structure in Port-au-Prince as Remy was coming of age attracted him to anthropology. Remy describes 1946 as a time when the consciousness of Haiti began to shift. The stigma of blackness was being removed: "The urban masses were mobilized around the slogan 'Un Noir au Pouvoir' (Power to the Black Man)" ("The Duvalier Phenomenon," 45). This transformation of color consciousness was due in no small part to the writing of Jean Price-Mars, the founder of the Haitian school of ethnology. Indeed, Remy describes Price-Mars as leading the revolution through his writing.[5] Thus, from the very beginning, Remy saw anthropology as a discipline of power and action, rather than of impotent ideas.

When Remy entered high school, he began to collaborate with the leftist movement and political party Mouvement ouvrier payson (Peasant Worker Movement, or MOP), which was at the time the most organized labor party in Haitian history (Smith, *Red and Black in Haiti*, 94). As the MOP was formed by a group of black intellectuals, Remy's involvement again foretells the brand of activist anthropology that he would come to practice. After high school, Remy worked for an American construction company to help his family. Two years later, after being laid off, Remy entered Université d'etat d'Haiti's Institut d'ethnologie, which had been founded by Price-Mars in 1941 and went from being a state subsidized institution to an official school of the University of Haiti in 1958, one year after Duvalier's election ("The Duvalier Phenomenon," 56). Remy became one of the first graduates of the state school. Yet cronyism was not Remy's modus operandi. Thus, despite his

Dual Identity of a Scholar-Activist

Like many Haitian students and activists during the Duvalier regime, Anselme Remy fled Haiti to seek asylum elsewhere.[6] Remy spent one year at the University of Puerto Rico's Institute of Caribbean Studies when he was twenty-eight years old, where he connected with James Blaut, a geographer, anthropologist, and activist who was serving as director of the Caribbean Research Institute and as professor and acting chairman of the geography department at the University of Puerto Rico.

More significant than Blaut's scholarship as an influence on Remy was his active membership in Henry A. Wallace's Progressive Party, his support of a variety of activist campaigns during the Vietnam War, and his support of the Puerto Rican independence movement. Ultimately, Blaut's impact on Remy's life was profound. Not only did Blaut model for Remy a life of scholarship that did not forsake activism, but part of Blaut's activist agenda was certainly realized through his support of a theretofore unknown brilliant Haitian anthropologist in the making, Anselme Remy. Subsequently, Blaut would help Remy to attain teaching posts at the Northeastern Illinois State University and Clark University. The pair remained colleagues over the years.

After his brief stint in Puerto Rico, including fieldwork in the Dominican Republic under the supervision of James Blaut and Howard Stanton, the former procured him a tuition scholarship to pursue a master's of art in anthropology at New York University. Remy describes his time in New York as eye opening. He says that in one month his professors covered what had been covered in one year in Haiti. At NYU, Remy was the only black student in the department, yet he reminisces on the experience fondly, without any trace of bitterness. In part, that contentment was due to Remy having been awarded a fellowship by the Research Institute for the Study of Man, founded in 1955 and contemporarily housed at NYU.

Remy remained emotionally and physically connected to Haiti, even while he focused on his studies. Not only did he have family and friends in New York, but there was a burgeoning community of Haitian migrants that participated in political organizations. When Remy graduated from NYU, his primary concern was his immigration status, as he was no longer on a student visa. He was delighted, then, when Jim Blaut recommended him for a job lecturing at Northeastern. As a lecturer, Remy

178 · ANGELA MCMILLAN HOWELL

began to take himself seriously as an anthropologist. After two years at Northeastern, he had made many friends and colleagues in the discipline. In fact, during this era he attracted the attention of Robert Alan Manners, professor emeritus and founding chairman of the Department of Anthropology at Brandeis University, who personally invited him to apply for the PhD program at Brandeis. Remy was excited about both the possibility of pursuing the PhD and moving to Boston, a city where the Haitian community was more populous than in Chicago and was engaged in the political struggles of the day.

The year 1968 was a pivotal one in Remy's life, then. Not only did he begin his PhD studies at Brandeis, where he "got anthropology in his blood," but he became connected with black intellectuals in the United States.[7] In addition, in 1968, the United States was in a process of social upheaval, a state of affairs that was familiar to Remy. The Vietnam War was in full swing, dividing the whole country. The black studies movement was spreading throughout the United States (Drake, "Reflections on Anthropology and the Black Experience," 101–2), and the Haitian opposition movement had a strong foothold in Boston. Remy began lecturing at Clark University in black studies in 1969. As a result of this teaching position, he would become a part of whole new scholarly community that would define the next twenty years of his career.

Fisk University and Diasporan Intellectual Life

In the political economy of anthropology, earning the PhD signifies that one has entered a new stratum. Anselme Remy never completed his PhD at Brandeis, but it certainly was not due to a lack of ability. In Remy's mind, leaving Brandeis was not a sacrifice. The PhD was a means to an end for him—and the end was doing the work of an engaged anthropologist, which he was already doing. By 1970, Remy had been teaching for four years. Further, he not only was researching and writing but was allied with colleagues both in anthropology and in black studies. Simply put, when he came to a crossroads, Remy simply determined that as much as anthropology was in his blood he was not just an anthropologist. He had a higher calling: to be a scholar-activist.[8]

The crossroads came in 1970 when he was thirty-six years old. While lecturing at Clark University in Massachusetts, Remy became a part of a community of black intellectuals. In 1969 he traveled to a black studies conference at Goddard College in Vermont, and the next year he traveled to another one at Jackson College in Jackson, Mississippi. There, he met Stanley Smith, dean at Fisk University, a historically black university in Nashville, Tennessee. Smith must have been a charismatic man, because when he met Remy and proclaimed that they needed a black anthropologist at Fisk, Remy decamped Boston immediately. During this first encounter, Smith challenged Remy to put his money where his mouth was, urging him to break away from the white ivory tower and come be a part of a dynamic cadre of black intellectuals that he was assembling at Fisk University. The next Wednesday Remy received an offer letter in the mail, and he left Boston shortly after to begin the next phase of his career at Fisk University.

Teaching at Fisk University was a dream. Smith had hired almost a dozen young black scholars who created their own multidisciplinary pan-Africanist community. Black studies powerhouse Abdul Alkalimat (formerly Gerald McWhorter) was a close colleague of Remy's and fondly remembers their time at Fisk together. According to Alkalimat, "Our days at Fisk University were the days of great intensity and optimism about the future. We formed a study group of faculty and students and focused on the relationship between Marxism and Black Liberation. Anselme brought a global perspective and his usual wit and charm to the discussion. . . . [H]e helped people know the importance of Haiti for all of us."[9]

Each Friday there were conferences at Atlanta's Institute for the Black World, directed by African American scholar Vincent Harding. Scholars and activists from all over the South and even scholars beyond the South, such as noted director of the Schomburg Center Howard Dodson, would converge there. Further, over the course of his five years at Fisk, Remy traveled all over the world, even completing a one-year position at the Center for Multiracial Studies at the University of the West Indies, Cave Hill, in Barbados. He completed fieldwork during this era in Grenada (1971), Barbados (1971–72), and Martinique (1971–72)—all of which was aimed at understanding facets of the sugarcane plantation system, from gender socialization to color and class conflict.

During his Fisk years, Remy published his first work. A thematic analysis of his scholarship reveals the impact that his status as a native anthropologist and diasporan intellectual had on his identity as a scholar. In December 1969, Remy participated in a conference on the family in the Caribbean on Aruba, where he delivered a timely and vindicationist critique of both British structuralist and American cultural assessments of the black family.[10] The next year, in November 1970, he was invited to attend Vanderbilt's sociology conference in Nashville, Tennessee. The published proceedings, entitled *Racial Tensions and National Identity*, includes an engaging collection of articles about creating and sustaining race as a concept that intersects with citizenship, kinship, and social class in diverse contexts.

Remy's contribution to the proceedings, "The Limitations of the Segmented Model in Explaining Race Relations in the Caribbean," criticizes the structural functionalist perspective that viewed society as made up of many different segments (racial, ethnic, class, and so on). Remy had already addressed the problems of applying this model to the Caribbean in an unpublished paper about Barbados that he wrote in 1970. Therein he argued against characterizing the social structure in Haiti as what James Leyburn referred to as a "caste" system, which renowned anthropologist Michel Rolph Trouillot would take up nearly two decades later in *Silencing the Past* (1995).

Remy's central argument in "The Limitations of the Segmented Model in Explaining Race Relations in the Caribbean," namely, that "present-day Caribbean social structure reflects the neocolonial character of the relations between the social classes within these countries, and with the industrialized societies" (48), was a forerunner to the dominant theoretical stance in the anthropology of the Afro-Caribbean and the critical study of Haitian political structures.[11] He further develops this idea in "The Unholy Trinity," where he uses the concept of ethno class to describe the negotiable and contested, yet materially and ideologically meaningful, social categories that define the Caribbean. He argues that the social categories in the Caribbean are not "mere reflection or product of economic conditions, but depend for their existence on the ideas and beliefs that people hold" (14). What he coined "ethno class" would later be analyzed alongside gender as "intersectionality." As both native anthropologist and scholar-activist, Remy also always assigned his subjects a degree of agency, a trend that was gaining steam alongside his writing (see Ortner, "Theory in Anthropology since the Sixties").[12]

Certainly, that Remy did not attain the PhD worked against his long-term recognition within the anthropological canon. His race, nationality, and decision to work at minority-serving institutions contributed to his underappreciation (Harrison, "Anthropology as an Agent of Transformation," 6–8; Harrison and Harrison "Anthropology, African Americans, and the Emancipation of a Subjugated Knowledge," 10–11). However, Remy's role as native anthropologist allowed him to be the corrective voice of an insider who knew better than to fall into traps set by etic observations, although at the same time, this status may have done him a disservice by situating him as reactive (Gordon, "Anthropology and Liberation," 154). Much of his written scholarship is comprised of critiques, reactions, and reviews, which have phenomenal insights tucked within them rather than advertised up front.[13]

The exception to that general pattern is "The Duvalier Phenomenon," published in *Caribbean Studies* in 1974. The article was written in English, published in an easily accessible journal, and has Duvalier in the title, which lends itself to a diverse readership. In it, Remy combines many of his past insights to illuminate the development and impact of Duvalierism, a nationalist ideology, and the Duvalier phenomenon, the implementation of that ideology in Haiti. Remy outlines the development of Duvalierism, its initial rejection of the mulatto bourgeoisie and later collusion with it, all against a backdrop of neocolonial and imperial foreign pressures. The article goes beneath the surface of the analyses of that time, which saw Duvalier as a maniacal dictator (a view Remy linked to the tendency to regard Haitians as savage, more generally). Instead, he shows how Duvalier's decisions were rational calculations and how his and his son Jean-Claude Duvalier's power was maintained through strategic acquiescence by the ethno classes in Haiti, who acted in various historical moments that presented a limited set of options. Despite its keen analytical insights, the article has only been cited a few times (in, for example, Rotberg, *State Failure and State Weakness in a Time of Terror*, and Stotzky, *Silencing the Guns in Haiti*), and not by prominent anthropologists studying Haiti or the Caribbean. As a result, Remy is much more widely known in the diasporan and Caribbean studies circles in which he traveled and worked, especially beginning during his years at Fisk. Due to its influence in Caribbean studies, "The Duvalier Phenomenon" was later translated into Spanish under the title "El fenómeno Duvalier."

Toward the end of Remy's tenure at Fisk, he began to reflect on some of the sacrifices that he had made as part of his "decolonizing anthropological praxis" (Gordon, "Anthropology and Liberation," 152–54). While Fisk was a stimulating environment, and Remy had gone there to do the work of an engaged anthropologist, he hadn't fully realized just how difficult it would be to do any writing at Fisk. Also, on a personal level, Remy had been married and divorced twice at that point, and he missed his Haitian community, from which he was isolated in Nashville. Finally, Fisk faced financial challenges, so it could no longer "afford a certain largesse" that had facilitated his diasporan connections and made his tenure there so meaningful.[14] Therefore, in 1975, Remy moved to the nation's capital, the center of the (Haitian) opposition movement.

Return to Haitian Activism

In 1975, Remy was contacted by a former classmate from Brandeis who said she had a job for him at Federal City College, now the University of the District of Columbia. At UDC, Remy was promoted to the rank of associate professor. More importantly, he arrived in DC just as Haitian immigration to the city began to accelerate. The center of Haitian migration and political opposition to the Duvalier regime had shifted from France to the United States—New York and Miami, especially. In addition, whereas previously Haitian immigrants, such as himself, had been primarily middle-class intellectuals, at that time, many more working, poor Haitian immigrants were flooding the northeast US corridor, bringing with them a host of social problems that Remy felt uniquely suited to help tackle.

Remy was seriously homesick and knew that any political pressure that he could apply from the United States to depose Jean-Claude Duvalier would facilitate his return to Haiti. Thus, with singular focus and renewed energy, Remy immediately immersed himself in the Haitian opposition movement. He rejoined the leftist organization in which he had previously been active. Further, Remy sought to create his own lobby that would pressure the United States to modify its policy toward Haiti, which supported Haiti's dictator in an effort to prevent another communist state from developing during the cold war era. Thus, in 1981 Remy cofounded the Haitian Center for Information, Documentation, and Social Action, which he directed and which served as a lobby center, a research center, and a community center, designed to serve the "boat peoples" in the areas of Washington, DC, Maryland, Virginia, and Delaware.

At UDC, Remy became known as the "head of the opposition movement." The dean would lighten his teaching load and give him credit for his activism. The State Department used to call Remy and his compatriots "the troublemakers." Every Tuesday from 9 AM to 12 noon they marched in front of the State Department in DC denouncing the US government's policy toward Duvalier. Over time they met with many US congresspeople and explained the dynamics undergirding the situation; gradually they went from being labeled troublemakers to being exclusive reception invitees.

This period of Remy's life as a grassroots activist was especially fruitful. From 1982 to 1985, he offered courses in English literacy to Haitian refugees living in and around Washington, DC. Remy's summers were devoted to bridging the gap between US-born Americans and Haitian migrants. Over the summers between 1981 and 1984, Remy served as the program coordinator for the Haitian American Training Institute in Washington, DC. During the summers between 1981 and 1983, he taught various Creole courses for the American staff of social service agencies in the Delmarva region. And, over the summers between 1982 and 1985, he conducted training seminars in cultural sensitivity for the employees of the social agencies that worked with the East Coast Migrating Workers Association.

Two of Remy's publications from this time typify his focus on public, applied, and/or activist approaches to the anthropology of Haiti. In

January 1979 the *Caribbean Monthly Bulletin* printed a commentary that Remy crafted entitled "Economic Dependence: U.S. Solutions to Haiti's Economic Problems," written in reaction to a memo the United States ambassador to Haiti had sent to Jean-Claude Duvalier in 1978. In his commentary, Remy outlines how the Duvalier regime would benefit from a proposed $125 million investment by the United States and the International Monetary Fund, the World Bank, and the InterAmerican Bank "unifying the Haitian bourgeoisie" at the expense of the masses (2).

Remy's culminating work aimed at bridging Haitian and American cultures was his 1984 book entitled *Sak Pase: A Haitian Creole-English Phonetic Guide for Health Personnel*, written in collaboration with Charles A. Cook and Gabrielle Kersaint. Published by the Department of Human Resources in Raleigh, North Carolina, *Sak Pase* translates and provides phonetic pronunciations for everything from quotidian questions and answers to very specific medical terminology. No doubt this work was incredibly helpful in preparing health workers to effectively treat the Haitian migrants who spoke little to no English.

Despite his focus on Haiti, Remy had not forsaken the pan-African perspective that he nurtured at Fisk. While at UDC, Remy collaborated with "the brothers" at Howard, completing a lectureship there from 1976 to 1977.[15] He published an article entitled "Anthropology: For Whom and What?" that was initially delivered at a symposium sponsored by the Anthropology Club at Howard University in November 1975. In 1978, he continued his comparative Caribbean research on class and color conflicts and their impact on socioeconomic transformations on sugarcane plantations in Barbados and Martinique.

At this time Remy also lent his activist training to the formation of a fledgling organization, now known as the Association of Black Anthropologists (ABA), which was in its infancy called the Caucus of Black Anthropologists (Harrison, "The Association of Black Anthropologists," 120). The impetus behind the ABA came from black scholars trying to identify other black scholars at the large American Anthropological Association (AAA) conferences, especially those with "black consciousness." What Remy recalls is that they began to have a reception at AAA's yearly meetings. After several years of those gatherings, they met in a hotel room in San Francisco in December 1975, spending all weekend long dialoguing about how they could organize themselves to address, among other issues, the lack of scholars of color in the AAA and the marginality of those scholars and their work, and to find ways to support people whose research had vindicationist, liberation, or diasporan focus. The contentious aspect of the meeting centered on whether creating and sustaining their own group would further isolate scholars

184 · ANGELA MCMILLAN HOWELL

of color, as some of the standard bearers within anthropology saw the assembling of affinity groups as acquiescence to a lesser, subjective, even racist brand of anthropology.[16]

In December 1975, the ABA was born. Remy not only helped to found the organization but also contributed to the newsletter *News from the Natives* ("Comments and Suggestions," "Our Core Task"), served as its first interim executive from 1975 to 1977, and served as president from 1978 to 1979. The ABA gave birth to many meaningful relationships for Remy; he became lifelong friends with Ira Harrison and enjoyed a brief marriage to fellow anthropologist Gwendolyn Mikell, out of which union came a beautiful daughter.

The Native Anthropologist Returns "Home"

Remy was a leader in the US-based opposition to the Duvalier regime. Thus, he was already making arrangements that would facilitate his return to Haiti when Jean-Claude "Baby Doc" Duvalier was pushed out of Haiti by popular uprising (Hallward, *Damming the Flood*, xi). In 1986 at fifty-two years old, the native anthropologist returned home, eager to help reshape an academic and political culture that had been dominated by the Duvaliers for twenty-nine years. When Remy returned to Haiti, he was saddened to discover the state of the School of Ethnology, which he says had been reduced to endless examinations of voodoo as part of Duvalier's agenda to reinforce Haitian-African links ("The Duvalier Phenomenon," 56).

The dean of the Faculty of Ethnology at the State University of Haiti, who had signed Remy's diploma in 1960, welcomed him back with open arms, and Remy quickly climbed the academic ranks. Over the years he has held many administrative offices, including chair of his department and dean of both the Faculties of Ethnology and the Faculty of Human Sciences at different times. In addition, he published two book-length studies of Port-au-Prince and various Haitian communities that examine how the people's thought processes, or social constructions of reality, influence their behaviors and correlate to their position in the global political economy.[17]

The significance of Remy's academic leadership notwithstanding, it was his role as activist that landed him at the center of international news. When Remy returned to Haiti, he became part of Lavalas, the popular democratic movement associated with "breaking the chains of dictatorship and foreign domination that had hobbled Haiti for decades" (Ives, "Haiti"). Meaning "flood" in Kreyòl, "lavalas" was an apt term for the movement that brought out rivers and seas of humanity in demonstrations that often ended with the chant "Yon sèl nou fèb, ansanm nou fò, ansanm, ansanm, nou se Lavalas" ("Alone we are weak, together we are strong, together, together, we are the flood") (Ives, "Haiti"). These were the central subjects of Remy's scholarship and activism, and, according to Remy, the 1990 elections, which resulted in an overwhelming victory for Jean-Bertrand Aristide, "were the crowning of my career."[18]

However, the 1990 elections and the years of political turmoil that followed represented an ideological compromise for Remy. Democratic elections were never his end goal; rather, "what was important [for him] was the radical transformation of Haitian society."[19] Obviously, the radical transformation of Haiti has yet to be achieved. The immensely popular political figure Jean-Bertrand Aristide, a former priest who worked for years with children in the slums of Port-au-Prince and went on to be elected president of Haiti with 67 percent of the popular vote in 1990 and reelected president in 2000 with 92 percent of the vote (Hallward, *Damming the Flood*, xi–xiii), was deposed twice in US-supported military coups (Chomsky, "'The Noble Phase' and 'Saintly Glow' of U.S. Foreign Policy," 8; Farmer, *The Uses of Haiti*). Remy's analysis of the insidiousness of foreign intervention in Haitian affairs and its interconnection with the competing economic and political agendas of Haiti's ethno classes played out in the contemporary context, and this time he was a central player.

A thorough examination of Remy's role in Haitian politics over the course of his lifetime and his influence as a social movement intellectual is beyond the scope of this chapter. However, it should be noted that during the first military coup from 1991 to 1994 in which Aristide was overthrown, Remy participated in organizing the opposition within the university to protest the military.[20] Because of his defense of President Jean-Bertrand Aristide and the constitutional order, he was beaten badly. Further, in 1994, Remy served as head of the Provisional Election Council, a position that placed him squarely in the center of a political firestorm before he was made a scapegoat and ultimately resigned.[21] Undeterred, Remy continues to speak truth to power, currently decrying the so-called democratic Haitian elections.

Remy has remained faithful to his commitment to shaping the future of his country from the front lines rather than from the sanctuary of an elite Western university. He has enjoyed a wonderful thirty-year professional career not only at the State University of Haiti but in Port-au-Prince more broadly. From August 1986 until February 1987, he served as director of the National Office for the Study of Participation and Popular Education. For a brief period in 1991, he served as chief executive officer of the Haitian National Archives, but he left that job in October 1991 because of his opposition to the military coup at that time. He completed the fieldwork for his two books between 1994 and

186 · ANGELA MCMILLAN HOWELL

1997 in the cities and rural areas of Port-au-Prince, Hinche, Cayes, Miragoane, St. Marc, Arcahaie, and Léogane. Currently, despite his advanced age, he teaches full time in the Faculty of Human Sciences, no doubt inspiring students with his knowledge and courage.

Recently, anthropologist Mark Schuller and Remy served on a panel on the history of anthropology in Haiti. Schuller describes Remy as an incredibly brave man who has produced old-school ethnographic work of the highest caliber, "one of few good resources in Haiti." Schuller said, "His story was in a word: riveting."[22]

Conclusion: Toward Anthropology of Liberation

Anselme Remy has labored on the front lines of political and social activism, devoted his career to minority-serving institutions in the United States, and created and sustained a network of scholar activists. He has collected and published ethnographic data from all over the Caribbean. He chaired the Department of Ethnology at the State University of Haiti and served on faculty, teaching there for almost thirty years. In short, Remy has traveled and survived a road full of ambushes and has had the satisfaction of witnessing several of his former students secure positions in academic, political, and national environments.

In "Anthropology and Liberation," Edmund Gordon argues that we must go one step beyond decolonizing anthropology. In order "to be an anthropology which no longer serves the interests of the oppressors, it must be one which actively serves those of the oppressed" (155). Anselme Remy should be lauded for going beyond decolonizing anthropology to engage in a genuine "anthropology of liberation."

Notes

1. Remy never refers to himself as a native anthropologist. However, I find that concept to suit him well because of his commitment to an anticolonial, anti-imperial agenda for all people and specifically for the people of Haiti. Bearing in mind Kirin Narayan's concerns about the essentializing nature of the term (see "How Native Is a 'Native' Anthropologist?"), I use it in a way suggested by Delmos Jones when he argues that "it is precisely by confronting, analyzing, and working through multiple social realities, dilemmas, constraints, and choices that native anthropologists participate in as actors and observers that the potential rewards of the undertaking exist" ("Anthropology and the Oppressed," 69). Indeed, Remy writes about the factors that inform the multiple competing identities of Haitians, which include not only color and class but also citizenship, education, and position vis-à-vis global capitalism.

Nina Glick Schiller delineates three forms of scholar activism: "direct political engagement," "acting as a public intellectual," and "creating a critical scholar-

13. ANSELME REMY · 187

ship that directly challenges the dominant theoretical frameworks, solipsisms, mystifications, and silences that underlie neoliberal regimes of truth" ("Scholar/ Activists and Regimes of Truth," 162). Any of these criteria would qualify Remy as a scholar activist.

2. Anselme Remy, phone interview with Angela McMillan Howell, November 15, 2013. To enable ease of reading, I have not inserted a citation each time that I include information about Remy that I obtained directly from him. Therefore, unless otherwise indicated, information connecting the details of his personal life was provided by him during this telephone interview. My own analyses, summaries, and conjectures are described as such. The sources of all other information presented have been cited.

3. See, for example, Gordon, "Anthropology and Liberation," and Harrison and Harrison, eds., *African American Anthropology Pioneers*.

4. Anselme Remy, phone interview with Angela McMillan Howell, November 15, 2013.

5. Anselme Remy, phone interview with Angela McMillan Howell, November 15, 2013. See also "The Duvalier Phenomenon," 44.

6. For an analysis of Haitian migration during Remy's lifespan and the phenomenon of long distance nationalism, see Schiller, *Georges Woke Up Laughing*.

7. Anselme Remy, phone interview with Angela McMillan Howell, November 15, 2013.

8. In "Anthropology: For Whom and What," Remy calls for anthropologists to "immerse themselves in the struggle of the exploited" (14). Shannon Speed argues that "the kind of critical engagement implied by activist research allows us to merge cultural critique with political action to create knowledge that is at once empirically grounded, theoretically valuable, and contributes to the ongoing struggle for greater social justice" ("At the Crossroads of Human Rights and Anthropology," 75.

9. Abdul Alkalimat, email to Angela McMillan Howell, July 4, 2014.

10. See Drake and Baber, "Further Reflections on Anthropology and the Black Experience."

11. See, for example, Clarke and Thomas, eds., *Globalization and Race*, Thomas, *Exceptional Violence*, Farmer, *The Uses of Haiti*, Hallward, *Damming the Flood*, and Trouillot, *Haiti, State against Nation*.

12. See Ortner, "Theory in Anthropology since the Sixties."

13. See Remy, "The Limitations of the Segmented Model in Explaining Race Relations in the Caribbean," Remy, review of *Haiti: The Politics of Squalor*, by Robert I. Rotberg, Remy, "Some Reflections on Caribbean Anthropology with Special Reference to the Family," Remy, review of *Lecture en anthropologie haïenne*, by Gerson Alexis and *Les marrons de la liberté*, by Jean Fouchard, Remy, review of *So Spoke the Uncle*, by Jean Price-Mars, and Valentine et al., "Brain Damage and the Intellectual Defense of Inequality."

14. Anselme Remy, phone interview with Angela McMillan Howell, November 15, 2013.

15. See Klugh and Howell, "Decolonization Continued" for a discussion of the long-standing, mutually beneficial, yet complex, relationship between the

discipline of anthropology and historically black colleges and universities. See also Remy, "Anthropology," for a critique of the politics in play in these institutions.

16. See "Anthropology." Anthropologist James Deetz, one of the fathers of historical archaeology, was, however, an early supporter of the caucus (Anselme Remy, phone interview with Angela McMillan Howell, November 15, 2013).

17. See Remy and Houtart, *Les référents culturels à Port au Prince*; Remy and Houtart, *Haïti et la mondialisation de la culture*.

18. Anselme Remy on the 1990 elections, Haiti Grassroots Watch, http://haitigrassrootswatch.squarespace.com/Dossier3Story3.

19. Anselme Remy on the 1990 elections, Haiti Grassroots Watch, http://haitigrassrootswatch.squarespace.com/Dossier3Story3.

20. Anselme Remy, phone interview with Angela McMillan Howell, November 15, 2013.

21. "At What Cost—Economic and Political?," Haiti Grassroots Watch, http://haitigrassrootswatch.squarespace.com/Dossier3Story2

22. Mark Schuller, email to Angela McMillan Howell, July 3, 2014.

Bibliography

Chomsky, Noam, "'The Noble Phase' and 'Saintly Glow' of U.S. Foreign Policy." In *Getting Haiti Right This Time: The U.S. and the Coup*, ed. Noam Chomsky, 1–9. Monroe, ME: Common Courage Press, 2004.

Clarke, Kamari Maxine, and Deborah A. Thomas, eds. *Globalization and Race: Transformations in the Cultural Production of Blackness*. Durham, NC: Duke University Press, 2006.

Drake, St. Clair. "Reflections on Anthropology and the Black Experience." *Anthropology and Education Quarterly* 9.2 (1978): 85–109.

Drake, St. Clair, and Willie L. Baber. "Further Reflections on Anthropology and the Black Experience." *Transforming Anthropology* 1.2 (1990): 1–14.

Farmer, Paul. *The Uses of Haiti*. Monroe, ME: Common Courage Press, 2006.

Gordon, Edmund T. "Anthropology and Liberation." In *Decolonizing Anthropology: Moving Further Toward an Anthropology for Liberation*, ed. Faye V. Harrison, 150–69. Washington, DC: American Anthropological Association, 1991.

Hallward, Peter. *Damming the Flood: Haiti, Aristide, and the Politics of Containment*. London: Verso, 2007.

Harrison, Faye V. "Anthropology as an Agent of Transformation." In *Decolonizing Anthropology: Moving Further Toward an Anthropology for Liberation*, ed. Faye V. Harrison, 1–14. Washington, DC: American Anthropological Association, 1991.

Harrison, Ira E. "The Association of Black Anthropologists: A Brief History." *Transforming Anthropology* 18.2 (2010): 120–27.

Harrison, Ira E., and Faye V. Harrison, eds. *African-American Pioneers in Anthropology*. Urbana: University of Illinois Press, 1999.

Harrison, Ira E., and Faye V. Harrison. "Anthropology, African Americans, and the Emancipation of a Subjugated Knowledge." In *African-American Pioneers in Anthropology*, ed. Faye V. Harrison, and Ira Harrison, 1–36. Urbana: University of Illinois Press, 1999.

Ives, Kim. "Haiti: Aristide's Party Fanmi Lavalas Taken Over by 'Macouto-Bourgeois Group.'" Global Research, December 12, 2013. www.globalresearch.ca/haiti-aristides-party-fanmi-lavalas-taken-over-by-macouto-bourgeois-group/5361350.

Jones, Delmos. "Anthropology and the Oppressed: A Reflection on 'Native' Anthropology." *NAPA Bulletin* 16.1 (1995): 58–70.

Klugh, Elgin, and Angela Howell. "Decolonization Continued: Anthropology and HBCUs." *Anthropology News*, June 2013.

Narayan, Kirin. "How Native Is a 'Native' Anthropologist?" *American Anthropologist* 95.3 (1993): 671–86.

Ortner, Sherry B. "Theory in Anthropology since the Sixties." *Comparative Studies in Society and History* 26.1 (1984): 126–66.

Remy, Anselme. "Anthropology: For Whom and What?" *Black Scholar* 7.7 (1976): 12–16.

———. "Comments and Suggestions." *News from the Natives* 1 (1975).

———. "The Duvalier Phenomenon." *Caribbean Studies* 14.2 (1974): 38–65.

———. "Economic Dependence: U.S. Solutions to Haiti's Economic Problems." *Caribbean Monthly Bulletin* 13.1–2 (1979): 1–4.

———. "El fenómeno Duvalier." Revista Interamericana 7.3 (1977).

———. "The Limitations of the Segmented Model in Explaining Race Relations in the Caribbean." In *Racial Tensions and National Identity*, ed. Ernest Q. Campbell, 45–55. Nashville, TN: Vanderbilt University Press, 1972.

———. "Men's Clique in a Barbados Community." Unpublished paper, 1970.

———. "Our Core Task: Response to a Presidential Address." *News from the Natives* 1 (1975).

———. Review of *Haiti: The Politics of Squalor*, by Robert I. Rotberg. Caribbean Studies 12.2 (1972): 119–29.

———. Review of *Lecture en anthropologie haïenne*, by Gerson Alexis, and *Les marrons de la liberté*, by Jean Fouchard. *American Anthropologist* 77.2 (1975): 401–2.

———. Review of *So Spoke the Uncle*, by Jean Price-Mars. *American Ethnologist* 14.3 (1987): 574–75.

———. "Some Reflections on Caribbean Anthropology with Special Reference to the Family." In *The Family in the Caribbean: Proceedings of the Second Conference on the Family in the Caribbean*, ed. Stanford N. Gerber, 51–64. Rio Piedras, Puerto Rico: Institute of Caribbean Studies, University of Puerto Rico, 1973.

———. "The Unholy Trinity." *Caribbean Review* 6.2 (1973): 14–18.

Remy, Anselme, Charles A. Cook, and Gabrielle Kersaint. *Sak Pase: A Haitian Creole-English Phonetic Guide for Health Personnel*. Raleigh, NC: Department of Human Resources, 1984.

Remy, Anselme, and François Houtart. *Haïti et la mondialisation de la culture: Etudes des mentalités et des religions face aux réalités économiques, sociales, et politiques*. Paris: L'Harmattan, 2000.

190 · ANGELA MCMILLAN HOWELL

———. *Les référents culturels à Port au Prince: Etude des mentalités face aux réalités économiques, sociales et politiques.* Port-au-Prince: CRESFED, 1997.

Rotberg, Robert I. *State Failure and State Weakness in a Time of Terror.* Cambridge, MA: World Peace Foundation, 2003.

Schiller, Nina Glick. *Georges Woke Up Laughing: Long-Distance Nationalism and the Search for Home.* Durham, NC: Duke University Press, 2001.

———. "Scholar/Activists and Regimes of Truth: Rethinking the Divide between Universities and the Streets." *Transforming Anthropology* 19.2 (2011): 162–64.

Smith, Matthew J. *Red and Black in Haiti: Radicalism, Conflict, and Political Change, 1934–1957.* Chapel Hill: University of North Carolina Press, 2009.

Speed, Shannon. "At the Crossroads of Human Rights and Anthropology: Toward a Critically Engaged Activist Research." *American Anthropologist* 108.1 (2006): 66–76.

Stotzky, Irwin P. *Silencing the Guns in Haiti: The Promise of Deliberative Democracy.* Chicago: University of Chicago Press, 1997.

Thomas, Deborah A. *Exceptional Violence: Embodied Citizenship in Transnational Jamaica.* Durham, NC: Duke University Press, 2011.

Trouillot, Michel-Rolph. *Haiti, State against Nation: The Origins and Legacy of Duvalierism.* New York: Monthly Review Press, 1990.

———. *Silencing the Past: Power and the Production of History.* Boston: Beacon Press, 1995.

Valentine, Charles A., Bettylou Valentine, Herbert Aptheker, Gerald D. Berreman, Santiago Genovés, Norman B. Henderson, Michael J. Hoffman, James R. Jaquith, Harry J. Jerison, Diane K. Lewis, Ashley Montagu, Michel Panoff, Anseleme Remy, and Michael R. Seltzer. "Brain Damage and the Intellectual Defense of Inequality." *Current Anthropology* 16.1 (1975): 117–50.

14

Vera Mae Green
Quaker Roots and Applied Anthropology

ANTOINETTE JACKSON

Vera Mae Green is recognized as an applied anthropologist. Although her contributions to the discipline are significant, they have often been underrepresented in discussions of persons of influence with respect to the professional canon of anthropology. This is especially evident when we examine the pantheon of intellectuals of influence presented to classes of new scholars at the university level in their initial immersion into anthropological theory.[1] For this reason, Green's work has to be sought out, studied, critiqued, and subsequently used to challenge and expand the canon.

This chapter presents an overview of Green's intellectual contributions to the discipline and provides an introduction to influences

Vera Mae Green
Courtesy of the University of Houston Archives

in Green's life that shaped her approach to applied anthropology, particularly focusing on her Quaker roots and her association with influential Quakers. In the Religious Society of Friends, Green found personal and intellectual acceptance, but she also faced challenges. She came of age during an era in which segregation, integration, and the civil rights movement in the United States impacted one's place in society on every level, informed economic status, and shaped political consciousness.[2]

Her identity was influenced by these experiences, and as an intellectual, she focused on the study of Black families and social/cultural influences impacting their construction. She identified gaps in existing research assumptions and approaches and proposed other ways of thinking. Previous research on this topic had been centered on a limited segment of communities, mainly urban ghettos and rural parts of the Deep South. According to Green, "A grave danger of biases exists in our present systematic knowledge, especially as we *insist* upon generalizing to the 'whole Black community' on the basis of two or three of the many lifestyles found among U.S. Blacks of different classes and geographical location" ("The Black Extended Family in the United States," 384). Green's work emphasizes diversity and variation among the Black community, both in the United States and abroad, and constitutes a major contribution to the field of anthropology. Her interest in studying Black families and communities in terms of complexity and dynamism stemmed from her upbringing in Chicago in poor and working-class communities (Bolles and Moses, "Vera Mae Green,"127).

Background and Academic Career

Green was born on September 6, 1928, in Chicago, Illinois. She was an only child. Terms that have most often been used to describe her upbringing include "poor" and "underprivileged." Green referred to her early years as "rented-room" poor, according to an article by Johnnetta Cole ("Vera Mae Green," 633). Green became interested in anthropology in her youth, her early criticism of Hollywood and its portrayal of Native Americans being a primary example of this burgeoning interest (Bolles and Moses, "Vera Mae Green," 127).

Throughout her academic career, Green was greatly influenced by her interest in Quakerism; it affected her choice of what colleges to attend and led her to collaborate with Quaker scholars. Green graduated from high school in 1946 and went on to William Penn College in Oskaloosa, Iowa, on a scholarship. At this Quaker-funded college, she became more aware of Quaker lifestyles and beliefs. Green joined an organization of

Quakers while at the college. In a letter years later requesting membership in the 57th Street Meeting of Quakers, Green explained that ever "since [I was a student at William Penn College], I have been associated with Friends and Friends' practices to the extent that I have felt myself a member of the 'wider' Circle of Friend."[3] ("Wider" refers to the wider body of Quakers.)

After leaving William Penn College, Green attended Roosevelt College in Chicago, Illinois, where she received a bachelor of arts in sociology. During her time at Roosevelt College, Green was mentored by African American sociologist Horace Cayton and anthropologist St. Clair Drake, a Quaker who encouraged her to continue her studies in a social science graduate program. Unfortunately, Green was unable to afford graduate school at that time and decided to work in the area of social welfare; during this time, she was employed by Chicago's Public Welfare Department (Bolles and Moses, "Vera Mae Green," 127–28). She eventually moved to New York to pursue graduate studies in cultural anthropology at Columbia University, receiving a master of arts in 1955 (Cole, "Vera Mae Green," 633).

When she failed to be admitted into the Columbia University doctoral program, Green got a job working with United Nations in the area of international community development (Adams, "Paying it Forward," 64). In 1956, Green became a fundamental educator under UNESCO after working in a mestizo community in Mexico. Green would later work with American anthropologist Oscar Lewis on his study of the poor; having previously conducted fieldwork on the poor in New York and having grown up poor herself, she had insight into Lewis's project.

Green was urged to enroll in a doctoral program by both Oscar Lewis and anthropologist Edward Spicer, who had a strong Quaker background. Spicer's father was a staunch Quaker who published in *The Friends Intelligencer* (Officer, *Edward Holland Spicer (1906–1983)*, 325). Spicer helped Green enter the anthropology doctoral program at the University of Arizona in Tucson and directed her dissertation research. For her doctoral study, Green examined interethnic relations on the island of Aruba, Netherlands Antilles. Her work in this area made her one of the first African American anthropologists to conduct research on interethnic relations in the Caribbean. During the time she was pursuing her PhD, Green decided to fully join the Society of Friends in 1961. In a letter to the 57th Street Meeting, Green wrote, "I never dared to think I could reach such a degree of perfection as to aspire to the 'inner circle' or actual membership, even though I knew that only Quakerism met all my religious needs."[4] In 1969, she received her PhD.

194 · ANTOINETTE JACKSON

Vera Green secured her first teaching job at the University of Iowa, although her time there was short lived. She moved on to the Department of Anthropology at the University of Houston, where she taught from 1969 to 1972. Green subsequently went to Rutgers University, where she served as chair and graduate advisor of the Department of Anthropology. She then became the chair of the undergraduate portion of the department at Livingston College, a college linked to Rutgers. Green's last position before her death was as director of Rutgers's Latin American Institute (Bolles and Moses, "Vera Mae Green," 129; Cole, "Vera Mae Green," 634; "Dr. Vera Mae Green").

Research

Green's research has contributed to the field of anthropology through her focus on heterogeneity and diversity within and across groups. Her research has influenced Black family studies, interethnic studies, Caribbean studies, as well as studies on less developed countries and the impact of development policies on affected populations. Green critiques previous methods of studying Black and Caribbean communities in her book *Migrants in Aruba* (1974), which was based on her dissertation research. She uses voluntary associations to examine such relationships, collecting cultural and societal data through her investigation. Based on the results of her study, Green argues that Aruba, Netherland Antilles, does not fit into the parameters of previous research conducted, which focused on Curacao and the Windward Islands. She asserts that there is a high level of positive interaction that occurs between nonnatives and natives, despite previous research suggesting otherwise ("Aspects of Interethnic Integration in Aruba, Netherlands Antilles," xi). Green concludes her study by stating that "it would seem that the use of voluntary associations as a tool for the study of interrelationships in heterogeneous and plural societies can be effective in the Caribbean as in West African and other areas, such as the United States" (225).

Additionally, Green criticizes previous research on Black communities in her article "The Confrontation of Diversity within the Black Community" (1970), arguing that contemporary scholars do not acknowledge diversity in the Black population but focus instead on the lower economic classes and then apply these findings universally. According to Green, focusing on one element or sector of the Black population and claiming on that basis that this is what is "truly Black" is a form of stereotyping, which limits ways of understanding a diversity of populations critically and has implications for policy making and administrative decisions that impact Black people (268).

In her book chapter "The Black Extended Family in the United States: Some Research Suggestions" (1978), Green further emphasizes the methodological problems concerning research on Black families. She critically reviews previous studies on Black extended families, arguing that the Black population and culture is more diverse than previously studied and identifying nine "cultural-ecological" areas that call for further research, including the Southeast coastal area (384). Today this area, which stretches from Wilmington, North Carolina, to Jacksonville, Florida, is called the Gullah Geechee Cultural Heritage Corridor and has been designated as a National Heritage Area by the federal government.[5] Projects undertaken for the Gullah Geechee Cultural Heritage Corridor, one of the first such areas of its size and focus in the nation, focus on the unique history of Africans in America.

Professional Organization Involvement

Vera Green was very dedicated to anthropology and provided service to professional organizations within this field. She was active on the executive board of the American Anthropological Association and served as president of the Association of Black Anthropologists from 1977 to 1978. Green was also active in the Society for Applied Anthropology and served as the director of the Mid-Atlantic Council for Latin American Studies. Lastly, from 1976 to 1979, Green was the convener of Quaker Anthropologists (Bolles and Moses, "Vera Mae Green,"131).

Death and Posthumous Publications

Green died after a long battle with cancer on January 17, 1982, at the age of fifty-three. She was an associate professor of anthropology at Rutgers University at the time of her death. Green's death was noted in the *New York Times*, which highlighted some of her accomplishments ("Dr. Vera Mae Green"). Additionally, scholars published various articles about Green following her death, showing her influence on the field.[6] Johnnetta Cole, an esteemed scholar of anthropology, wrote about Green in *American Anthropologist* (1982), outlining not only Green's academic achievements but also her personal interests, such as her karate skills. Green was a black belt in karate. A. Lynn Bolles, Green's mentee, wrote an article in memory of the scholar ("African-American Soul Force: Dance, Music, and Vera Mae Green" [1986]) in which she examines Green's love for dance while exploring the concept of "soul force." Bolles integrates Green's social dancing and academic interests into her discussion of African American dance and music and their ties to Africa. She also mentions how Green loved to wear "non-Euro-Western" clothing (32). Green's head would be "wrapped in tie-dyed polished cotton from the Ivory Coast, while on her wrists would be bracelets of Navajo turquoise and silver" (32–34). Bolles provides an insight into Vera Green's personal interests and her love for dance, specifically the rhumba, in a letter published in "Paying It Forward: Making Thirty Years of the Association of Black Anthropologists" by Robert Adams Jr.

Finding Vera Green's Material Legacy Today—Searching the Archives

Vera Green willed all of her papers, which included well over 150 boxes, to Tuskegee Institute, now called Tuskegee University. Bolles notes this gift in her letter to Green (Adams, "Paying it Forward," 64). Unfortunately, her archives are challenging to locate and review at Tuskegee University. In order to access her information, a researcher must locate the main holding list after getting onto the Tuskegee library's archival page and look for Vera Green, listed as number 210. However, Green's extensive holding of documents have yet to be digitized. Additionally, her papers have not been indexed; therefore, there is currently no database indicating what is included in the boxes. There is also no means of requesting materials from her holdings via interlibrary loan. In order to view her documents, researchers must go to the Tuskegee University library and look through the boxes. Green has done tremendous work that has contributed to the field of anthropology. Scholars are encouraged to seek out her papers at Tuskegee University and help make them accessible to a broader audience.

Quaker Influence

Green's research expanded beyond academia and into her religious affiliations. In 1973, she was asked by the Friends General Conference to conduct an anthropological study as to why there was such a small number of Black Quakers and what should be done to attract more Blacks to Quakerism. In the study, entitled "Blacks and Quakerism: A Preliminary Report" (1973), Green states that the Blacks she interviewed believed that the majority of blacks are not well informed about Quakerism and also would question Quakers' belief in nonviolence. This opposition to Quakerism by Black people, especially the younger generation, was thought by Green to be mainly due to the political and social climate of that time period—the Jim Crow period and transition to integration.

Academically, Vera Green was nurtured and influenced within a circle of intellectuals that were deeply committed to Quakerism as a way of life, one aspect of which was the use of philosophical persuasion to encourage public engagement and corrective action aimed at disrupting injustice through nonviolent means. The basic aspect of a Quaker community is the meeting, which is not only a form of worship but a time for the members to bond and work collectively. This collective group shares testimonies, also known as their beliefs, which guide their spirituality (Plugh, "Meaning in Silence and the Quaker Tradition"). Howard Brinton, a renowned scholar of Quakerism, explains that there are four basic testimonies: simplicity, harmony, community, and equality. Simplicity refers to the simple aspect of truth and integrity among members. Harmony means being peaceful not only during the meetings but also when interacting with those outside of the faith (*The Nature of Quakerism*, 10). Community is a collection of individuals who are a "living whole" (7). The last aspect or tenet of Quakerism is equality with respect to sex, race, and class (10). Green's research and life's work mirrored these practices, as she encouraged African Americans and other underrepresented groups to go into the field of anthropology.

Conclusion

In revisiting Green's work, I have concluded that we ought to rethink the work of other pioneers, other African American women with intellectual traditions in African diaspora theory who have conducted anthropological research in the Caribbean.[7] It is time to visit the archives at Tuskegee where Green's work is stored and open the box containing her files. It is time to examine those hundred plus unexplored papers and items in her file to find out what they tell about this pioneer in African American anthropology that can help us today. Vera Green's life and work sits at the intersection of applied anthropology, African diaspora research, and community engagement. There is much more to learn.

Notes

I would like to thank my graduate research assistant, Kaniqua Robinson, a PhD candidate in the University of South Florida Department of Anthropology, for her help with this chapter.

1. See Harris, *The Rise of Anthropological Theory*, McGee and Warms, *Anthropological Theory*, and Layton, *An Introduction to Theory in Anthropology*.

2. See Brinton, *The Nature of Quakerism*, Ezra, *Civil Rights Movement: People and Perspectives*, and Chafe, Gavins, and Korstad, *Remembering Jim Crow*.

198 · ANTOINETTE JACKSON

3. Green to the Society of Friends, August 3, 1961, 57th Street Meeting of Friends Library, Chicago.

4. Green to the Society of Friends, August 3, 1961, 57th Street Meeting of Friends Library, Chicago.

5. See National Park Service, Gullah/Geechee, www.nps.gov/guge/parkmgmt/publicinvolvement.htm.

6. See Cole, "Vera Mae Green," Bolles and Moses, "Vera Mae Green," and Adams, "Paying it Forward."

7. See Hurston, "Dance Songs and Tales from the Bahamas," Hurston, *Mules and Men*, Hurston, *Tell My Horse*, Dunham, "Form and Function in Primitive Dance," Dunham, *Island Possessed*, Cole, "Vera Mae Green," Bolles, "African-American Soul Force," and Moses, "Female Status, the Family, and the Male Dominance in a West Indian Community."

Bibliography

Adams, Robert, Jr. "Paying It Forward: Marking Thirty Years of the Association of Black Anthropologists." *Transforming Anthropology* 15.1 (2007): 63–76.

Bolles, A. Lynn. "African-American Soul Force: Dance, Music, and Vera Green." *Sage* 3.2 (1986): 32–34.

Bolles, A. Lynn, and Yolanda T. Moses. "Vera Mae Green." In *Women Anthropologists: A Biographical Dictionary*, ed. Ute Gacs, 127–30. New York: Greenwood Press, 1988.

Brinton, Howard. *The Nature of Quakerism.* Wallingford, PA: Pendle Hill, 1949.

Chafe, William Henry, Raymond Gavins, and Robert Korstad. *Remembering Jim Crow: African Americans Tell about Life in the Segregated South.* New York: New Press, 2011.

Cole, Johnnetta. "Vera Mae Green." *American Anthropologist* 84.3 (1982): 633–35.

"Dr. Vera Mae Green." *New York Times*, January 18, 1982.

Dunham, Katherine. "Form and Function in Primitive Dance." *Educational Dance* 4.10 (1941): 2–4.

———. *Island Possessed.* Chicago: University of Chicago Press, 1994.

Ezra, Michael. *Civil Rights Movement: People and Perspectives.* Santa Barbara: ABC-CLIO, 2009.

Green, Vera M. "Aspects of Interethnic Integration in Aruba, Netherlands Antilles." PhD diss., University of Arizona, 1969.

———. "The Black Extended Family in the United States: Some Research Suggestions." In *The Extended Family in Black Societies*, ed. Demitri B. Shimkin, Edith M. Shimkin, and Dennis Frate, 379–90. Paris: Mouton, 1978.

———. "Blacks and Quakerism: A Preliminary Report." In *Black Fire: African American Quakers on Spirituality and Human Rights*, ed. Harold D. Weaver Jr., Paul Kriese, and Stephen W. Angell, 233–41. Philadelphia: Friends General Conference Quaker Press, 1973.

———. "The Confrontation of Diversity within the Black Community." *Human Organization* 29.4 (1970): 267–72.

14. VERA MAE GREEN · 199

———. *Migrants in Aruba*. Assen: Van Gorcum, 1974.

Harris, Michael. *The Rise of Anthropological Theory: A History of Theories of Culture*. Lanham, MD: Rowman and Littlefield, 2001.

Hurston, Zora Neale. "Dance Songs and Tales from the Bahamas." *Journal of American Folklore* 43.169 (1930): 294–312.

———. *Mules and Men*. Reprint, New York: Harper Perennial Modern Classics, (1935) 2008.

———. *Tell My Horse: Voodoo and Life in Haiti and Jamaica*. Reprint, New York: Harper Perennial Modern Classics, (1938) 2008.

Julye, Vanessa. "Vera Green (1928–1982): Educator, Social Scientist, Author." Friends General Reference. www.fgcquaker.org/sites/www.fgcquaker.org/files/attachments/Vera%20Green.pdf.

Layton, Robert. *An Introduction to Theory in Anthropology*. Cambridge: Cambridge University Press, 1997.

McClaurin, Irma, ed. *Black Feminist Anthropology: Theory, Politics, Practice, and Poetics*. New Brunswick, NJ: Rutgers University Press, 2001.

McGee, R. Jon, and Richard Weems. *Anthropological Theory: An Introductory History*. New York: McGraw-Hill, 2011.

Moses, Yolanda. "Female Status, the Family, and Male Dominance in a West Indian Community." *Signs* 3.1 (1977): 142–53

Nelson, Jack L., and Vera M. Green, eds. *International Human Rights, Contemporary Issues*. Standfordville, NY: Human Rights Publishing Group, 1980.

Officer, James. *Edward Holland Spicer (1906–1983)*. Washington, DC: National Academies Press, 1995.

Plugh, Michael H. "Meaning in Silence and the Quaker Tradition." *ETC: A Review of General Semantics* 69.2 (2012): 204–15.

15

Claudia Mitchell-Kernan
Sociolinguistic Anthropologist, Administrator, and Innovator

BETTY J. HARRIS

Claudia Mitchell-Kernan received her PhD in anthropology from the University of California, Berkeley, in 1969 at the age of twenty-seven. Her research specialties include urban anthropology, sociolinguistics, African American culture, and field research in American Samoa, the Caribbean, and Rwanda. Mitchell-Kernan's first academic appointment was as assistant professor of anthropology at Harvard. However, in 1973, she accepted a faculty position in anthropology at the University of California, Los Angeles (UCLA). Shortly after her arrival at UCLA, she was appointed director of the Ralph Bunche Center for African American Studies (1976–1989). In 1989, Mitchell-Kernan was appointed vice chancellor for graduate studies and dean of the Graduate Division at UCLA, a position she held until 2010.

Claudia Mitchell-Kernan
Courtesy of Ira E. Harrison

Mitchell-Kernan was born and educated through high school in Gary, Indiana. She received her BA and MA degrees in anthropology from Indiana University, Bloomington. In 1968, while at Berkeley, she married fellow Berkeley anthropology graduate student Keith T. Kernan, also a linguistic anthropologist, and the couple did field work together in Samoa and in Belize. Early in his career, Keith Kernan was appointed assistant professor of social relations at Harvard in 1969, and at the time of his passing in March 2017, he was UCLA professor emeritus of psychiatry and biobehavioral sciences. The couple are the parents of Ryan James Kernan, assistant professor of English at Rutgers University, and Claudia Leafa Kernan, who maintains a neuropsychology practice in Los Angeles and also holds a position as clinical assistant professor at UCLA, and the grandparents of Olivia Irene Kernan.

Sociolinguist of Urban Black English

As a member of the second generation of Black anthropologists, Mitchell-Kernan's entry into the discipline was contemporaneous with the emergence of the New Anthropology in the late 1960s. Contributors to Dell Hymes's edited volume *Reinventing Anthropology* (1972) cited profound challenges to anthropology as a discipline and described anthropologists' efforts to positively respond to those challenges. Hymes's introduction emphasized the integration of the four-field orientation; the discipline's role in educating people to be nonsexist and nonracist; the importance of maintaining the discipline as an academic profession; the discipline's role in articulating the relationship between scientism and humanism; the role of participant-observation and ethnographic representation; the importance of political activism; and the role of the discipline vis-à-vis ethnic studies and international studies. This was a period in which more Blacks and other minorities were receiving PhDs in anthropology and entering into academic positions. As a reflection of the increasing Black presence in the discipline, the Association of Black Anthropologists (ABA), founded in 1970, was recognized as a society within the American Anthropological Association (AAA) in 1975.

Anthropological linguistics, one of four subdisciplines of American anthropology, also underwent a transformation in moving away from structural linguistics and toward the "ethnography of speaking" (later, "ethnography of communication") as manifested within particular speech communities. Mitchell-Kernan characterizes Hymes's notion of the ethnography of speaking as emphasizing setting or scene, participants or personnel, ends, art characteristics, key, instrumentalities, norms of interaction and interpretation, and genre (*Language Behavior in a Black Urban Community*, 4–5).

202 · BETTY J. HARRIS

Mitchell-Kernan's dissertation committee at Berkeley included William Gumperz, a leading scholar in the emerging field of sociolinguistics, and Susan Ervin-Tripp, a psychologist whose research focused on language acquisition and bilingualism. Mitchell-Kernan's scholarly direction was influenced by the interests of her dissertation committee members. Gumperz's collaboration with Dell Hymes (*Directions in Sociolinguistics* [1972]) in the ethnography of communication was central to Mitchell-Kernan's earlier work, and she later coauthored an article on language acquisition with Ervin-Tripp. Thus, Mitchell-Kernan was at the center of the development of sociolinguistics and published with leading scholars. Her early work on the relationship between Black English (BE) and Standard English (SE) provides a West Coast counterpart to Labov's East Coast research on BE. Her 1971 monograph *Language Behavior in a Black Urban Community* served as a basis for her publication of a number of articles and chapters.

Mitchell-Kernan did sociolinguistic, ethnographic research in a working-class African American community in West Oakland, in northern California, from June to September 1965 and October 1966 to August 1967. She characterized the socioeconomic status of the community as follows:

> Of the 50,000 individuals who reside in this area 70% are non-White. In 1960 the median family income was just over $4,500; four out of every ten families earn under $3,000 while only one out of ten earned over $7,000. Family income in nine-tenths of the area is less than $4,000. West Oakland contains some 30% of the city's welfare recipients and in 1960 close to 20% of the defined labor force is unemployed. (*Language Behavior in a Black Urban Community*, 12)

Culturally, she does not view Black Americans as being integrated into the American "melting pot" in the way White immigrants have been (18). Yet they are connected to American society more distantly, and patterns of language use reflect interactions in different speech communities.

Mitchell-Kernan interviewed informants in different contexts, choosing two key informants, with differential use of BE and SE, to establish a continuum of language usage between the two poles. The key informants were given the pseudonyms Rita and Esther. Both were in their twenties and had some education beyond high school. Rita and Esther had children born out of wedlock and had at some point been welfare recipients. Rita's English was viewed by others in the community as average to poor and Esther's as good. After taping extensive interviews with each informant, Mitchell-Kernan analyzed their speech vis-à-vis the BE structural differences of copula deletion and deletion of the auxiliary "have" and other patterns not considered here. As an example of the former, she provides the following: "He _____ the one who had to go try pick up the peacock." "Is" has been deleted here. As an example of the latter, she provides the following: "I think he done gave her the rest." In this case, "done" replaces "have." Rita engages in both types of deletions a higher percentage of the time than does Esther (32–35). The author also found that there was substantial variation in BE/SE usage throughout the Black community in Oakland (36). Her work challenges scholarly perspectives that viewed Black students as being linguistically and culturally deprived and provides a relativistic perspective on Black language and culture.

Mitchell-Kernan considers the variations in BE across the United States that arose due to migration of southern blacks to urban areas in different regions of the United States, the stereotypes associated with the use of BE with regard to race, gender, educational attainment, social class, and southern rural residence/origins, and the commonly held view that BE does not meet "prestige norms" (56).

In the classroom context, Mitchell-Kernan asked students to edit BE utterances into SE. However, the different corrections did not always result in SE utterances. She argues that although BE surface structure might vary from SE, these utterances had the same meaning in the deep structure (57–58). Furthermore, she points to code switching between BE and SE in changing from casual to more "careful" speech and argues that one could, in her view, conclude that BE and SE are not two different languages but that BE is a dialect.

Mitchell-Kernan, raised in Chicago, could also provide an "emic" perspective on BE, as she ably demonstrated in an interchange with mainly one young Black male interlocutor in Oakland, which follows (R is "researcher" and I, II, III are interlocutors):

> The following interchange took place in a public park. Three young men in their early twenties sat down with the researcher, one of whom initiated a conversation in this way:

> I: Mama, you sho is fine.
> R: That ain't no way to talk to your mother.
> (*Laughter.*)
> I: You married?
> R: Um hm.
> I: Is your husband married?
> (*Laughter.*)
> R: Very.

> (*The conversation continues with the same young man doing most of the talking. He questions me about what I am doing and I tell him about my research project. After a couple of minutes of discussing "rappin," he returns to his original style.*)

I: Baby, you a real scholar. I can tell you want to learn. Now, if you'll just cooperate a li'l bit, I'll show you what a good teacher I am. But first we got to get into my area of expertise.

R: I may be wrong but seems to me we already in your area of expertise.

(*Laughter.*)

I: You ain't so bad yourself, girl. I ain't heard you stutter yet. You a li'l fixated on your subject though. I want to help a sweet thing like you all I can. I figure all that book learning you got must mean you been neglecting other areas of your education.

II: Talk that talk! (*Gloss: Olé!*)

R: Why don't you let me point out where I can best use your help.

I: Are you sure you in the best position to know?

(*Laughter.*)

I: I'mo leave you alone, girl. Ask me what you want to know. Tempus fugit, baby.

(laughter)

(106–7)

Mitchell-Kernan shows her skill not only in speaking BE in this interview but also in keeping the interview focused on its scholarly purposes.

Using Labov's sociolinguistic work on BE in New York, she prefers the term "monitoring" to Labov's notion of hypercorrection, in which BE speakers generate nonstandard grammatical forms in their attempts to conform to perceived SE rules of grammar and pronunciation. In trying to speak SE in a more formal setting, BE speakers experience embarrassment when they make a mistake (67). In choosing the term "monitoring," she captures the speaker's decision making in determining whether to shift from BE to SE and then back to BE (60). In monitoring, the hearer must determine the motives of the speaker in order to decide how to respond. The speaker usually signals with his or her tone of voice, posture, speech rate, or facial expression (126). While a speaker may "monitor" BE to a Black hearer to promote solidarity, he or she may also "monitor" SE to a White hearer while ignoring a Black person who is present by "deleting linguistic markers which would serve to underline their different identities" (75). She views monitoring as an indigenous process (148).

Mitchell-Kernan concludes that BE is a variant of SE structurally and not a separate language. However, she examines aspects of BE performance that indicate its differences from SE. Her work, along with that of other sociolinguists, was heavily influenced by Erving Goffman's notion of individuals as actors who conduct "impression management" while engaging in a speech act, keeping aspects of themselves that they do not want to reveal "backstage." With regard to the Oakland community, Mitchell-Kernan identifies the following speech acts as representing an array of types of BE artistic performance: "signifying, rapping, sounding, playing the dozens, woofing, marking, loud-talking, shucking, jiving" (8).

In the monograph, she focuses on signifying, marking, and loud talking as speech acts. Signifying is verbal dueling or a way of encoding messages and meanings that features an element of indirection; examples would be delivering a grave insult as a form of censure or exhibiting joking behavior (127–29). It can also mean that one is "making fun" of an individual (88). It is incumbent on the listener/recipient to respond in order to save face (89). A "change in posture, speech rate, tone of voice, facial expression, etc., may signal a change in meaning" (126). These changes are often used to indicate that signifying is taking place (123). Signifying is formulated on the basis of shared cultural knowledge. Abrahams and Kochman interviewed mostly men for their studies of Black folkloric speech acts, while Mitchell-Kernan interviewed mostly women (90). This raises questions as to whether signifying is different for men and women. Loud talking is defined by the volume of speech (129). The speech act, which can take the form a statement, question, or imperative, requires an audience: the interlocutor(s) and other hearers or overhearers. The volume of speech produces unwanted attention, which is perceived negatively by the hearer and could lead to permanent antagonism and, possibly, a physical altercation (133, 134, 136). Marking, which is the BE equivalent of SE mocking, is a mode of characterization of an individual. The interlocutor mimics what the individual has said and how it was said, reflecting the marked person's "background, personality, or intent" (137).

In "Signifying and Marking: Two African-American Speech Acts," Mitchell-Kernan elaborates on her analysis of signifying and marking. She suggests that signifying as a form of verbal dueling is manifested in one interlocutor's expectation of invoking his or her superiority over the other (168–69). She adds that a defining feature of signifying is "its indirect intent or metaphorical reference" (173). The marker, however, is the replaying of a scene, which the interlocutor has knowledge and cultural understanding of, for his or her hearers (176). In signifying and marking, the performance must be skillfully orchestrated to be perceived as being an effective speech act.

As to language acquisition under age five, Mitchell-Kernan observes that parents do not intervene in the sorting of BE and SE because they assume that their children will sort out variants on their own in learning the major aspects of SE, particularly through their exposure to mass media (*Language Behavior in a Black Urban Community*, 83–84). After age five, they experience pressure to use SE variants in kindergarten and primary school, with the idea that it is necessary to use SE at school being firmly entrenched by age nine. Middle-class Black communities would have stricter SE/BE co-occurrence restrictions (85). Mitchell-Kernan notes that there is pressure from teenagers to use BE in everyday speech in the Black community. They also attempt to eliminate gross differences between BE and SE (86). In the classroom setting, she suggests that teachers exhibit more tolerance of BE by accommodating a more diverse speech environment (151–52).

In 1996, a controversy emerged in Oakland public schools concerning the teaching of Ebonics, or BE, as a form of bilingual education for Black students. While language acquisition is not the primary focus of Mitchell-Kernan's monograph, she does consider it in a volume she coedited with Susan Ervin-Tripp entitled *Child Discourse* (1973). Central themes of the volume, which includes a chapter by Mitchell-Kernan and her husband on African American children, are that natural conversation can serve as a source of data, that sentences do not constitute the highest level of analysis, that social context is relevant to linguistic rules, that variability is a component of linguistic rules, and that language is diverse.

Ervin-Tripp and Mitchell-Kernan discuss different anthropological approaches to the child's acquisition of linguistic competence. A common strategy is to observe how children interact with adults in learning the adult system. However, a number of contributors to *Child Discourse* adopt an alternative method, namely, studying the oral culture of the child separately from adults, and often interactions with other children (introduction, 6–7). This approach is relevant to Hymes's notion of the ethnography of speaking. The contributors to *Child Discourse* selected a variety of speech events on which to conduct ethnographic research, including play, narratives, arguments, and teaching in comparative context. Structured role-playing was introduced into play (12–13). Contributors examined sequencing and turn taking by children, and, in the case of Mitchell-Kernan and Kernan, focused on the use of directives in role-playing and perceived status as other factors influencing directive form (21). A directive is a speech act that "has the special property that it requires work on the part of the addressee, so its form is sensitive to issues of social cost, face, and politeness" (20). Mitchell-Kernan and Kernan studied the use of directives among a group of seven- to twelve-year-old African-American children and came to the conclusion that directives in children's role-playing are used to reach an instrumental goal and as a means of expressing social rank ("Pragmatics of Directive Choice Among Children," 191). Directives are most frequently delivered by a dominant person to a subordinate person and, in this study, often by parent to child (201).

Architect of Twenty-First-Century Ethnic Studies and Graduate Education

UCLA experienced the sociopolitical turmoil of the 1960s like other colleges and universities throughout the United States, as California was undergoing significant demographic changes. However, the university seems to have exhibited more foresight in developing transformative structures to create a diverse, intellectually vibrant, and socially responsible institution of higher learning. In 1969, when the UCLA faculty was overwhelmingly White, students of color began engaging in activism around issues of representation on the faculty and among students, around social and research ties to communities of color in southern California, and around the integration of research and teaching on Asian Americans, African Americans, Chicanos, and Native Americans into the curriculum. Chancellor Charles Young (1968–97) insisted that each ethnic studies center be structured as an organized research unit. Mitchell-Kernan comments in the foreword to *The Long Road Home: 40 Years of Ethnic Studies at UCLA* that

> the idea that African Americans, Asian Americans, American Indians, and Chicanos should enjoy the same rights as other Americans, including a voice in higher education, had considerable difficulty taking root. Over many years, some faculty associates of the centers have felt they were in a no-win situation, judged by traditional academic criteria of "publish or perish" while at the same time being expected to do far more in terms of teaching, mentoring, and university/community service. (6)

In precipitating the formation of the UCLA ethnic centers, minority undergraduates made demands for curricular changes, graduate students developed syllabi, taught courses, and conducted research in their respective communities, and new faculty members were hired to institutionalize curricular changes and to carry out innovative and engaged research. There was considerable creativity in each center and crossfertilization among them. Japanese American ethnic studies scholar Ron Takaki taught the first African American history course (12). Mexican American students developed the High Potential Program (later, the Academic Advancement Program) for the recruitment and college preparation of underrepresented minorities.

Organized research units elsewhere on the UCLA campus functioned as spaces where faculty from different disciplines collaborated on externally funded research projects. Due to the initial paucity of faculty and financial resources, the ethnic studies centers experienced difficulties in developing scholarly activities (13). Nevertheless, Mitchell-Kernan argues that the organized research unit model has benefited these units in the long term. All four ethnic studies centers established libraries, archives, lecture series, and scholarly journals. *Aztlan, American Indian Culture Center Journal*, and the *Journal of Black Studies* were founded at UCLA. The *Amerasian Journal* was moved from Yale University. Three centers—African American, American Indian, and Asian American— developed master's programs shortly after their inception.

When Mitchell-Kernan became director of the Bunche Center for African American Studies in 1976, she sought to create a distinctive orientation that would result in its national visibility. As an anthropologist, her conception of African American studies was "hemispheric,"; she saw it as encompassing the study of African Americans in North, Central, and South America vis-à-vis slavery and its legacy, class, caste, and so forth. The Bunche Center's first bachelor's degrees were awarded in 1978. In 2002, Nicole Johnson-Ahorlu received a five-year, $70,000 Ford Foundation grant to fund the College Access Project for African Americans to identify factors contributing to a precipitous decrease in African American undergraduate enrollment throughout the University of California system after the passage of Proposition 209, which prohibited affirmative action in state programs and was implemented in 1997 (56). UCLA had the largest decrease in African American students, with 65% fewer freshmen between 1996 and 2006. The College Access Project for African Americans report revealed that UCLA was basing its undergraduate admissions decisions on slight differences in GPA and SAT scores, the latter of which have low predictive value regarding academic performance, and this had an "adverse impact" on minority student admissions.

Mitchell-Kernan left the directorship of the Ralph Bunche Center for African American Studies in 1989 to assume the position of vice chancellor for graduate studies and dean of the Graduate Division, a position in which she served until 2010. She became the advocate for the advancement of graduate education for the entire UCLA campus; her duties included ensuring that "standards of excellence, fairness, and equity" were consistently maintained across graduate programs. In her position of academic administration and leadership, she managed strategic planning and budgeting for graduate programs, conducted program planning and review, and engaged in external relations. In addition, the four ethnic studies centers reported to her under the rubric of the Institute of American Cultures.

Mitchell-Kernan served as dean at a time when California, the most populous US state, was undergoing tremendous demographic changes, changes we are currently grappling with in the United States as a whole. UCLA was a predominantly White campus in 1969, but in a 2009 survey only 33 percent of undergraduates who participated in the survey identified as White or Caucasian. Although 75 percent of UCLA undergraduates were born in the United States, less than 60 percent indicated that English was their native language. Thirteen cultural categories were provided in the survey, reflecting the broad range of course offerings and the extensive research activity conducted at UCLA (10). This provides some evidence of the efficacy of the four ethnic studies centers as vehicles for transforming UCLA into an institution of higher education whose student body better reflected California's changing demographics, despite the passage of Proposition 209. In fact, UCLA is a national model for diversity in higher education, although its transformation process is still a work in progress with regard to the representation of Blacks and other disadvantaged minority students at the undergraduate and graduate levels.

Among Vice Chancellor Mitchell-Kernan's accomplishments in her twenty-one-year tenure are that she increased graduate student stipends substantially (by 300 percent) and increased enrollment moderately; identified additional placement opportunities in nonacademic areas, particularly in industry; reduced the time it took for students to earn the PhD; increased external fellowship funding from the National Science Foundation, the Fulbright Program, and so forth; provided data for the program review process to identify problems and strategize solutions; and organized the celebration of the fortieth anniversary of the four UCLA ethnic studies programs (Lee, "Ten Questions for Graduate Division's Claudia Mitchell-Kernan").

President Bill Clinton appointed Mitchell-Kernan to one term on the National Science Foundation Board (2000–2006). She also served on the board of directors of the Consortium of Social Science Associations, on the government relations advisory committee of the Council of Graduate Schools, on the Board of Higher Education and Workforce of the National Research Council, and on the advisory board of the National Security Education Program. She served as chair of the Council of Graduate Schools advisory committee on minorities in graduate education and the board of directors of the Graduate Record Examination.

Scholar of Ethnic and Family and Marriage Studies

In the 1990s, while she was vice chancellor and dean of the Graduate Division, Mitchell-Kernan began to collaborate with former Bunche

Center associate director M. Belinda Tucker on an edited volume and a number of articles in the field of marriage and family studies, focusing on women of color. Tucker, a social psychologist with a PhD from the University of Michigan, is a professor of psychiatry and bio-behavioral sciences. She has directed or codirected a number of national surveys, including the National Survey of Black Americans and the 21-City Survey of Families and Relationships, and has received substantial funding from the National Institute of Mental Health. Tucker collaborated with Mitchell-Kernan extensively in her capacity as associate director of the Ralph Bunche Center and as an associate dean in the Graduate Division (2007–11). Since Mitchell-Kernan stepped down as vice chancellor, Tucker accepted the newly established position of vice provost of the Institute of American Cultures, representing the four ethnic studies centers.

In a coauthored article titled "New Trends in Black American Interracial Marriage," Tucker and Mitchell-Kernan (1990) examine interracial marriage in southern California among African American, Latina, and White women, aiming to identify both factors that constrained and were conducive to the contracting of interracial marriages. To contextualize the problem, they considered the antimiscegenation laws that were enforced by many states prior to the Supreme Court's *Loving v. Virginia* ruling in 1967, striking down all antimiscegenation laws, and other historical, regional, and sociological factors. Black women have the lowest rates of interracial marriage of women in all racial groups, and their rates of interracial marriage are also lower than that of Black men. People who marry interracially tend to be older, to have been married previously, and to live in urban areas (211). The West is the region with the highest percentage of interracial marriages in the United States.

Tucker and Mitchell-Kernan reviewed 1990 census data to identify members of couples with at least one Black partner; the sample consisted of 7,328 Black males and 7,023 Black females (212–13). In the sample, Black married men were significantly more likely to be employed, were at a higher income level, were older on average, and were also older than Black women at first marriage. Married Black women were slightly more educated, more likely to have been married previously, and more likely to be significantly older or younger than their spouses. Black men and women were equally likely to have had a previous marriage, to have been born in the same regions proportionally, to have professional occupations, and to exhibit the same spousal age differences. Black women who were married interracially tended to be younger, were more likely to have had a previous marriage, were older or significantly younger than their spouses, and were more likely to have been born in the Northeast or north central United States or abroad.

Black women and men who were interracially married exhibited similar tendencies: being younger, having been married previously, being older or younger than their spouses, and more likely to have been born in northeastern or north central areas of the United States or abroad. While Black males married interracially at a higher rate than females, 6.6 percent as compared to 2.6 percent, they married below the western states' total of 12.3 percent but higher than the 1985 national rate of 3.4 percent. At the time of the study, 64.4 percent of Los Angeles County Black residents were born in the South, the most conservative region with regard to rates of interracial marriage. Tucker and Mitchell-Kernan conclude that it is not simply where one lives that determines one's likelihood of marrying interracially but where one was born (215–16). To account for discrepancies between Black male and female interracial marriage, the authors suggest that women are more likely to choose men based on "earning capacity" or "ambition," and that men choose women on the basis of more Eurocentric aspects of "physical attractiveness." White men may judge Black women according to European standards that define blonde hair and blue eyes as physically superior and thus find them less attractive.

Mitchell-Kernan coauthored another article with Tucker entitled "Psychological Well-Being and Perceived Marital Opportunity Among Single African American, Latina and White Women" (1998). The co-authors explore the decline in Black marriage, the availability of Black men, and changing family formation by comparing single African American, Latina, and White women. In the article, they seek to determine whether perceived availability of potential partners has a pronounced psychological impact, whether it be depression, anxiety, and/or life satisfaction. Tucker and Mitchell-Kernan highlight the central value placed on marriage in African American culture (57). Census data from 1890 attests to the strong marital bonds of African American adults, with 92 percent of Black women and 88 percent of Black men between the ages of thirty-five and forty-four being married or widowed. In the second half of the twentieth century, Black marriage rates declined significantly.

Before 1950, Black women and men tended to marry earlier than Whites, a pattern that has recently been reversed. Tucker and Mitchell-Kernan point out that in 1970, Black women had slightly higher marriage rates than White women and Latinas. By 1990, Black women had the lowest marital prevalence rate of the three groups, with White women and Latinas maintaining 1970 marriage rates. To account for the decrease in Black women's marital prevalence, the authors observe that since 1920, Black males have had proportionately higher death rates, which has led to a steady decline in sex ratios. In 1990, there were 88.2 males to every 100 females. Black male economic marginalization is an additional factor. Black women tend to marry older men. For baby boomers, that male cohort they would likely marry into was smaller (58).

African Americans are now marrying later, are experiencing a higher divorce rate, and are more likely to remain single. There is a gender discrepancy in which only 70 percent of Black women born in 1954 will ever marry as compared to 86 percent of Black men, and 90 percent of Whites of both genders. They also suggest that growing acceptance of lesbian, gay, and bisexual partnerships may be a factor in lower marriage prevalence. However, at the time of this study, in 1998, gay marriage was not legal in California. The focus of this study is mate availability with regard to Black women's expectation of marital role fulfillment, or perceived marital opportunity, and well-being (59–60). Some of the relevant literature indicates that male shortages are accompanied by increased rates of "singlehood, divorce, out-of-wedlock births, adultery, and transient relationships," with marriage and family being devalued and with the rise of feminism. A good marriage might be a source of emotional well-being, although that could vary with age and degree of financial independence.

The Southern California Social Survey was administered by phone to a stratified random digit-dialed sample in predominantly Black and Latino geographical areas of Los Angeles, Ventura, and Orange counties. Mate availability was negatively correlated with some indicators of well-being for White and Latina women, but not generally for Black women. Black women, instead, experienced anxiety associated with "date availability" rather than "mate availability" (67). Singlehood was viewed as resulting from more systemic factors and was becoming more normative in Black culture despite the strong cultural emphasis on marriage. More potential partners were viewed as already being married. Nevertheless, most African Americans were (and are) involved in some sort of romantic relationship. Tucker and Mitchell-Kernan conclude that "there was no relationship between expectation of marriage and psychological well-being" for the three groups of women (68).

In focusing on marriage and family studies of different racial groups, and particularly of African-Americans using large data sets, phone surveys, and statistical analysis rather than the qualitative approaches of interviewing and participant-observation that Mitchell-Kernan engaged in when she was conducting sociolinguistic research, Mitchell-Kernan, Tucker, and other collaborators have been able to interrogate changes in family formations that accompany migration, marriage, social mobility, and other life circumstances. Nevertheless, these studies are comparative across ethnic groups, including Whites, who are no longer the majority of California's population. This highlights the broad range of

Mitchell-Kernan's research and her adaptation to a changing research environment.

Postscript: More Emphasis on International Research

Vice Chancellor Mitchell-Kernan decided to leave the position she had occupied for twenty-one years to return to teaching and research in 2010. She and her husband decided to return to American Samoa where they had conducted sociolinguistic field research early in their careers. Mitchell-Kernan also began a new research project in Rwanda that appears to be more ethnographic than her other work under the auspices of the UCLA African Studies Center and Kigali Teachers' College in Rwanda, with funding from the US Agency for International Development. The project focuses on improving girls' access to primary and secondary education by training teachers to engage girls in learning in a classroom that has been traditionally male-child focused. This has required that she spend substantial periods of time in Rwanda.

Clearly, Claudia Mitchell-Kernan has had a successful career as a professor, researcher, and academic administrator in a variety of contexts. An early innovator in sociolinguistic and family studies research, she has proven to be an innovative administrator and in a period of tremendous social change. Certainly, having a Black female anthropologist appointed at such a high level in the administrative hierarchy at UCLA has had an impact on the nine-campus University of California system. Because California is the most populous state and, if it were an independent country, would have the eighth largest economy in the world, the United States and other countries monitor the innovations in the state in higher education and other areas.

Bibliography

Ervin-Tripp, Susan, and Claudia Mitchell-Kernan. Introduction to *Child Discourse*, ed. Susan Ervin-Tripp and Claudia Mitchell-Kernan, 1–23. New York: Academic Press, 1973.

Goffman, Ervin. *The Presentation of Self in Everyday Life*. New York: Doubleday, 1959.

Gumperz, John J. Introduction to *Directions in Sociolinguistics: The Ethnography of Communication*, ed. John J. Gumperz and Dell Hymes, 1–25. New York: Holt, Rinehart and Winston, 1972.

Hymes, Dell. Introduction to *Reinventing Anthropology*, ed. Dell Hymes, 3–79. New York: Vintage, 1974.

Lee, Cynthia. "Ten Questions for Graduate Division's Claudia Mitchell-Kernan." *UCLA Today*. December 16, 2010.

214 · BETTY J. HARRIS

Mitchell-Kernan, Claudia. *Language Behavior in a Black Urban Community.* Monographs of the Language-Behavior Research Laboratory. Berkeley: University of California, Berkeley, 1971.

———. "Signifying and Marking: Two African-American Speech Acts." In *Directions in Sociolinguistics: The Ethnography of Communication*, ed. John J. Gumperz and Dell Hymes, 161–79. New York: Holt, Rinehart and Winston, 1972.

———. "Studies in Sociolinguistics." *Reviews in Anthropology* 1.3 (1974): 380–87.

Mitchell-Kernan, Claudia, and Keith T. Kernan. "Pragmatics of Directive Choice among Children." In *Child Discourse*, ed. Susan Ervin-Tripp and Claudia Mitchell-Kernan, 189–208. New York: Academic Press, 1973.

Tasch, Jacqueline, and Claudia Mitchell-Kernan, eds. *The Long Road Home: 40 Years of Ethnic Studies at UCLA*. Los Angeles: University of California, 2010.

Tucker, M. Belinda, and Claudia Mitchell-Kernan. "New Trends in Black American Interracial Marriage: The Social Structural Context." *Journal of Marriage and the Family* 52.1 (1990): 209–18.

———. "Psychological Well-Being and Perceived Marital Opportunity among Single African American, Latina, and White Women." *Journal of Comparative Family Studies* 29.1 (1998): 57–72.

Contributors

ALICE BALDWIN-JONES received her BA in liberal arts from the City College of New York, her MA in anthropology from Hunter College, and her PhD in applied anthropology from Columbia University. Her ethnographic research focuses on the social structure of Jamaican Accompong Maroons.

RICHÉ J. DANIEL BARNES received her BA in political science from Spelman College, her MS in urban studies from the Andrew Young School of Policy Studies at Georgia State University, and her MA and PhD in cultural anthropology, with a certificate in women's studies, from Emory University. Barnes is the author of *Raising the Race: Black Career Women Redefine Marriage, Motherhood, and Community* (2016), an ethnographic study of black women's strategies for family and communal survival, which was considered for an NAACP image award and winner of the Distinguished Book Award for the Race, Gender and Class Section of the American Sociological Association (2017). Her research has appeared in numerous scholarly collections, including *The Changing Landscape of Work and Family in the American Middle Class* and *The Gender, Culture, and Power Reader*. Her research builds on the conceptual framework she calls Black strategic mothering, which she describes as a way to discuss the insurmountable odds Black mothers have historically faced that force them to continuously navigate and redefine their relationship with work to best fit the needs of their families and communities. Barnes previously taught at Spelman College and Smith College, was the assistant dean of social sciences and associate professor of anthropology at Endicott College, and is currently dean of Pierson College at Yale.

216 · CONTRIBUTORS

DALLAS L. BROWNE received his PhD in cultural anthropology from the University of Illinois in 1983. He is the former president of the Mid-West Alliance for African Studies and a member of the National Association of African American Studies, the Society for Urban Anthropology of the American Anthropological Association, and the Council on Foreign Relations, as well as former chair of the Department of Anthropology at Southern Illinois University.

BETTY J. HARRIS is a professor of anthropology and women's and gender studies at the University of Oklahoma. She received her PhD from Brown University in 1982. Harris is the author of *The Political Economy of the Southern African Periphery: Cottage Industries, Factories, and Female Wage Labor in Swaziland Compared* (1993), the coauthor of *Some Problems and Possibilities of Sustainable Development* (2017) with Edward Sankowski and Jozef Hernik, and the author of a variety of articles and chapters. She was coeditor of the *NWSA Journal* special issue "Women, Tenure, and Promotion" (Fall 2007). She is editorial board president of *Feminist Formations* (formerly *NWSA Journal*), published by Johns Hopkins University Press. Harris has had two Fulbright fellowships (Swaziland; South Africa). She is chair of the Elliott P. Skinner Book Award Committee in the Association for Africanist Anthropology.

ANGELA MCMILLAN HOWELL is a cultural anthropologist and associate professor at Morgan State University who specializes in African American identity, youth culture, and education. She earned her bachelor's degree from Morgan State University and her AM and PhD from Brown University. Her 2013 book *Raised Up Down Yonder: Growing Up Black in Rural Alabama* explores the everyday lives of young African Americans who live in a small Black Belt town in rural Alabama. Presently, she co-coordinates the Benjamin A. Quarles Humanities and Social Science Institute Undergraduate Scholars Program in Interdisciplinary Perspectives on the African-American Legacy, funded by the Andrew W. Mellon Foundation.

JANIS FAYE HUTCHINSON is a professor in the Department of Comparative Cultural Studies at the University of Houston–University Park. As a medical anthropologist, her research interests include condom use, HIV/AIDS, racism and health, family talk about chronic illnesses, and health issues among people of color. Her many publications focus on these topics. She is the former president of the Association of Black Anthropologists, cochair of the Commission on Race and Racism in Anthropology, and consultant for the National Institutes of Health, the National Science Foundation, and the Ford Foundation.

CONTRIBUTORS · 217

ANTOINETTE JACKSON earned a PhD in anthropology from the University of Florida, and an MBA from Xavier University in Cincinnati. She is an associate professor in the Department of Anthropology at the University of South Florida. Her interests include issues of identity and representation at National Heritage sites. Her research focus is heritage tourism and the business of heritage resource management in the United State and the Caribbean. Antoinette directs the University of South Florida Heritage Research Lab. *Speaking for the Enslaved: Heritage Interpretation at Antebellum Plantation Sites*, her most recent book, was published in 2012.

DEBORAH JOHNSON-SIMON is the founder and CEO of the Center for the Study of African and African Diaspora Museums and Communities in Savannah, Georgia. She is also an adjunct professor of anthropology at Savannah State University. She is a former adjunct professor of anthropology at Santa Fe Community College in Gainesville, Florida, and the University of Florida, Department of African American Studies. She received a PhD in anthropology from the University of Florida, Gainesville, an MA in anthropology and museum studies from Arizona State University, Tempe, and a BA in anthropology and sociology from Rollins College in Winter Park, Florida.

ELGIN L. KLUGH is an associate professor and chair of the Department of Applied Social and Political Sciences at Coppin State University, in Baltimore, Maryland. He is an urban anthropologist with research interests in urban/suburban communities, community revitalization, heritage, cultural landscapes, and cultural resource management. After graduating from Morehouse College, he earned an MA and a PhD in applied anthropology from the University of South Florida. Grounded in oral history methodology, he is active in research related to community revitalization and heritage in Baltimore, Maryland. Additionally, he is involved in collaborative projects aimed at increasing the presence of anthropology at HBCU institutions.

BERTIN M. LOUIS JR. is vice chair of Africana Studies and associate professor of anthropology and Africana studies at the University of Tennessee, Knoxville, where he teaches courses in Africana studies and cultural anthropology. He is a 2015 University of Tennessee, Knoxville, Quest Scholar of the week, a 2013 Southeastern Conference travel grant award recipient, and a 2012 American Anthropological Association Leadership Fellow. He received his PhD in 2008 from the Department of Anthropology at Washington University in Saint Louis, and he studies the growth of Protestant forms of Christianity among Haitians transnationally. His book, *"My Soul Is in Haiti": Protestantism in the Haitian Diaspora of the Bahamas* (2015), was a finalist for the 2015 Haitian Studies Association Book Prize in the Social Sciences. He also studies human rights and statelessness among Haitians in the Bahamas.

CHERYL R. RODRIGUEZ is a cultural anthropologist and an associate professor of Africana studies. She is also the director of the Institute on Black Life at the University of South Florida. Her teaching and research focus on feminisms in Africa and the African diaspora, community ethnography, black women's grassroots activism, and community-based programs for youth. Rodriguez has carried out a range of anthropological projects and has published articles on issues related to the intersection of gender, race and class, including scholarship on black women and public housing and the complexities of black motherhood.

RACHEL WATKINS is an associate professor of anthropology at American University. She received her BA in anthropology from Howard University, her masters in applied anthropology from the University of Maryland, College Park, and her PhD from the University of North Carolina, Chapel Hill. Her research focuses on the biological and social history of African Americans in urban areas of the United States in the nineteenth and twentieth centuries, as well as the history of American physical/biological anthropology. Her investigations include the analysis of human skeletal remains ("Variation in Health and Socioeconomic Status within the W. Montague Cobb Skeletal Collection") and archival/historical research on the use of black bodies in shaping bioanthropological practices ("Biohistorical Narratives of Racial Difference in the American Negro"). She also contributes to the academic and public documentation of first generation pioneer W. Montague Cobb's work in the field.

ERICA LORRAINE WILLIAMS is an associate professor and chair of the Department of Sociology and Anthropology at Spelman College in Atlanta, Georgia. She earned her MA and PhD in cultural anthropology from Stanford University and her BA in anthropology and Africana studies from New York University. Her research has focused on the cultural and sexual politics of the transnational tourism industry and Afro-Brazilian feminist activism in Salvador, Bahia, Brazil. Her book *Sex Tourism in Bahia: Ambiguous Entanglements* (2013) won the National Women's Studies Association/University of Illinois Press First Book Prize. She teaches courses on issues of gender, sexuality, globalization, and the African diaspora. She received the Vulcan Materials Teaching Excellence Award in 2013. She currently serves as secretary of the Association for Feminist Anthropology.

ALISHA R. WINN is an applied cultural anthropologist whose community-engaged work focuses on race, identity, language, historic preservation, museums, and heritage education for youth. She is a consultant in preservation and community building efforts for West Palm Beach's Community Redevelopment Agency, the Spady Cultural Heritage Museum, and the Storm of '28 Memorial Park Coalition. She received BA degrees from Bethune-Cookman University in sociology and Florida Atlantic University in anthropology. She earned her MA in anthropology from Georgia State University and her PhD in applied anthropology from the University of South Florida. A former assistant professor of anthropology at Fayetteville State University in North Carolina, Winn teaches anthropology to community and religious institutions, helping individuals outside of the classroom gain an appreciation for the discipline's usefulness and relevance.

Index

57th Street Meeting, 193

AAA (American Anthropological Association): awardees and fellows, 80, 96n3, 123; Committee on Minorities, 38; conferences, xiii, 60, 65, 80, 115, 116, 120–21, 123, 183; Ethics Committee, 59–60; executive board, 59, 68, 195; Minority Caucus, xiii, 65, 88, 120; and race, xiii, xxiii, 137, 138, 183; Task Force on Poverty and Homelessness, 65

AAMA (African American Museums Association), 108

ABA (Association of Black Anthropologists), 108, 121; archivists, 114, 115, 121; awardees, 95, 96n3, 123; becomes part of AAA, 120, 201; creation and development of, xiii, 88, 114, 120, 124n2, 183–84; and native anthropology, 110; as presenting marginalized voices, 126; presidents of, xiii, 88, 120, 184, 195

Addis Ababa, Ethiopia, 32, 33, 35. *See also* Ethiopia

African-American Pioneers in Anthropology (Harrison and Harrison), ix–x, xv–xvi

African American speech acts, 205

African American studies, as hemispheric, 208

African diaspora, xx, xxi; extended families in, 68–70, 75–77; as field of study, 85, 181, 197; intellectual life, 178–79; and systems of oppression, 87

African states, 147, 156

Aggrey, James, 143, 146; Yombe knowledge of speech by, 145, 146, 150

agnatic kinship structure, 151

Airhihenbuwa, O., 119

Algerians, 129

American Graves Registration Service, 17, 19

American missionaries, beliefs of, 132–33

anthropology, xxi, 48; applied, 115, 191, 196; black feminist, 39, 40, 45–46, 87, 89–91; feminist, 75, 77, 85, 90; forensic, 16, 17, 18–22, 25; of liberation, 186; medical, 118–19, 123, 167; militarized, 56–57; military forensic, 15–22; native, 41, 52, 61, 87, 100, 110, 175, 184; physical, 17, 19–21, 24, 41; social and cultural, 68, 86, 132

Anthropology News (magazine), 121

antiestablishment thought, 53, 54

antiracism, 127. *See also* racism

apartheid: policies in United States, 39; in South Africa, 10

applied anthropology, 115, 191, 196

archivist, ABA's first, 114

Aristide, Jean Bertrand, 185

Asian black populations, 16, 23–25

Atlanta, GA, 116

Australian Aboriginal communities, 61, 63, 65

Bahamas, 69

BAM (Black Action Movement), 71–72

Barbados, 165, 174, 179–80, 183

222 · INDEX

Batak people, 23–24. *See also* Asian black populations
BE (Black English), 100, 201–6
Bedford-Stuyvesant, NYC, 165
Bennett College for Women, 85, 92
Beyer, Henry Otley, 17, 24, 25
bilingualism, and Black English, 206
Birdsell, Joseph, 41
Birom people, 133
black church research, 114, 117
Black English (BE), 100, 201–6
Black family studies, 192, 194
black intellectual inferiority, notions of, 40, 138
blindness. *See* Gwaltney, John Langston
"boat peoples," 182
Bohannon, Paul, 135
Bolles, A. Lynn, 40, 195
Bond, George Clement: analytical frameworks, 145–47; and anthropology, 155–57; childhood and family, 143; at Columbia University, 144; as editor, 152–55; education, 143; photo, 142; research in Zambia, 143–44 (*see also* Yombe people of Northern Zambia)
Boston University, 143
Brinton, Howard, 197
Brooklyn, NY, 165
Bunche, Ralph, 41, 121. *See also* Ralph Bunche Center for African American Studies

Caribbean: immigration to US from, 68; research in, 89, 177, 181, 183, 186, 193–94, 197; social activism in, 174; social structures in, 180. *See also specific countries*
carving, ritual, 111–12
Center for Multiracial Studies, University of the West Indies, 179
Chiang Mai, Thailand, 58
Chicago, IL, 192; South Side, 28, 31
chiefdoms, leadership of, 145, 148–49
Chinantec people, 106
churches, black, 114, 117
CIA, 56, 58
class, socioeconomic, 156; biases around, 62; and Black English, 203, 206; black middle, 30, 206; conflict of, 179, 183; educated, 154; and equality, 197; ethno, 180, 181, 185; intersections with race and gender, 37, 64, 89, 90, 122, 176, 179–80; lower middle, 176; middle, 4, 28, 30,

45, 166, 182; and oppression, 92; and privilege, 43, 86; and socialization, 37; upper, 85–86; working, 1, 192, 202. *See also* elites
Coast Guard, 30
Coatesville, PA, 115
code switching, 203
Cole, Johnnetta Betsch, 69; and ABA, 88; and Black feminist anthropology, 89–91; childhood and family, 85–86; and class-based oppression, 92; as college president, 73, 85, 92, 94; education, 85, 86–88; faculty positions, 88–89; and marriage and family, 92–95; photo, 84; as public anthropologist and educator, 95–96; at Smithsonian Museum of African Art, 95, 97n13
colleges, black. *See* HBCUs
colonialism: anthropology and, 37, 41, 44–45; anti-, 146, 159n17, 186n1; as context, 153; economic and political options under, 134; European, in Africa, 106, 129–30, 133, 147; and genealogical disputes, 149; ideology of, 44; neo-, 180–81; Eslanda Robeson on, 4. *See also* mission schools; postcolonialism
colonial narratives, 146
Columbia University, 106, 144
conviviality, as element of "core black culture," 101
core black culture, 101, 110
Cornell University, 5, 42, 55
critical native anthropology, 62–64
Cuba, 176
cultural authenticity, 65
cultural change, 131
cultural ecological approach, 133, 195

Dallas County Training School, 53
Davis, Allison, 156
dependent associates, African states as, 147
diaspora. *See* African diaspora
Diggs, Ellen Irene, 122, 156
Dillard High School, 69
"do goodism," 92
Dominican Republic, 89, 174, 177
Drake, St. Clair, 31, 41
Duvalier, François "Papa Doc," 174, 176–77, 181
Duvalier, Jean-Claude "Baby Doc," 181, 182, 183, 184

Duvalierism, 181
Dwight, Thomas, 18

Ebonics, 206. *See also* Black English
eco-adaptive relationship, 136–37
ecology: culture and, 133, 195; perspective of, 131
education, 2, 95, 172; and Black English, 203, 206; of elites in Africa, 149, 154, 155–56; extended family and, 76; funding for, 170; and gender, 46–47, 78, 85, 95, 213; mission schools, 148, 149–51; of racial minorities, 3, 37, 39, 76, 85, 92, 155, 209; of women inmates, 48. *See also profiled individuals*
Eggan, Fred, 31, 32, 33
elites: African American, 3, 85, 155; Amharic, 35; in Botswana, 11; and education, 149, 154, 155–56; "indigenous," 63; Yombe, 144–45, 146, 148, 149–50, 155. *See also* class, socioeconomic
emic perspective on Black English, 203
English language, variants of, 201–6
ensete (food crop), 33–34
environmental changes (El Niño), 152
esus (economic practice), 70
Ethiopia, 29, 31, 32–33, 35
ethnic studies, 207
ethno class, 180, 181, 185
ethnographic research, 17, 35, 40, 59, 114, 145, 202, 206, 213; data from, 54, 147–48, 149, 151, 186
evolutionary theories, 131–32, 133
extended families, 69, 75, 86; in African diaspora, 68–70, 75–77

families, research on: black, 37, 192, 194; extended, 69, 75 (*see also* extended families)
family and marriage studies, 209–12
female-headed households, 75–77
feminism, 39, 47, 48–49, 78, 133–34; black women and, 46, 47, 48, 64; and family, 212; ideology of, 135; and intersectionality, 79; and Western ideas, 78, 135–36. *See also* anthropology: black feminist; anthropology: feminist
feminist consciousness, 45, 133
Fisk University, 69, 178
folk seminars, 109
Ford Foundation, 42, 69
forensic anthropology, 16, 17, 18–22, 25
Foucault, Michel, 145

Fox, Robert, 16, 17
Franklin, John Hope, 121
Frazier, E. Franklin, 76–77, 121
Frazier-Herskovits debate, 76–77
Ft. Lauderdale, FL, 68

Gary, IN, 201
gender: and economic activities, 74, 78, 133; and education, 78, 150; and family, 70, 92–95, 133, 212; and fieldwork, 71; and interactions and relations, 151–52, 167–68; intersections with race and class, 64, 89, 90, 180; and migration, 68, 78; roles, 37, 77, 134, 135; and socialization, 37, 179; and sociopolitical transition, 145; stereotypes about, 40, 203; as structuring experiences, 71; and wealth, 86. *See also* feminism
genealogy, and power, 147–48, 149
Georgia Poetry Society, 123, 124
Ghana, 75
Gibbs, Huldah Hortense Dabney, 3
Gibbs, James Lowell, 3
Gibbs, James Lowell, Jr.: childhood and family, 1–3; education, 3, 5–7; faculty and administrative positions, 8–11; in Liberia, 3, 8; photo, 2; professional service, 11–13; Eslanda Robeson's influence on, 4
Gibbs, Jewelle Taylor, 7
Gluckman, Max, 7, 132, 135
Gramsci, Antonio, 145–46
Greater Harvest Baptist Church, 87, 88
Green, Vera Mae: background and academic career, 192–94; legacy, 195–96; and music and dance, 195; organizations, 195; photo, 191; Quaker influence, 192, 196–97; research, 194–95
Grenada, 174
Gullah Geechee Cultural Heritage Corridor, 195
Gurage people, 31–35
Guy-Sheftall, Beverly, 91
Gwaltney, John Langston: career, 106–7, 110–11, 112; childhood and family, 99–104; *The Dissenters*, 105; *Drylongso*, 100, 103; education, 105–6; marriage, 104–5; organizations, 108–9; photo, 100; and ritual carvings, 111–12; in a sighted household, 103; *The Thrice Shy*, 104, 107
Gwaltney, Judith, 105
Gwaltney, Mable Harper, 101, 102

224 · **INDEX**

Gwaltney, Stanley, 101, 103

Hackenberg, Robert, 54
Haiti: Bond's childhood years in, 143; bourgeoisie in, 181, 183; ethnographic portrayals of, 174; MOP in, 176; opposition movement, 178, 181–82; overthrow of Lescot in, 176; social and political structures in, 180; University of, 176, 184, 185; US immigrants from, 177–78, 181–82, 183. *See also* Duvalierism; Remy, Anselme
Haitian Center for Information, Documentation, and Social Action, 180
Haitian National Archives, 185
Hampton Institute, 119
Harrison, Ira E.: and ABA, 114, 120–21; activism, 116–17; awards, 123–24; childhood and family, 115; and churches, research on, 117–18; education, 116; and HBCUs, 119; photo, 114; and public health, 118–19; and vindicationism, 121–23
Harvard University, 5
HBCUs (historically black colleges and universities): and ABA, 108; anthropology at, 115, 119; black women presidents of, 73; professors from, 3
healers: faith, 102; traditional, 34, 119, 168
health: beliefs and education, 119; of minority women, 48; public and community, 118–19, 123, 153, 168; racial disparities in, 138; soldiers' records, 19; of women inmates, 48; women's role in family's, 94–95. *See also* HIV/AIDS; medical anthropology; mental health
health care: and migrants, 183; and patriliny, 135; and poverty, 46; systems of, 167–68, 169, 171
Herskovits, Melville, 70, 76–77, 85, 87–88
heterosexism, 89, 91
historically black colleges and universities. *See* HBCUs
HIV/AIDS, 48, 152, 153
homophobia, 89
Howard University Anthropology Club, 37, 183
Human Ecology Fund, CIA, 56
humanism, 169, 201

Hunter College, 89
Hymes, Dell, 201, 202

imperialism, and anthropology, ix, 37
Inas (Malaysian village), 42
income: and gender, 75, 210; multiple streams of, 172. *See also* class, socioeconomic
inequality, 47
InterAmerican Bank, 183
interethnic studies, 193–94
International Monetary Fund, 183
international research, 213
intersectionality, 79, 174, 180. *See also* class, socioeconomic: intersections with race and gender
Ithaca, NY, 55

Jim Crow South, 53, 85, 86
Jones, Delmos: childhood and family, 53; and the CIA, 56–57, 58; education, 53–56; and ethics of anthropology, 59–61; faculty positions, 57, 59; and McCarthyism, 54; and native anthropology, 61–64; photo, 52; research in Arizona, 54–55; research in Australia, 63–64; research in Thailand, 55–56, 57–58
Junior Youth League, 54

kgotla (meetings), 10
kinship: African, and female-headed households, 76–77; agnatic, 151; and Kouri people, 63; matriliny and patriliny, 133–36; and Yombe descent groups, 147–48
Korean War, 16, 17–18, 19
Kouri people, 63, 65
Kpelle people, 7, 8–9, 10, 11

laboratories, military. *See* military forensics
Lahu people, 55–58, 60–61
Lewis, Diane K.: and black feminist anthropology, 45–48; on colonialism, 44–45; education, 38, 39, 40, 41–42; faculty positions, 38 42; photo, 38; publications, 37–38, 43–44, 46–47; and public health, 48; research in Malaysia, 42
LGBTQ community, 89
liberation: anthropology of, 174, 186; black, 179; and imperialism, 37; as

INDEX · 225

process, 95; and racism, 41; as research focus, 183; women's (*see* feminism)
Liberia: Barnes in, 92, 93; Bond in, 143; Gibbs in, 3, 7, 8
Lincoln University, 68, 73–74, 79, 115, 156
Livingstonia mission and school, Zambia, 143, 149, 150
London School of Economics, 4, 31, 33, 35–36, 143

Malaysia, 38–39, 42, 45
Malinowski, Bronislaw, 4, 35–36, 143
marriage studies, 209–12
Marshall, Gloria. *See* Sudarkasa, Niara
Martinique, 174, 179, 183
matriliny, 133–34
Mays, Benjamin, 116
McCarthyism, 53–54
Mead, Margaret, 59, 105, 106, 109
medical anthropology, 118–19, 123, 167
mental health: and context for mental illnesses, 171; nursing, 167–69; and systems of care, 169
mestizo community, 193
middle class. *See* class, socioeconomic
militarized anthropology, 56–57
military forensics, 15–22
mining: diamond, 10; tin, 132–33
missionaries, American, beliefs of, 132–33
mission schools, 148, 149–51
Mitchell-Kernan, Claudia: appointments, 209; and Black English, 202–6; *Child Discourse* (ed.), 206; education, 200–201, 202; ethnic studies, 207–9; faculty and administrative positions, 200, 208, 209; family and marriage studies, 209–13; international research, 213; and language acquisition, 205–7; marriage and family, 201; photo, 200
Morehouse College, 116
Morocco, 129
Moses, Yolanda, 40
multigenerational families. *See* extended families
museum anthropology, 108, 112
Museum of the African Diaspora in San Francisco, 12
museum professionals, 108, 112
museums. *See specific museums*

NAACP, 2, 3, 12
Nash, Dorothy, 28–29, 32
National Institute of Mental Health, 17, 65, 169, 210
National Museum of African Art, 13, 95
National Museum Philippines, 15
National Office for the Study of Participation and Popular Education, 185
National Science Foundation (NSF), 18, 108, 209
native anthropology, 41, 52, 61, 87, 100, 110, 175, 184
Negrito groups. *See* Asian black populations
neocolonialism, 180–81. *See also* colonialism
neo-evolutionist view, 131, 132
New York University, 68
Nigeria, 70, 119, 132
non-Tumbuka speakers, 149
nonviolence, 196–97
North Africans, 129
Northwestern University, 17, 93
nursing, 167–72

Oakland Technical High School, 53
Oakland University, 135
Obama, Barack Hussein, 91, 126
Obama, Michelle, 91
Oberlin College, 69, 86
Operation Baby Lift, 21
opposition movement, Haitian, 178, 181–82
oppression: anthropology and, 52, 58, 61, 62–65, 186; and class, 92; and ethic of care, 171; of the Gurage, 32; multiple systems of, 84, 85, 87, 89, 95–96; racial, 43, 46; in Thailand, 58; of women, 90, 91, 133–35
Orange, NJ, 99
Osborne, Oliver: and AAPPN, 170; childhood and family, 165–66; faculty and administrative positions, 167, 168, 169–71; as institution builder, 169; multiple jobs, 166, 172; as nurse anthropologist, 171; photo, 166; and psychiatric nursing, 167–68; and psychosocial nursing, 168–69, 171; research in Nigeria, 167–68; retirement, 171
outsider and insider, perspectives of, 62

Palawan, Philippines, 17, 23, 24

Papago, 54
Paris, 129
patriliny, 133–36
Peabody Museum, 6
Philippines, 17, 22–23, 24–25. *See also*
   Warren, Charles Preston, II
physical anthropology, 17, 19–21, 24, 41
physical characteristics, 17, 24, 130–31;
   and interracial marriage, 211
Port-au-Prince, Haiti, 175–76, 184, 185,
   186
postcolonialism, 144, 146, 148
postmodernism, 138, 147
poverty: black women and, 46; healing
   rituals and, 34; impact of, 55; study of,
   193; task force on, 65. *See also* class,
   socioeconomic
psychiatric nursing, 167–69. *See also*
   mental health
psychosocial nursing programs, 168–72
public and community health, 118–19,
   123, 153, 168

race: idea of, 127, 135, 136–37; legacy
   of, 139; purpose of, 136
race relations: in the Caribbean, 180; and
   misinformation, 43
racial bias, 129
racial stratification, 166
racism, 55; as area of study, 80, 138–39;
   in Australia, 63; and black women,
   46–47, 79, 91; covert, 48; in forensic
   anthropology, 20; ideology of, 44, 138;
   role of anthropology in eliminating,
   201; in schools and organizations, 128,
   166; in twenty-first century, 126; in
   universities, 31, 42
Ralph Bunche Center for African American Studies, 200, 208, 210
religion: coexistence of, 154–55; ensete
   and, 33; Gurage, 35; old-time, 110–12;
   and women, 133, 151;Yombe, 151–52.
   See also black church research
Religious Society of Friends, 192
religious studies, 122
Remy, Anselme, 37, 49; and ABA, 183–
   84; childhood and family, 175–76;
   education, 176, 177, 178; faculty positions, 177–78, 179–80, 181, 184, 186;
   as a native anthropologist, 179, 180,
   184, 186–87n1; photo, 175; publications, 174–75, 179, 180–81, 182–83;

as scholar-activist, 177, 178–79, 182,
   184–85; summer positions, 182
revitalization, storefront churches and,
   117–18
ritual carving, 111–12
Robeson, Eslanda, 4, 5
Roosevelt, Eleanor, 102, 105
Rosaldo, Michelle, 77
Rutgers Latin American Institute, 194

sacred motifs, 111. *See also* religion
Sagwara (traditional healers), 34
Sahlins, Marshall, 131
San Francisco, CA, 53
San Francisco State University, 53
San Francisco Writers Workshop, 54
San Pedro Yolox, Mexico, 106
scholar-activist, dual identity of, 177–78
Schuller, Mark, 186
scientism, 201
SE (Standard English), 202–6
sexism, role of anthropology in eliminat-
   ing, 201. *See also* gender
Shack, Dorothy Nash, 28–29, 32
Shack, William Alfred: as an Africanist,
   35; childhood and family background,
   27–28, 30; courtship and marriage,
   29, 32, 33; education, 27, 30–32, 33;
   Fred Eggan and, 31, 32, 33; photo,
   28; as radio operator and technician,
   30; research in Ethiopia, 31–35; at UC
   Berkeley, 32, 33
Skinner, Elliot, 70
Smedley, Audrey: childhood and family,
   127–28; education, 128, 131–32; in
   Europe and Morocco, 129–30; faculty positions, 134, 135; and family
   structure, 133–35; photo, 127; *Race in
   North America*, 127, 131, 136–38; and
   racism in anthropology, 138–39; research in Nigeria, 132–33
Smedley, Brian, 136
Smedley, Ulysses, 127
Smithsonian National Museum of African Art, 13, 95
social justice, 12, 52, 54, 63, 174
social organization, 133
socioeconomics, 202. *See also* class, socioeconomic
sociolinguistics, 200, 201–6, 212–13
soji (unbaptised person), 110–11
Soul Force, 195

INDEX · 227

Sou Sou (economic arrangement), 86
Spelman College, 85, 92
spirituality, 197. *See also* religion
Stanford School of Law, 9
State University of Haiti, 176, 184, 185
State University of New York, 136
structural functionalism, 35
Sudarkasa, Niara: activism, 71–72;
awards and appointments, 80; childhood and family, 69; education, 69–70, 71; faculty positions, 71, 72–73; and feminist anthropology, 77–79; name, 68; photo, 69; as president of Lincoln University, 73–74; research in West Africa, 70–71, 74–75; research on families, 75–77
Syracuse, NY, 115

Thai aboriginal peoples, 23; Lahu, 55–58, 60–61
Thailand, 23, 56, 58–59, 64; US laboratories in, 18, 19, 21. *See also* Jones, Delmos: research in Thailand
Thomas, Clarence, 79
tin mining, 132–33
traditionalism, 146
Treganza, Adan, 53
Tucker, M. Belinda, 210
Tumbuka language, 149. *See also* Yombe people of Northern Zambia
Tuskegee University, 196

UDC (University of the District of Columbia), 181–82, 183
UNESCO (United Nations Educational Scientific and Cultural Organization), 193
UNIP (United National Independence Party), 144, 145
universities, black. *See* HBCUs
University of Arizona, 54, 193
University of California system, 38, 208, 213; Berkeley (UCB), 7, 29, 32, 33, 48, 200; Los Angeles (UCLA), 39–42, 200, 201, 207–9, 213; Riverside (UC Riverside), 42; Santa Barbara (UC Santa Barbara), 42
University of Chicago, 31, 36
University of Ibadan, Nigeria, 70
University of Massachusetts, 89
University of Michigan, 68, 71, 128

University of Tennessee, 122
University of the District of Columbia (UDC), 181–82, 183
University of the West Indies, 179
urban black English. *See* Black English (BE)
urban ethnography, 100, 200

Vietnam War, 16, 18, 178; activist campaigns during, 177; and social science research, 57; US displeasure over, 21
Vincent, Joan, 153
vindicationism, xv, 121–23, 142, 146

Warren, Charles Preston, II: at American Graves Registration Service, 17; army/military work, 16–17, 18, 19–22; and Asian black populations, 16, 23; education, 16–18; exclusion from Association of American Physical Anthropologists, 20; and Philippines National Museum, 17; photo, 15; as researcher and teacher, 18, 20, 22–25. *See also* forensic anthropology
Washington State University, 88
Western education, 78, 150, 154. *See also* education
West Indies. *See* University of the West Indies; *and specific countries*
White, Leslie, 131
white immigrants, 202
William Penn College, 193
World Bank, 183
World War I, 19, 101
World War II, 3, 16, 19, 30, 101. *See also* military forensics
Wowo clan, 144, 149

Yombe people of Northern Zambia, 141, 144–46, 148–52. *See also* Zambia
Yoruba people, 70–71, 74–75, 77–78; and mental illness, 167–68
Youth Recorder (leftist group), 54

Zambia: Aggrey's speech in, 143; Bond's dissertation research in, 143–46; education in, 143, 148, 149–51; gender in, 151–52; reflections on Western society, 152; religion in, 148–51, 154–55; transitions in, 141, 145, 148, 151, 156

The University of Illinois Press
is a founding member of the
Association of American University Presses.

Composed in 10.5/12.5 Plantin Std
with Trade Gothic LT Std display
by Lisa Connery
at the University of Illinois Press
Cover designed by Jennifer S. Fisher
Cover illustration: *African Woman* (2018), oil painting by
Anastasiya Valiulina (valartgallery.etsy.com)

University of Illinois Press
1325 South Oak Street
Champaign, IL 61820-6903
www.press.uillinois.edu